Whisk, Toss, and Enjoy these
unique and delicious salads
from TikTok's beloved recipe creator
The Salad Lab!

Salad is now taking its rightful place at the center of the dinner table with the incredibly creative recipes you'll find in this book. Darlene Schrijver first created The Salad Lab when she was compiling her favorite salad recipes for her daughter to take to college and a friend asked, "Why don't you film the directions for making these salads and post them on TikTok? She's always on there anyway." Darlene started out making videos of classic and retro salads and thought it would be fun to measure the ingredients with test tubes and beakers, since her daughter was a science major. She called her TikTok account The Salad Lab to encourage a spirit of experimentation. The Salad Lab's following began to grow rapidly as Darlene attempted to re-create a celebrity's favorite salad, a recipe inspired by a dish from a restaurant, or a follower's request, and soon she had millions of fans.

There are salads for every occasion in this beautiful cookbook, including many of those celebrity-inspired favorites and restaurant re-creations—mouthwatering dishes like Chicken and Avocado with Honey Hot Sauce Vinaigrette, Lemon Basil Pasta Salad, and Bibimbap Salad. There's a chapter devoted to proving that anything can be turned into a salad, with recipes like Breakfast Burrito Salad and Burger and Fries Salad. There's a whole section devoted to delicious salad dressings like Ginger Miso Tahini and Darlene's viral Green Goddess Dressing, as well as beloved salad-making elements like Sourdough Garlic Croutons. And if you want a dish for serving on the side, like American Potato Salad or a classic Niçoise, Darlene has you covered.

In true Salad Lab tradition, every recipe includes an accompanying drink suggestion, and there are tips throughout for experimenting and taking your salad creations to the next level. Darlene includes a salad pantry guide, tips on equipment you need, and more, making this the last book that salad lovers may ever need.

The Salad Lab
Whisk, Toss, Enjoy!

I dedicate this book to my daughter, Athena; my son, Morgan;
and The Salad Lab community.

SIMON
ELEMENT

An Imprint of Simon & Schuster, LLC
1230 Avenue of the Americas
New York, NY 10020

First Simon Element hardcover edition June 2024

SIMON ELEMENT is a trademark of Simon & Schuster, LLC

Simon & Schuster: Celebrating 100 Years of Publishing in 2024

For information about special discounts for bulk purchases, please contact Simon & Schuster Special Sales at 1-866-506-1949 or business@simonandschuster.com.

The Simon & Schuster Speakers Bureau can bring authors to your live event. For more information or to book an event, contact the Simon & Schuster Speakers Bureau at 1-866-248-3049 or visit our website at www.simonspeakers.com.

Food Stylist: Amanda Anselmino

Prop Stylist: Glenn Jenkins

Photo Assistant: Vanessa Solis

Interior design by Kristina Juodenas

Manufactured in China

1 3 5 7 9 10 8 6 4 2

Library of Congress Cataloging-in-Publication Data has been applied for.

ISBN 978-1-6680-2524-6

ISBN 978-1-6680-2525-3 (ebook)

The Salad Lab
Whisk, Toss, Enjoy!

RECIPES FOR MAKING FABULOUS SALADS EVERY DAY

Darlene Schrijver

Photography by Erin Kunkel

SIMON ELEMENT

New York | London | Toronto | Sydney | New Delhi

Contents

Start Out with the Basics

Introduction   10

My Salad Philosophy   14

Let's Go Shopping!   17

Essential Lab
Equipment   25

Salad-Making
FUNdamentals   29

Arugula Salad   36
House Salad   38
Greek Salad   40
Spinach Salad   42
Tabbouleh   44
Coleslaw   46
American Potato Salad   48
Orzo Pasta Salad   50
Vegan Cobb   54
Niçoise   56
Caesar   58
Kale Salad   60
Not-So-Chinese Chicken Salad   62
Wedge   64
Chopped Salad   66
The Original Cobb Salad   68

Celebrity-Inspired Favorites

Supermodel's Arugula Salad 72

First Lady's Spring Pea Salad
with Asparagus and Pea Shoots 74

Controversial Fake Cobb Salad 76

Famous Sisters-with-a-K's Favorite 78

My First Celebrity's Creamy,
Lemony Cobb 80

Viral Sesame Chicken 82

Let's Travel: Destination-Inspired Recipes

Chicken and Avocado with
Honey Hot Sauce Vinaigrette 86

Beverly Hills McCarthy Salad 88

Fancy Italian Caesar 90

Arizona Chopped Salad 92

Smoked Jalapeño Mexican Grill 94

Fisherman's Wharf Shrimp Louie 97

Maurice Salad 100

French Fry Salad 102

Tropical Salad with Fruit
and Creole Chicken 105

Poke Bowl Salad 108

BBQ Salad 112

Windy City–Style Chopped 114

Cowboy Caviar 116

Jamaican Coleslaw 118

Steak and Chimichurri 120

Ceviche 123

Esquites Salad 126

Across-the-Pond Irish Salad 128

Panzanella 132

French-Style Potato Salad 134

Tapas Salad 136

Fattoush 138

West African Avocado
and Citrus Salad 140

Kani (Kanikama) Salad 142

Bibimbap Salad 144

Southern Hemisphere
Sweet Potato Salad 147

Seasonal and Holiday Favorites

Pea Salad 152

Lemon Basil Pasta Salad 154

Strawberry Jicama Salad 156

Pub Salad 157

Brunch Salad 158

Grilled Peach Salad 160

Watermelon Feta Salad 162

Hot Girl Salad 164

Summer Wedding Salad 166

Red, White, and Blue Potato Salad 168

Chicken Pesto Pasta Salad 170

Roasted Vegetable Salad 173

Autumn Fruit Salad 176

Fall Chopped Salad 178

Harvest Salad 180

Waldorf Salad 182

All in One Thanksgiving Salad 184

Beet Salad 187

Winter Wedge 190

Supreme Citrus Season Salad 193

New Year's Celebration Salad 196

Everything Is a Salad

Breakfast Burrito Salad 200

Lox and Bagel Salad 203

Avocado Bruschetta 205

Doradito Salad 206

Potato Skin Salad 209

Spring Roll Salad 212

Soba Noodle Salad 214

Fish Taco Salad 218

Grinder Salad 220

Burger and Fries Salad 222

Pizza Salad 225

Corned Beef and Cabbage Salad 228

Salad Lab Elements

Classic Homemade Croutons 232

Polenta Croutons 233

Pita Croutons 233

Sourdough Garlic Croutons 235

Everything Bagel Croutons 236

Parmesan Crisp "Croutons" 237

Cheesy Tortilla Croutons 238

Vinaigrette 242

Caesar Dressing 243

Ranch Dressing 244

Blue Cheese Dressing 245

Balsamic Dressing 246

Ginger Miso Tahini Dressing 247

Vegan Better-than-Caesar Caesar 248

Green Goddess Dressing 249

Carrot Ginger Dressing 250

Cilantro Lime Dressing 251

Thousand Island Dressing 252

Creamy Peanut Dressing 253

Basil Mustard Dressing 255

A Few More Salad
Lab Elements 256

Periodic Table of Salad 259

Acknowledgments 265

Index 267

The Salad Lab

Introduction

Welcome to The Salad Lab,
where we're making
fabulous salads every day!

Have a passion for making salads? Me too! As a kid, I would make salad for our family dinners. As an adult, when I go out to lunch with friends, my regular question is, "Who has the best salad?" The buffet signup sheet in hand, I head straight for the salads, and always show up with my big wooden bowl of leafy greens, but as a main dish. A fabulous salad and a beautiful glass of wine or cup of tea is forever my ideal meal.

"Mom, can you write down all your recipes?"

It all started with that question. I consider myself one of those who functions well in "organized chaos" and I kept all my recipes in an old-school recipe box and an overflowing binder, both of which we lost in the Northern California fires of 2017. My daughter, Athena, was headed off to college after spending most of her childhood on the road as a Youth and Junior Team USA Olympic weightlifting athlete. During those years we worked with nutritionists, calibrating the optimal healthy diet for a young athlete that promoted a fun and delicious relationship with natural proteins and lots of vegetables, staying clear of protein shakes and sports drinks.

I procrastinated writing the recipes all back down for my daughter, and on a call one bright and sunny day in spring 2020, my best friend suggested I film them instead. "Why don't you put the recipes on TikTok? She's always on there anyways." It didn't hurt that I was craving some fresh content (pun intended) during that time that *wasn't* sourdough bread. And that's how The Salad Lab was created.

Initially the videos were only for Athena and maybe a few of her friends. In the beginning they were really rough. I had just replaced my beloved hand-carved wooden bowl, the original I had received for a wedding gift from my parents. I was able to rig my iPhone 3 above, and so it began. I had the bowl, a few ramekins for ingredients, and a measuring cup for the dressing to go alongside. After a few weeks, I wanted to make the videos more fun so I thought: let's make it "major" themed. Since my daughter is a molecular biology major, I went for the "lab" concept, both in the fun, science-influenced way I styled the videos and in experimenting with lots of different ideas beyond our family favorites. She was eating up the content. Turns out, lots of other people were too.

I challenged myself to post every day for thirty days when I first joined TikTok. With every new salad I posted, the numbers started growing. I noticed The Salad Lab was really taking off when I started getting requests from followers who were definitely *not* my daughter or her friends. What they wanted more than anything else was the recipe for the Kardashians' go-to salad (see page 78) that they were constantly shaking on every episode of their show. I researched and developed the recipe, and when I posted it, that's when I knew I had found my niche: fabulous salads with great stories. Over the first few weeks I hit a thousand followers, then ten thousand; then it just started growing exponentially.

Salad is so much more than just a healthy meal: it's comfort food, and I think that's why The Salad Lab has been so popular since the beginning. People have a lot of personal connection with these recipes! From salads inspired by places they've traveled to, to their favorite celeb's orders, and ones that remind us of a special time of year, the community connects to that feeling of being excited to eat something delicious, healthy, and nostalgic. If I've learned anything from these past few years, it's that salads offer a common ground for many types of people.

Now that I have this thriving, engaged salad community, I love searching through the comments, restaurant menus, farmers' markets, produce aisles, food magazines, and social media platforms to find my next "experiment." I have so much fun researching different requests, traveling and visiting restaurants, meeting chefs and owners of small businesses. All while learning the history of each salad, how to prepare them, the background of any unusual ingredients, and the stories of how they were invented. There's even a little drama sometimes: Who made it first, what were the original ingredients, when was it created, even "what ingredient in that dressing was so good that her ex lay in front of her car so she couldn't take it to her new lover?" (If you know, you know.) Creating phenomenal salads for my followers allows me to explore my creative and curious scientific sides. It may take a couple tries and some experimenting until I get the recipe just right, but when I do, I get to share it with my fellow salad enthusiasts.

The energy of the now multimillion-strong community is contagious. I'm always amazed how passionate people are about salads! From one group telling me I cannot call a salad "classic" if I dare to put a new ingredient in it (I won't do that again) to the outpouring of gratitude when I posted a very retro one that allowed hundreds of people to reminisce about eating it with a grandparent on a special occasion. The encouragement and support make my heart full—and are a tiny bit overwhelming at times.

I always say I'm forever on the learning curve, and hopefully this book will help you on yours. It is for our salad community, to have fun making salads and experimenting!

My goal for you, the reader, above all, is to have fun while dancing and laughing around the kitchen, with music playing, while you prepare healthy, delicious food that makes you feel good long-term and makes you smile inside and out. I want you to take that joy and spread it around *your* community. Support the "soil" in your neighborhood, and get to know who is growing your food, what goes into it, and where it's coming from. Show the children (and adult children) in your life that not everything you eat comes delivered to your front door in a box. When my town was damaged by wildfires in 2017, we all came together to support one another however we could. That's why I pair my salads with Sonoma County wines: it's a small way for me to give back to those that helped me. And it doesn't hurt that the wines are some of the best in the world.

I am not a nutritionist or dietician and by no means is this a diet recipe book. I do hope your next delicious salad can support your own health, and the health of your community. With this book, you can learn something new, have fun, spread a little love, and eat something fantastic. I'm so excited that my experimenting with The Salad Lab has resonated with so many people, and I'm thrilled to help you discover more delicious, healthy, spectacular recipes to enjoy alone, or with friends or family, every day.

My Salad Philosophy

1. WHEN YOU CAN, BUY YOUR PRODUCE AT A FARMERS' MARKET OR A MARKET THAT SOURCES VEGETABLES LOCALLY.

This is the not-so-secret key to both getting the tastiest, freshest food and supporting your community. Research where your local farmers' markets are and when they're open. Many cities and towns now have markets year-round. If yours doesn't, talk to the farmers during the market season and see who they sell to and how you can support them in the off season, or ask where they get their produce in the winter.

2. OR, EVEN BETTER, GROW YOUR OWN PRODUCE.

It's surprisingly easy and rewarding to grow your own vegetables, fruit, and herbs. At-home hydroponic kits make your kitchen truly feel like a science lab, or a small potful growing outside your door will keep a fresh supply of herbs nearby (a lifesaver!). In the spring and summer, start some herbs, grow a tomato plant in a large pot, or plant a Meyer lemon tree if you live in a warmer climate. You'll appreciate your salads so much more, and the sense of accomplishment will make them taste even better.

3. EMBRACE VARIETY.

We live in a time in which we have almost too many options, and I am so grateful for such abundance. The produce aisle is my happy place. There are many types of produce, greens, and herbs we can buy now, anywhere, anytime of the year. The advancement of hothouse growing and faster time to markets means we can have flavorful tomatoes all year round, so if you can't find decent beefsteak tomatoes, use whatever looks tastiest at the market or grocery store. Amazing quality cheeses and grass-fed beef are easy to find in supermarkets now. Always keep trying new things; they'll make your salads sing.

4. TASTE, TASTE, TASTE!

When all your ingredients are full of flavor it only enhances the finished product. Make sure your grilled chicken is seasoned properly, onions have mellowed enough in ice water, and jalapeños are as spicy as you like them. Bring it all together with just enough dressing to elevate and marry all the flavors. That said, I have learned that many people's view of "the perfect amount of dressing" is relative. I like to think the amount in these recipes is just right, but if you go heavy on the sauce, feel free to double the recipe or alternatively, if you tend to go light, make the dressing separately and serve it on the side for individual tastes.

5. EXPERIMENT.

I hope every recipe will teach you a new trick or get you to try something new. Through the powers of social media, I have discovered that there are many ingredients people don't eat or can't find. That's why an "Experiment" section follows every recipe in this book. It's where I recommend how to swap out polarizing ingredients, seasonal produce, animal products for plant-based products, and more.

6. MAKE IT FUN!

Turn on some good music while you prep all your ingredients. Encourage others to join in and dance in the kitchen while gathering all the ingredients, washing, chopping, whisking, tossing, and enjoying. If you're a visual learner or just want some inspo, head to your favorite social media platform and watch a video for the recipe first (many of these are on my page)! Please laugh and don't take life so seriously while you make your marvelous salad.

7. SHARE THE JOY!

Most of these salad recipes are for four as a meal. Not because I have spent most of my life with four humans in the house or because four is the standard for recipes. Rather, sitting at a table with family or friends or even strangers with a glass of my favorite beverage and a plate piled high with a flavorful salad in front of me is my "happy place." I hope you discover it as one of yours too, as you invite friends and family to join you.

Let's Go Shopping!

My grocery MO is all about finding minimally processed, fresh, local, and community-based seasonal ingredients. I find those foods are the freshest, tastiest, healthiest, and best for the environment—everything that goes into a great salad. That means my first choice is going to farmers' markets for produce and then to my locally owned market for almost everything else when I can. I'm really lucky to have a wonderful store at the heart of my community stocked with local products. If you are fortunate enough to still have a real butcher and/or fish market in your area, do not hesitate to shop there. If nearby options don't include those, it's all good—you just need to divide and conquer your shopping a little. Try nationwide markets like Whole Foods or budget-friendly ones like Trader Joe's for produce and proteins or big-box stores like Target for pantry items. Ethnic markets are great for pantry items and can carry some harder-to-find produce. I would recommend ordering online when you know it's the only option.

Some people collect designer bags; I have multiple types of extra-virgin olive oil in my pantry. What can I say, I love good ingredients! So I've broken my pantry must-haves and control group (i.e., everything else) into basic items that will get the job done deliciously, and some nonessentials that I can't cook without (Maldon flaky sea salt: believe the hype). I've included drinks in my pantry list so I have everything on hand to turn a salad into a nice meal. I recommend keeping a supply at home so you can do the same. Finally, because I go to the market so often, I've included shopping lists for essential salad produce. I hope you'll find them helpful!

My Top Five Must-Haves

OLIVE OIL AND AVOCADO OIL

I have been told by multiple sports nutritionists to steer clear of anything other than extra-virgin olive oil or avocado oil, and some will go as far as to suggest finding out exactly where the olives were harvested. I try a more relaxed approach and prefer California olive and avocado oils and experiment with what is on sale that month (I go through a lot of it). You want to purchase the ones that are bottled in darker glass containers and pressed within the last two years. For a bougie option, try McEvoy Ranch or O Olive oils: both are delicious California oils.

VINEGAR

Generally, stick to quality basics like red and white wine, balsamic, champagne, apple cider, and rice vinegar, and perhaps white balsamic and sherry wine vinegar when you're feeling fancy. Only have a few flavored ones (if I do keep them around, I like tarragon and raspberry vinegars) because they will take up valuable pantry space. Rice vinegars can be sweetened or seasoned, so always taste and adjust your dressing accordingly. Lemon or lime juice is a great substitute if you discover the bottle is empty. The amount and flavor of vinegar often sets the overall tone of the salad, so buy what you love.

SALT AND PEPPER

I discovered Maldon flaky sea salt and never looked back. I put it on *everything*. If I'm out, I revert back to my old faithful granulated Hawaiian sea salt, which can be saltier. Whatever salt you use, if you love it, use it. Salt amounts and types are personal preferences. It can really enhance the flavor of ingredients or overpower a whole dish if you aren't careful. Always take that into consideration and taste ingredients along the way to get your salt levels just right. Same with pepper. I use freshly cracked black pepper whenever possible, and my family rolls their eyes when we are out at restaurants because I always ask for it. White pepper, usually finely ground, is also good to have, as it's used a lot in Asian-style salads. Oftentimes you can find local salts (and other spices) on your travels, which make a fun souvenir.

MUSTARD

Just because they call it Dijon doesn't mean it's good. I enjoy Maille brand mustards, and they are used in more than half my recipes. If you are American, you most likely have a bottle of French's yellow mustard somewhere in the pantry and maybe some type of brown German-style for sandwiches, and that's all you really need for cooking (unless you are a mustard connoisseur and attend the Napa Valley Mustard Celebration every year). Condiments are another category that can unnecessarily "occupy" pantry/refrigerator shelf space, so buy what you know you'll use to the end, which for me is quality, Maille brand mustards, both Dijon-style and whole-grain.

SWEETENERS

To balance most dressings, I like to add a little sweetener. Local honey is my first choice. You've probably heard someone say if you eat local honey, it helps with allergies? I don't know if there is any science behind it, but our local honey tastes great and doesn't have a bunch of fillers or additives. Maple syrup is a close second, great for vegan and fall dressings. Palm sugar is nice for Asian-style salads, and granulated sugar sometimes just hits right. It all depends on your personal taste and dietary restrictions.

Pantry Control Group

INGREDIENT	BASIC	LUXURIOUS
Other Oils and Fats	Toasted sesame oil (in addition my must-haves; see page 18)	Nut oils (walnut, almond, hazelnut, peanut), ghee, coconut oil
Dried Herbs and Spices	Basil, ground cumin, oregano, garlic powder, onion powder, sweet paprika, tarragon, ground mustard, cinnamon, red pepper flakes, citric acid, everything bagel seasoning, chili powder, Italian seasoning, furikake, nutritional yeast	Harissa seasoning, curry powder, herbes de Provence, rosemary, ground coriander, turmeric, cardamom, cayenne, taco seasoning, Jamaican jerk, za'atar, sumac, McCormick Salad Supreme
Condiments	Good-quality mayonnaise, sweet and dill pickle relish, ketchup, hot sauce, sriracha, soy sauce, low-sodium soy sauce, Worcestershire, barbecue sauce, teriyaki sauce, tomato paste, white and red miso, wasabi	Kewpie mayonnaise, avocado mayonnaise, cocktail sauce, sweet chili sauce, pickled ginger, sambal oelek, sweet soy sauce, gochujang, hot chili oil, regional barbeque sauce, plum sauce, pomegranate molasses, tamari
Grains	Quinoa, farro, cracked wheat, short-grain white rice, medium- or long-grain brown rice (For many grains, there are now good shelf-stable premade options!)	Bulgur wheat, winter wheat berries, barley, wild rice, buckwheat, tri-colored quinoa, brown and white sushi rice, millet, freekeh, jade pearl rice, forbidden rice, red rice, premade polenta
Pasta and Noodles	Couscous, pearl couscous, vermicelli, orzo, soba noodles, bite-size pasta (such as macaroni or penne)	Brown rice noodles, whole wheat pasta, seasonal shaped pastas, tubetti, orecchiette, pre-fried chow mein, pad thai noodles, ramen, soba rice noodles, gluten-free pasta
Dried Legumes	Chickpeas, green lentils, pinto beans, kidney beans, Great Northern beans	Red lentils, black lentils, soybeans, black-eyed peas, yellow lentils, marrowfat beans, orca beans
Salad Toppings	Pita chips, tortilla chips, won ton wrappers, Italian bread crumbs, panko bread crumbs	Plantain chips, sweet potato chips, black corn chips, rice crackers, cheese crisps

Canned/ Jarred Beans and Vegetables	Pitted black olives, pitted Kalamata olives, chickpeas, black beans, cannellini beans, pinto beans, pepperoncini, capers, water-packed artichokes, canned chipotle peppers in adobo sauce	Spanish olives, niçoise olives, canned black-eyed peas, jarred imported beans, roasted bell peppers, diced chiles or pimentos, hearts of palm, banana peppers
Canned or Smoked Fish	Anchovies in oil, anchovy paste, jarred oil-packed tuna, smoked salmon	Italian or Spanish anchovies
Freeze-Dried and Dried Produce	Raisins, dates, cranberries, coconut flakes	Freeze-dried corn, freeze-dried apples, freeze-dried strawberries; dried mango, dried papaya, dried blueberries, prunes, dried apricots, and dried cherries; sun-dried tomatoes
Nuts and Seeds	Almonds, walnuts, cashews, pecans, peanuts, pistachios, sesame seeds, sunflower seeds	Macadamia nuts, hazelnuts, Brazil nuts, black walnuts, pine nuts, candied pecans, honey-roasted sliced almonds, Spanish peanuts, chia seeds, hemp seeds, flax seeds, poppy seeds
Nut and Seed Butters	Tahini, peanut butter, almond butter, mixed nut butter	Cashew butter, sunflower seed butter, macadamia butter
Dairy and Dairy Substitutes	Buttermilk, oat milk, full-fat coconut milk, Greek yogurt, plain yogurt, sour cream	Coconut cream, light coconut cream, whipping cream, crème fraîche, coconut yogurt
Wines	Sonoma County sparkling, sparkling rosé, pinot gris, sauvignon blanc, chardonnay, rosé, red table blend, merlot, pinot noir, zinfandel, cabernet	Sonoma County and Napa Valley wines (whatever you like!)
Nonalcoholic Beverages	Lemonade, limeade, orange juice, coconut water, sparkling water, black tea, herbal teas	Yerba maté, kombucha, fancy elixirs, fresh juices (mango, pineapple, tangerine, cherry, pomegranate, watermelon, yuzu, guava, carrot, cranberry), apple cider
Frozen	Corn, garlic purée, ginger purée, peeled edamame, peas, green beans, quinoa, white rice, French fries, bagels, sourdough bread, chicken (or vegan chicken), shrimp, salmon, imitation crab, ground beef	Sweet potato fries, brown rice, grilled corn, bell peppers, leeks, pineapple, naan, focaccia, turkey breast, sushi-grade ahi tuna, lobster, filet mignon

Perishable Variables

Keeping your refrigerator full of fresh, local produce, meat, cheese, and more really doesn't take much planning with these grocery list templates. I divide my shopping into daily, weekly, and monthly trips so I make sure I use up what I need before it goes bad, never run out of fresh essentials, and always have what I need close by to pull together a great salad. I have to make a list before I leave and check recipes twice; otherwise, I am guaranteed to forget something. There are many grocery apps with shopping lists that can be helpful. At the time of writing this book, I work with Amazon and Instacart and have pantry lists on both.

When you get home from the store or market, remember that certain fruits and vegetables do better out on the counter and taste better if they're at room temperature. Avocados are best refrigerated until a day or two before use. Get yourself a few beautiful fruit bowls or baskets in which to ripen fruit, tomatoes, and citrus and to hold potatoes, onions, garlic, and shallots. I treat herbs like fresh-cut flowers: I put them into a vase or glass half-filled with water, cover them with a plastic bag, and refrigerate. You could leave them out and they make great kitchen counter decorations too. Lettuce doesn't need to be prepped right after shopping; you can store it for a few days and chop it right before serving (see page 30 for my tips).

STAY INFORMED: It's important to be aware of food recalls, especially for produce that isn't cooked, such as salad greens. It seems every time I walk into a supermarket lately there is a recall taped up by the door. Big recalls may hit the news, but there are all sorts of smaller ones we are not informed about.

Be in the know. Regularly check https://www.fsis.usda.gov/recalls for updates. The many problems plaguing our national food system are another reason to try to shop for local produce as much as you can.

DAILY SHOPPING LIST

- ☐ Lettuces, kale, and other leafy greens
- ☐ Cucumbers
- ☐ Tomatoes (whatever looks best)
- ☐ Bell peppers
- ☐ Chiles
- ☐ Carrots
- ☐ Herbs
- ☐ Scallions
- ☐ Lemons
- ☐ Fresh fish
- ☐ Fresh cheeses (like feta, goat, cheddar, and fresh mozzarella)

BI-WEEKLY SHOPPING LIST

- ☐ Cabbage
- ☐ Avocados
- ☐ Mushrooms
- ☐ Cauliflower, romanesco, broccoli, and/or broccolini
- ☐ Brussels sprouts
- ☐ Eggplant
- ☐ Celery
- ☐ Zucchini and yellow squash
- ☐ Perishable fruit (like berries, melon, and other seasonal fruit)
- ☐ Bread
- ☐ Sprouts
- ☐ Peas and pea shoots
- ☐ Green beans

WEEKLY SHOPPING LIST

- ☐ Radishes
- ☐ Onions

- ☐ Shallots
- ☐ Potatoes
- ☐ Garlic
- ☐ Hardy fruit (such as apples and mangoes)
- ☐ Citrus
- ☐ Eggs
- ☐ Fresh chicken
- ☐ Tofu
- ☐ Tortillas
- ☐ Longer-lasting cheese (like Parmesan, blue cheese, Pecorino Romano, and extra-sharp cheddar)
- ☐ Other dairy (sour cream, crème fraîche, and yogurt)

MONTHLY SHOPPING LIST

- ☐ Buttermilk
- ☐ Extra-virgin olive oil
- ☐ Avocado oil
- ☐ Mayonnaise
- ☐ Sesame oil
- ☐ Dijon mustard
- ☐ Miso paste
- ☐ Local honey

ANY OTHER PANTRY ITEMS THAT NEED REPLACING:

- ☐ _____
- ☐ _____
- ☐ _____
- ☐ _____
- ☐ _____
- ☐ _____

Essential Lab Equipment

People ask me every day where I get my beakers and test tubes! With so many requests, I now sell them (along with my big, beautiful salad bowls and many other items on this list) on my website, www.thesaladlab.net. If you want to turn your kitchen into your very own salad lab, you can get a set for measuring. Everything else on this list is just as essential. If you don't already own something mentioned below and want to add one to your kitchen, my rule is: if it's something you're going to use every day, buy the best quality you can.

TEST TUBES

They come in all different sizes; the size I use holds about 75ml. Get a set that comes with a stand so you can safely store them without breaking. If you don't want test tubes or beakers, a set of nonplastic measuring cups and spoons are great substitutes.

BEAKERS

Get a graduated glass set with several sizes that are stackable, and make sure the pour spouts are all in the same direction when you store them so they don't get stuck. The tiny 5-ml size I use to measure salt and pepper is my favorite!

PETRI DISHES

I love them to show off ingredients, but if you find you're not using them much, they make great storage containers for salt and dried herbs, or you can use them as coasters.

KNIVES

I use five knives in my kitchen: a small paring knife, a medium utility knife, a large chef's knife, a rectangular cleaver, and a serrated knife.

CUTTING BOARDS

Get a silicone board with a well around the edge to collect juices and use it for meat. For everything else, I love my beautiful wood cutting boards.

DISH TOWELS

I can't stop collecting tea towels. They add flair to my kitchen (and cleanup).

SALAD SPINNER

I'm very passionate about my stainless-steel OXO Good Grips spinner! The metal is heavier than plastic, so it's more stable and falls off the track less. The rubber bottom prevents it from spinning off the counter, and the bowl is big enough that you can use it as a salad bowl.

PEPPER GRINDER

One of my recent Christmas gift guides included the Peugeot pepper mill. Sometimes called the "sports car of pepper grinders," it has four different granule sizes. Get one; it will last forever.

SALT BOX

Storing salt in a box makes it easier to measure and pinch. The exact one you buy matters less than making sure it's got a lid that protects the salt from things flying around in the kitchen. I use my petri dishes in a pinch (pun intended).

ZESTER

I use my Microplane zester every day, not only for zesting fresh citrus but also as a cheese grater. It's a must for freshly grated Parmigiano-Reggiano.

GARLIC PRESS

This is how I make my pressed garlic while preventing my hands and cutting board from smelling. Buy one that you can flip over to push the excess garlic out of the bottom for easy cleaning.

FOOD PROCESSOR

Great for when you're in a hurry and need to do a lot of chopping, slicing, shredding, or grating. I use the grating attachment for vegetables and the adjustable slicing blade for radishes or shaved Parm.

IMMERSION BLENDER

I call it my "emulsifier." I have a cordless version, which takes up a lot less space than a corded one. I highly recommend this easy-to-clean tool, but you can also use a regular blender or mini food processor to make dressings.

BLENDER

You need a blender to make margaritas, but it also works when you don't have an immersion blender. A small cordless blender is a good substitute (either an all-in-one type or one with a removable cup), especially for meal prepping. Make your dressing in the blender and store the whole thing in the refrigerator.

SPATULA

Get a set of silicone spatulas in varying sizes. I use the little ones way more often than I thought I would, to scrape sauces out of the blender or get the last bit of mustard in the jar.

THERMOMETER

To properly prepare meat it is essential to have an instant-read meat thermometer. I like one that has cooking temperatures for the different meats printed right on it.

LAB COAT (OR APRON)

I wear lab coats to protect my clothes in the kitchen, and I love the full coverage. Everything is protected and I get a kick out of the *Breaking Bad* vibes when the delivery person stops by!

COMPOST BIN

In California it's all about composting. Convenience is the most important thing when it comes to buying a bin. Find something that is easy to clean (so you'll actually use it) and that has a filter on top to help with any smell.

BIG BEAUTIFUL WOODEN SALAD BOWL AND FOOD-SAFE MINERAL OIL/WAX

The bigger the better. You need plenty of room when tossing a salad, otherwise it's difficult to keep your counters clean and get everything well combined. For serving one or two people I suggest a 12-inch (30-cm) bowl; for three or four people, a 15-inch (38-cm) bowl; and for any more people, a 17-inch (43-cm) bowl. Wooden bowls are a family tradition and I love them because they're made from a natural material that has a weight I like, and the stunning woodgrain is unique to each piece. Mine come from different craftsmen using ecologically friendly wood or naturally fallen trees. To keep them looking their best, wash immediately after use with soapy warm water and towel dry. Never leave a wooden bowl sitting full of liquids for a long period or it can crack. Treat it with beeswax or mineral oil about once every five washes, or anytime it starts to dull (I like a blend of the two from the brand Bee's Oil), to keep it looking beautiful.

TOSSERS

Another thing I collect when I'm on vacation; who can pick just one pair? I look for utensils with style, character, charm, a large surface area (so that they grab a lot of the ingredients when tossing), and Goldilocks handles—not too long, not too short.

MEAL-SIZE SERVING BOWLS

The standard salad plate is too small to hold a meal's worth of salad, but a pasta bowl is the perfect size: it's wide and has depth too. There are some quality hand-thrown ones made by local craftspeople. Alternatively, a beautiful dinner plate also works if you don't have a pasta bowl.

MEAL PREP CONTAINERS

If you like to pack a salad for lunch, you need a fairly large container (that holds at least four cups), preferably glass or metal, with separate sections or small containers for dressing and croutons to keep everything crisp.

STORAGE CONTAINERS

You can never have enough glass food storage containers in my opinion. Stock all different sizes for storing leftovers and salad components prepped ahead of time.

Salad-Making FUNdamentals

If you follow me on social media, you know my salad-making process is "Whisk, Toss, and Enjoy!" For this book I added two more that are just as important: Start Out and Experiment. I've broken those steps out into more detail here.

Start Out

Salads take some prep work. This is the step where I make any cooked ingredients like croutons or roasted vegetables (and even before that, I may start marinating meat or fish). If there are roasted or boiled components you like to use often, prepping large batches in advance will save you time here.

While my ingredients are in the oven or simmering, I'll also get my vegetables ready. In recipes with shallots and onions, I always recommend soaking them in ice water for ten minutes. This will remove some of the sulfides that cause that harsh bite, bad breath, and onion burps. Another step you will see a lot is straining chopped tomatoes. Most vegetables are at least ninety percent water, and tomatoes have a habit of releasing a lot of liquid when cut. If you like your dressing on the thinner side you can add the strained juice to it, otherwise save it for something else.

This is a perfect time to pay special attention to your lettuce and leafy greens. I don't prepare my greens until right before I plan to eat them, because lettuce browns so quickly. Here's what I do:

- Break off the individual leaves from a head of lettuce and rinse them.

- Fill a salad spinner (see page 26) with water and a few ice cubes and add the leaves. Like flowers, lettuce will drink up a lot more water from a fresh cut, and the ice helps keep everything crisp. I let the lettuce soak for 10 minutes. (If I have time and I'm using it, I will soak bagged lettuce, which helps separate out any bad leaves and crisps up the rest.)

- Drain the lettuce, rinse it again, and if it was a particularly muddy specimen from the market, rinse once more.

- Spin the lettuce dry in the spinner, and it's ready to add to a salad. If I have any extra, I'll store it in an airtight container in the refrigerator with a paper towel or clean dish towel for a few days.

Whisk

Why do I have you make the dressing first and make it at the bottom of the bowl? I started preparing dressing directly in the serving bowl for demonstration purposes, but I usually make the dressing first anyway, because it gives the flavors a chance to mingle and herbs—especially dried—to release their flavors. Added bonus: it saves on dishes. That said, if you wish to control the amount of dressing in your salad or you are meal prepping, prepare the dressing separately.

I begin by rinsing the pressed garlic to mellow the flavor. Then, I often add the oil. "Aren't you supposed to drizzle it in at the end to emulsify the dressing?" I get asked a lot. After filming and preparing hundreds of salads, I've learned that not only does the oil create an extra protective barrier for the wood of my salad bowl but it also emulsifies just fine no matter when you add it.

My only two rules for dressing are: remember to taste, taste, taste; and the classic 3:1 ratio of fat to acid is a thing of the past. Like anything, it's all personal preference. Do what you like, like what you do.

Toss

With the dressing at the bottom of the bowl, I add my cooked and raw ingredients and toss until everything is evenly combined and distributed—so everyone gets the same mix of ingredients and dressing. I could just toss and be done. But I like to take a minute or two before serving to make sure my salad looks its best before bringing it to the table. Even if you're only serving yourself, I think it's important to take the time to make it beautiful.

If I'm serving family-style, my big, beautiful salad bowl and tossers are my serving pieces. I'll reserve some of the "special" ingredient in the salad—plump shrimp, big crumbles of cheese, extra croutons—for garnish and set aside. After tossing, I wipe any dressing off the rim or the exposed sides for a clean look. Then I'll arrange the reserved garnish in the middle of the bowl.

If I'm plating the salad, sometimes it's easier to serve up individual portions before bringing the salad to the table. If that's the case, I'll toss the salad, pile it high onto large, deep serving bowls or plates (see page 27 for my recommendations), and sprinkle a nice little garnish on top (extra croutons, herb sprigs, etc.). Some salads may need to be assembled on the individual plates, like a Wedge (page 64). Make sure each serving looks intentional. Depending on the diners or when we're eating, I may serve the dressing on the side so my guests can customize their salad. Wipe any stray dressing or ingredients off the sides of the plates before bringing them to the table (you don't want Gordon Ramsay throwing it in the garbage).

Enjoy

Every meal should feel special! Make sure you've got a delicious beverage to pair with your salad. I give suggestions for nonalcoholic as well as adult beverages for each salad: both can add that missing element to your experience. What beverages to stock is a personal preference thing (see page 21 for my recommendations). Juice, loose-leaf teas, sparkling water (you can flavor it yourself), affordable wines you know you like, and a bottle or two of something you want to try are great options. All locally produced if available.

Experiment

When you're choosing a recipe, don't be discouraged if there are ingredients in the salad you can't find or don't eat. If some of the produce isn't in season, there are often great hothouse options from the grocery store, or other vegetables that make excellent swaps. A big part of my philosophy is encouraging substitutions and creativity. So definitely don't skip a salad just because it has something you don't like in it (for example, blue cheese)! For vegetarians and vegans, there are tasty options for plant-based cheese and meat substitutes. I'm not a fan of processed foods, so I lean toward the homemade options or very simple products like the ones below. Any salad can still be amazing without animal products.

One thing I've learned from my community is that there are certain ingredients a lot of people do *not* want in their salads! Here are my top substitution requests, and what to do if you also don't love these ingredients:

- If you don't like **raw egg** in your Caesar dressing . . . use **coddled egg** (see page 243).

- If you don't like **cilantro** . . . use **parsley**.

- If you don't like **anchovies** . . . use **capers**.

- If you don't like **blue cheese** . . . use **feta** or **fresh goat cheese**.

- If you don't like *any* **cheese** . . . use **nutritional yeast** or a **cashew-based cheese**.

- If you don't like **bacon** . . . use **turkey bacon** or **carrot bacon**.

- If you don't like **meat** . . . use **Roasted Tofu** (page 258) or **cooked portobello mushrooms** (see pages 261 and 263).

- If you don't like **kale** . . . **try massaging it really well in the dressing** and let it marinate for at least ten minutes, or **cut it super fine** (or both). If it's just not your thing, experiment with **baby kale varieties, cabbage, endive,** or **other hearty greens**.

And now you're ready to Whisk, Toss, and Enjoy!

Caesar Salad (page 58)

Start
Out
with the
Basics

Arugula Salad

This may be my favorite side or lunch salad; I regularly crave its refreshing flavors. It's so simple and takes only a few minutes to prepare. Arugula is a small, pretty, deeply colored, narrow-leafed peppery green. "Rocket," as the other half of the world calls it, has gained popularity in recent years and is now found in everything from gourmet sandwiches and wraps to piadina (a small flatbread with a salad on top). The tart, lemony dressing and peppery greens contrast well with the salty Parmigiano-Reggiano and crunchy sour-sweet of the pomegranate in this salad, making it one of my effortless favorites.

EXPERIMENT:

If you are new to arugula, taste it. Some prefer a 50-50 combination of spring mix or baby spinach to arugula for a lighter, less peppery version. If you can't find pome-granate molasses, use pomegranate juice and add honey to taste. Ex-periment with skipping the pomegranate and replacing the pista-chios with walnuts, pecans, or other nuts you already have. If you're serving this to children, or the child in all of us, serve with a Shirley Temple (grena-dine is also made with pomegranates) and it may take you back to a simpler time. Use this salad to top pizza or naan for an easy light meal.

START OUT	WHISK	TOSS
Ice water	⅓ cup (80 ml) extra-virgin olive oil	8 cups (1,900 ml) lightly packed arugula
2 tablespoons (30 ml) very finely diced shallot	¼ cup (60 ml) fresh lemon juice	¾ cup (175 ml) freshly shaved Parmigiano-Reggiano
½ cup (120 ml) coarsely chopped, toasted (see page 257) pistachios	3 tablespoons (45 ml) pomegranate molasses	¾ cup (175 ml) pomegranate seeds
	1 tablespoon (15 ml) honey	
	Flaky sea salt and freshly cracked black pepper	

START OUT: Fill a 250-ml beaker or a small glass bowl halfway with ice water and add the shallot. Soak for 10 minutes, then drain and pat the shallot dry. Toast the pistachios.

WHISK: In a large salad bowl, combine the shallot, oil, lemon juice, pomegranate molasses, and honey and season with salt and pepper. Whisk until emulsified, then taste and adjust the seasoning if needed.

TOSS: In the bowl with the dressing, add the arugula, Parmigiano-Reggiano, pomegranate seeds, and pistachios. Toss until all the ingredients are evenly combined and coated with dress-ing and serve.

ENJOY: I'm having it with a sparkling brut rosé or iced black tea with lemon.

SCIENCE IN THE KITCHEN: As you'll see in this recipe and all the rest, I include volume measurements in both imperial units and milliliters, the official measurement of science experiments. I also include grams for weights, centimeters for inches, and Celsius for temperatures since that's how everything is measured in a lab. However, I've rounded them to make measuring easier for the home cook. That way you can use tablespoons and cups if you prefer, or committed salad scientists can reach for their beakers and test tubes without needing a calculator too.

House Salad

House salads are a salad fanatic's gateway drug. In restaurants, house salads are usually a smaller portion of a meal salad on their menu and if you're lucky you get to choose a specialty dressing or from a few of the classics. I used to always order the house salad when I was in school. I loved to go out to lunch with friends and it was usually the least expensive thing on the menu. These days, I get a lot of requests for house salad recipes from my followers' favorite restaurants. It usually starts out with romaine, tomatoes, cucumbers, some cheese, and onions. The "house" will then add a little bit of their own style to it, whether it is a special dressing, croutons, beans, or a few bites of meat. This is my house salad.

START OUT

2 cups (475 ml) Sourdough Garlic Croutons (page 235)

4 Perfect Boiled Eggs (page 257)

Ice water

½ cup (120 ml) diced red onion (¼-inch/6-mm pieces)

1 cup (240 ml) cubed beefsteak or Roma tomatoes (½-inch/1.3-cm pieces)

WHISK

½ teaspoon (2.5 ml) pressed garlic

¼ cup (60 ml) extra-virgin olive oil

2 tablespoons (30 ml) red wine vinegar

2 tablespoons (30 ml) finely chopped fresh basil

1 tablespoon (15 ml) fresh lemon juice

1 tablespoon (15 ml) honey

2 teaspoons (10 ml) Dijon mustard

1 teaspoon (5 ml) McCormick Salad Supreme seasoning

¼ teaspoon (1.5 ml) red pepper flakes

Flaky sea salt and freshly cracked black pepper

TOSS

4 cups (950 ml) torn butter lettuce (bite-size pieces)

4 cups (950 ml) torn baby gem or romaine lettuce (bite-size pieces)

1 cup (240 ml) sliced English cucumber

½ cup (120 ml) grated sharp cheddar

START OUT: Prepare the croutons and eggs. When the eggs are cool enough to handle, chop them.

Meanwhile, fill a 500-ml beaker or a small glass bowl halfway with ice water and add the onion. Soak for 10 minutes, then drain and pat the onion dry. Place the diced tomatoes in a colander and gently press down with a spoon to drain off excess liquid.

WHISK: Rinse the pressed garlic in a very fine mesh strainer and shake off any excess water. In a large salad bowl, combine the garlic, oil, vinegar, basil, lemon juice, honey, mustard, Salad Supreme, and red pepper flakes and season with salt and pepper. Whisk until well combined, then taste and adjust the seasoning if needed.

TOSS: In the bowl with the dressing, add the butter lettuce, baby gem lettuce, cucumber, cheese, croutons, eggs, onion, and tomatoes. Toss until all the ingredients are evenly combined and coated with dressing and serve.

ENJOY: I'm having it with a nice rosé or sparkling water with lemon.

EXPERIMENT:
Use any of the dressings in Salad Lab Elements (pages 242–55) that speak to you. If you can't find Salad Supreme, add ½ teaspoon (2.5 ml) sweet paprika and ½ teaspoon (2.5 ml) toasted sesame seeds. I encourage you to adapt this one to what is in season. If your zucchini crop is out of control, use them in place of the cucumbers. If you, like me, have beets (and carrots) in the back of your veggie drawer, add grated raw beets for a nice texture (and less "overpoweringly earthy" flavor than roasted or boiled). Rinse them after grating so they are less likely to stain everything they touch. Same with herbs: if you bought fresh dill and forgot the basil . . . have fun with it!

Greek Salad

You see Greek salads on many restaurant menus for good reason: they are flavorful and refreshing with just a few quality ingredients. I usually say buy local, but in this case you may want to experiment with real Greek feta made either from sheep's milk or a mixture of sheep's and goat's milks. It's lighter and tastier than domestic cow's milk feta. Once I posted a "Classic Greek Salad" that included romaine lettuce. I soon discovered that my Greek followers were very passionate about their salad not having lettuce in it! I've learned so much from my community and I'm even happier with this version.

EXPERIMENT:
Quality ingredients are key for this salad. It is fabulous when tomatoes are in season, so use whatever looks best at the market. It is also good with English or Persian cucumbers. For a pretty presentation, try removing only half the cucumber skin by running the peeler down the length of the cucumber every other inch (2.5 cm) so it looks striped before slicing. To plate the salad individually, instead of cubing the feta, cut it into four 2-ounce (55-g) slices and place one piece on each serving, drizzled with olive oil and sprinkled with oregano. If you like it extra garlicky, sprinkle more pressed garlic on top.

START OUT

Ice water

½ cup (120 ml) halved and thinly sliced red onion

4 cups (950 ml) quartered cherry tomatoes, or substitute what looks best at the market

WHISK

1 tablespoon (15 ml) pressed garlic

⅓ cup (80 ml) extra-virgin olive oil

2 tablespoons (30 ml) red wine vinegar

2 tablespoons (30 ml) dried oregano or 3 tablespoons (45 ml) finely chopped fresh oregano

½ teaspoon (2.5 ml) flaky sea salt

½ teaspoon (2.5 ml) freshly cracked black pepper

TOSS

4 cups (950 ml) peeled, halved lengthwise, and sliced cucumber

1½ cups (360 ml) chopped green bell peppers (¾-inch/2-cm pieces)

1 cup (240 ml) pitted and halved Kalamata olives

1½ cups (360 ml) cubed sheep's milk feta cheese (1-inch/2.5-cm pieces)

4 teaspoons (20 ml) extra-virgin olive oil

2 teaspoons (10 ml) dried oregano or 1 tablespoon (15 ml) finely chopped fresh oregano

START OUT: Fill a 500-ml beaker or a small glass bowl halfway with ice water and add the onion. Soak for 10 minutes, then drain and pat the onion dry. Place the tomatoes in a colander and gently press down with a spoon to drain off excess liquid.

WHISK: Rinse the garlic in a very fine mesh strainer and shake off any excess water. In a large salad bowl, whisk together the garlic, oil, vinegar, oregano, salt, and pepper until combined.

TOSS: In the bowl with the dressing, add the cucumber, peppers, olives, onion, and tomatoes. Toss until all the ingredients are evenly combined and coated with dressing. Top with the cubed feta, drizzle the olive oil over the top of the cheese, sprinkle with the oregano, and serve.

ENJOY: I'm having it with a merlot or bubble water.

Spinach Salad

I usually make this salad around Valentine's Day and also for hot summer days. It has renewed my faith in raw spinach. High in iron, spinach is great for athletic women that are more likely to have low iron levels and need it for muscle recovery. Be like Popeye (or Ariana Grande, who reportedly loves a spinach salad) and eat your spinach with a little Olive Oyl. If you notice a chalky metallic feeling on your teeth when you eat raw spinach (from the oxalate crystals that bind to the calcium in your teeth when chewing), try finely slicing or chopping the spinach before it goes into the salad, which reduces the amount of oxalate released.

EXPERIMENT:
You can make this salad with all spinach or all spring mix. Date syrup is a wonderful sweetener that's popping up in markets everywhere. If you find it, taste it, and experiment with replacing the maple syrup, honey, or other sweeteners in dressings. It has a rich, caramelized flavor. I prefer to buy frozen shelled edamame and just take it out of the freezer, rinse it, strain, and you're good to go, or use blanched, shelled fresh eda-mame if that's what you have.

START OUT

2 cups (475 ml) Roasted Tofu (page 258)

½ cup (120 ml) Honey-Roasted Sliced Almonds (page 257), or store-bought

Ice water

1 tablespoon (15 ml) very finely diced shallot

1½ cups (360 ml) shelled frozen edamame

WHISK

⅓ cup (80 ml) extra-virgin olive oil

¼ cup (60 ml) fresh lemon juice

¼ cup (60 ml) maple syrup

1 tablespoon (15 ml) apple cider vinegar

1 tablespoon (15 ml) chia seeds

TOSS

6 cups (1,400 ml) lightly packed baby spinach

2 cups (475 ml) lightly packed spring mix (baby lettuce blend)

1½ cups (360 ml) sliced strawberries (sliced lengthwise)

½ cup (120 ml) crumbled feta cheese (see opposite)

⅓ cup (80 ml) chopped pitted dates (½-inch/1.3-cm pieces)

START OUT: Prepare the roasted tofu and almonds (if making) and let them cool. Meanwhile, fill a 250-ml beaker or a small glass bowl halfway with ice water and add the shallot. Soak for 10 minutes, then drain and pat the shallot dry. Defrost the edamame.

WHISK: In a large salad bowl, whisk together the shallot, oil, lemon juice, maple syrup, vinegar, and chia seeds until well combined.

TOSS: In the bowl with the dressing, add the spinach, spring mix, strawberries, feta, dates, tofu, almonds, and edamame. Toss until all the ingredients are evenly combined and coated with dressing and serve.

ENJOY: I'm having it with sparkling rosé or iced coffee.

PERFECTLY CRUMBLED CHEESE:

If your salad calls for a crumbled soft cheese like blue, feta, or fresh goat cheese, stick it in the freezer for 30 minutes, then try crumbling it by hand or with a fork. It will break apart much more easily, leave less on your hands, and be thawed by the time you Toss and Enjoy!

Tabbouleh

I first discovered tabbouleh (also spelled tabouli) when visiting a friend who grew up in Lebanon. She served it along with hummus, kabobs, and freshly made pitas. You could taste the love and passion for cooking in everything she made that day, and she was happy to share the recipe with anyone who asked. Tabbouleh dates all the way back to the Middle Ages, from somewhere in the Syrian and Lebanese mountains. I don't know how many generations this recipe was passed down, but I added a few little "extras" to make it my own. This salad is a good one to whip up on a hot summer day when unexpected guests arrive, especially if you already have herbs and tomatoes at home. Do some chopping, add a few pieces of marinated meat, seafood, or tofu on a skewer, and you're good to go.

EXPERIMENT: I love curly leaf parsley for tabbouleh. Sumac is a complex red dried herb that is used in many Middle Eastern dishes that adds a nice tang. This is one salad for which I don't soak the onion in ice water before adding it because I enjoy the bite, but feel free to soak it if you don't. In a hurry? I prepped this with the food processor one time, right before heading to the airport. Grate the onion, tomatoes, and cucumbers with the grating attachment, then transfer them to a sieve to drain. Throw the parsley and mint in with the chopping blade. Purists call it blasphemy, but it was great to have something refreshing to eat while waiting for a flight and it cleaned out the fridge—a win-win.

START OUT

2 cups (475 ml) water

1 cup (240 ml) bulgur wheat (I use Bob's Red Mill)

3 cups (720 ml) diced Roma, hothouse, or Campari tomatoes (¼-inch/6-mm pieces)

WHISK

½ cup (120 ml) extra-virgin olive oil

⅓ cup (80 ml) fresh lemon juice (remember to zest first)

1 teaspoon (5 ml) granulated sea salt

½ teaspoon (2.5 ml) ground sumac

½ teaspoon (2.5 ml) lightly packed grated lemon zest

½ teaspoon (2.5 ml) freshly cracked black pepper

TOSS

6 cups (1,400 ml) finely chopped curly parsley (3 to 4 large bunches, see Note)

3 cups (720 ml) diced seeded Persian or English cucumber (¼-inch/6-mm pieces)

¾ cup (175 ml) finely chopped fresh mint

½ cup (120 ml) finely diced red onion (¼-inch/6-mm pieces)

½ cup (120 ml) pomegranate seeds (optional)

Flaky sea salt and freshly cracked black pepper

START OUT: In a small pot, combine the water and bulgur wheat. Bring to a boil, cover, and adjust the heat so the water simmers. Cook until the bulgur is tender, about 12 minutes. Drain off any excess liquid and fluff the bulgur with a fork. Let cool. (Alternatively, follow the package cooking directions.)

Place the tomatoes in a fine mesh strainer and gently press down with a spoon to drain off excess liquid.

WHISK: In a large salad bowl, whisk together the oil, lemon juice, granulated sea salt, sumac, lemon zest, and pepper until well combined.

TOSS: In the bowl with the dressing, combine the parsley, cucumber, mint, red onion, pomegranate seeds (if using), bulgur, and tomatoes. Toss until all the ingredients are evenly combined and coated with dressing. Taste and adjust the seasoning if needed, then serve.

ENJOY: I'm having it with sauvignon blanc or iced black tea.

NOTE: Herb bunches can vary in size and intensity from season to season and farm to farm. You need a lot of parsley for this one! Err on the side of buying too much, and you can always use extra to make a parsley chimichurri dressing (see page 120) or in other dressings.

Coleslaw

Have you noticed almost every culture has some type of coleslaw recipe? With good reason: the simple sour, sweet, fatty, salty, crunch of this salad makes it so good, and it's top-notch for an outdoor barbecue. I was first introduced to this style when I helped prep for my then-boss's wedding and couldn't stop eating it. Yes, there is a good amount of sugar. You can use any sweetener you like, but substitutions won't hit quite the same. Make as many batches as you want a day ahead of time for your outdoor barbecue to go with sliders and sandwiches, or as a side for any event. It will keep for days.

START OUT

8 cups (1,900 ml) shredded green cabbage

1 tablespoon (15 ml) granulated sea salt

WHISK

1½ cups (360 ml) mayonnaise

½ cup (120 ml) grated yellow onion

½ cup (120 ml) sugar

¼ cup (60 ml) apple cider vinegar

½ teaspoon (2.5 ml) flaky sea salt

½ teaspoon (2.5 ml) freshly cracked black pepper, or to taste

START OUT: Place the shredded cabbage in a large colander, sprinkle with the granulated sea salt, and toss to distribute. Let drain for an hour, then rinse the cabbage and pat dry.

WHISK: In a large salad bowl, whisk together the mayonnaise, onion, sugar, vinegar, flaky sea salt, and pepper until well combined.

TOSS: In the bowl with the dressing, add the cabbage and toss until evenly combined and coated with dressing. Cover and refrigerate for at least an hour, or up to a few days. Drain off excess liquid right before serving.

ENJOY: I'm having it with sauvignon blanc or a cola.

EXPERIMENT: Add some red, napa, or savoy cabbage or a little grated carrot. Try mango or pineapple and cilantro to give it a tropical flavor. Shredded green apples add tang and flavor. To keep it light, try using a balsamic dressing (like the one on page 246) instead. The variations are endless but you can't go wrong with this base. If you'd like to serve the coleslaw sooner, mix the dressing and cabbage right away and season with salt to taste. Let sit for 30 minutes, drain if necessary, and serve.

American Potato Salad

Why is potato salad so controversial? In some American cultures, attendance at social gatherings is based on who is bringing the potato salad. Family recipes are specific, down to the brand, shape, and size of ingredients. It's *the* essential side dish for picnics, barbecues, and celebrations. It was first introduced to Europe by Spanish explorers in the sixteenth century. Those salads were made by boiling potatoes in wine or a mixture of vinegar and spices. The American version of potato salad is rooted in German cuisine and came to the United States with European settlers in the 1800s. This is definitely a salad that has what I call "sentimental flavors" that go deeper than the simple ingredients listed below. I remember my mom would require us to taste it to ensure it was just right. My dad would always have to try it again, and again, to "make sure," when really, he just couldn't wait to dig in. This is how I make my family's traditional potato salad.

EXPERIMENT: The original family recipe was russet potatoes and this recipe is perfectly good with them, or with other varieties you may find at your local farmers' market. Yukon golds have more of a buttery flavor and russets are a little earthy. You may have to double or triple this recipe for larger gatherings.

START OUT

Flaky sea salt

3 pounds (1.4 kg) Yukon gold potatoes, or substitute russet potatoes

6 Perfect Boiled Eggs (page 257)

WHISK

1¼ cups (300 ml) Best Foods (Hellmann's) mayonnaise

¾ cup (175 ml) finely chopped Claussen dill pickles (¼ inch/6 mm or less)

2 tablespoons (30 ml) Claussen dill pickle brine

1 tablespoon (15 ml) French's yellow mustard

1 tablespoon (15 ml) Star red wine vinegar

½ teaspoon (2.5 ml) flaky sea salt

½ teaspoon (2.5 ml) freshly cracked black pepper

TOSS

1½ cups (360 ml) diced celery (¼- to ½-inch/6-mm to 1.3-cm pieces; 4 or 5 celery stalks)

1 cup (240 ml) chopped scallions (green and white parts)

1 tablespoon (15 ml) sweet paprika

START OUT: Fill a large pot half full of water and lightly salt it. Over high heat, bring to a boil, then add the potatoes, cover, and adjust the heat so the water boils softly. Cook until the potatoes are easily pierced with a fork all the way to the center, 20 to 30 minutes. Remove the potatoes from the pot and let cool completely before peeling. Cut into 1-inch (2.5-cm) cubes. You need 6 cups (1,400 ml) for the salad (save any extra for another use).

Meanwhile, prepare the eggs, and when they're cool enough to handle, dice them or use an egg slicer, rotating the egg 90 degrees and slicing again.

WHISK: In an extra-large bowl, whisk together the mayonnaise, pickles, brine, mustard, vinegar, salt, and pepper until well combined.

TOSS: In the bowl with the dressing, add the potatoes, diced eggs, celery, and scallions. Toss until all the ingredients are evenly combined and coated with dressing. Sprinkle with paprika, cover, and refrigerate for at least 2 hours (or even better, overnight) before serving.

ENJOY: I'm having it with a pinot gris or cola.

Orzo Pasta Salad

SERVES 3 TO 4 AS A MEAL OR 8 TO 10 AS A SIDE

Not a whole grain—though it looks like one—orzo is a mini, versatile pasta that makes this easy, fun salad a crowd-pleaser. It's packed with flavor from the sun-dried tomatoes, rich olives, salty feta, and fresh herbs. It travels well, is better the second day, and keeps for a few days in the refrigerator. A departure from your usual bow tie– or fusilli-based option, it's a great one for picnics and potlucks, accompanying grilled meats or deli sandwiches. Added bonus: you can eat it with a spoon.

EXPERIMENT:
Have fun with other small pastas like ditalini. Experiment with adding other finely chopped vegetables including red or yellow bell pepper, finely diced seeded cucumbers, a little arugula, or chopped fresh spinach. Garnish with a drizzle of balsamic and more torn fresh basil leaves if you have them handy.

START OUT

Flaky sea salt

3½ cups (830 ml) orzo

1 cup (240 ml) quartered cherry tomatoes

WHISK

1 teaspoon (5 ml) pressed garlic

½ cup (120 ml) extra-virgin olive oil

¼ cup (60 ml) red wine vinegar

2 tablespoons (30 ml) finely chopped fresh flat-leaf parsley

1 tablespoon (15 ml) fresh lemon juice (remember to zest first)

1 tablespoon (15 ml) honey

2 teaspoons (10 ml) dried oregano

1 teaspoon (5 ml) lightly packed grated lemon zest

½ teaspoon (2.5 ml) red pepper flakes

Freshly cracked black pepper

TOSS

1 cup (240 ml) coarsely chopped fresh basil

1 cup (240 ml) crumbled feta cheese (see page 43)

⅔ cup (160 ml) finely chopped pitted Kalamata olives

⅔ cup (160 ml) finely chopped scallions (green and white parts)

½ cup (120 ml) drained and finely chopped oil-packed sun-dried tomatoes

Flaky sea salt (optional)

START OUT: Fill a large pot with water and generously salt it. Bring to a rolling boil, then add the orzo. Return to a boil and cook according to the package directions until al dente. Drain, lightly rinse the orzo, and let cool. Meanwhile, place the tomatoes in a colander and gently press down with a spoon to drain off excess liquid.

WHISK: Rinse the pressed garlic in a very fine mesh strainer and shake off any excess water. In a large salad bowl, combine the garlic, oil, vinegar, parsley, lemon juice, honey, oregano, lemon zest, and red pepper flakes and season with black pepper. Whisk until well combined.

TOSS: In the bowl with the dressing, add the cooked orzo, fresh tomatoes, basil, feta, olives, scallions, and sun-dried tomatoes. Toss until all the ingredients are evenly combined and coated with dressing. Taste and season with salt if necessary (it may not be with the other salty ingredients). Refrigerate for at least an hour, or up to overnight, so the pasta marinates before serving.

ENJOY: I'm having it with sauvignon blanc or Italian soda.

Vegan Cobb

Sometimes I get so excited with all the varieties of produce at the farmers' market, I forget what I came there for. That's how this colorful salad came to be. It's perfect for a hot summer day and has something for everyone. Is this your typical vegan Cobb salad with fake eggs, fake cheese, and fake bacon? No, and it's not trying to be; but if you are looking for something delicious, hydrating, and hearty this might be the one. Added bonus: you just may feel great after eating it.

EXPERIMENT:

Try a different grain: quinoa has been trending for years and there are so many other ancient grains available now. Farro has become popular and buckwheat isn't just for pancakes anymore with its rich texture and flavor. Barley is a delicious, underrated grain. Change it up: head to the bulk section and try new ones you've never had before. Stock up on all the seeds called for, or use more of what you do have at home. If you find yourself unpacking an unintended beautiful vegetable from the farmers' market like I often do . . . experiment!

START OUT

2 cups (475 ml) Roasted Tofu (page 258)

1 cup (240 ml) roasted cubed golden and red beets (see page 262; ½-inch/1.3-cm pieces)

1 cup (240 ml) cooked quinoa (see page 264)

1 cup (240 ml) blanched green beans (see page 260)

Ice water

1 tablespoon (15 ml) very finely diced shallots

1 cup (240 ml) quartered cherry tomatoes, or substitute what looks best at the market

1 small ripe plantain (yellow and just starting to brown)

2 tablespoons (30 ml) coconut oil

WHISK

½ teaspoon (2.5 ml) pressed garlic

⅓ cup (80 ml) extra-virgin olive oil

2 tablespoons (30 ml) balsamic glaze

2 tablespoons (30 ml) water

2 tablespoons (30 ml) nutritional yeast

1 tablespoon (15 ml) white miso paste

1 tablespoon (15 ml) fresh Meyer lemon juice, or substitute regular lemon juice (remember to zest first)

1 tablespoon (15 ml) whole-grain mustard

½ teaspoon (5 ml) lightly packed grated Meyer lemon zest, or substitute regular lemon zest

Flaky sea salt and freshly cracked black pepper

TOSS

4 cups (950 ml) lightly packed spring mix (baby lettuce blend)

4 cups (950 ml) lightly packed baby kale

1 cup (240 ml) cubed avocado (½-inch/1.3-cm pieces)

1 cup (240 ml) cubed cucumber (½-inch/1.3-cm pieces)

1 cup (240 ml) peeled, shaved carrot ribbons, cut into 1-inch (2.5-cm) pieces (rainbow carrots are fun)

¼ cup (60 ml) finely chopped fresh chives

¼ cup (60 ml) coarsely chopped Marcona almonds

2 tablespoons (30 ml) finely chopped fresh flat-leaf parsley

2 tablespoons (30 ml) hemp seeds

2 tablespoons (30 ml) sunflower seeds

1 tablespoon (15 ml) chia seeds

1 tablespoon (15 ml) flax seeds

START OUT: Prepare the tofu and roasted beets. Prepare the quinoa and let it cool. Blanch the green beans.

Fill a 250-ml beaker or a small glass bowl halfway with ice water and add the shallot. Soak for 10 minutes, then drain and pat the shallot dry. Place the tomatoes in a colander and gently press down with a spoon to drain off excess liquid.

Peel the plantain by cutting off both ends and cutting a slit down the side just through the peel, not the fruit. Remove the peel and cut into ¼-inch (6-mm) thick diagonal slices. Line a plate with paper towels. Heat a cast-iron skillet on medium-high heat. Add the coconut oil, and when it begins to shimmer, add the plantain slices. Fry on one side until lightly golden, about 1½ minutes, flipping the slices as they brown, then cook on the other side until golden, about 1 minute, removing the slices as they finish. Transfer to the paper towels and let cool. The plantains should turn slightly brown like really ripe bananas after frying.

WHISK: Rinse the pressed garlic in a very fine mesh strainer and shake off any excess water. In a large salad bowl, add the garlic, shallot, oil, glaze, water, nutritional yeast, miso, lemon juice, mustard, and lemon zest and season with salt and pepper. Whisk until well combined, then taste and adjust the seasoning if needed.

TOSS: In the bowl with the dressing, add the spring mix, kale, avocado, cucumber, carrots, chives, almonds, parsley, hemp seeds, sunflower seeds, chia seeds, flax seeds, tofu, beets, quinoa, green beans, plantains, and tomatoes. Toss until all the ingredients are evenly combined and coated with dressing and serve.

ENJOY: I'm having it with a yerba maté.

NOTE: Once opened, nuts and seeds can go stale or rancid quickly. Kept in an airtight container in the refrigerator, they will last up to six months. Look for ones grown in the United States.

Niçoise

Even salad history has a little controversy. The Niçoise salad was said to be inspired by locally grown ingredients (not just the olives) and created by a chef in Nice, France, named Bigot. Some reports say Jean Bigot made the dish in 1860, others say it was André Bigot in 1903, and some believe that it was created at the Hôtel de Paris Monte-Carlo in Monaco. It first appeared on menus in both Nice and Paris, and was called Salade Niçoise. Following the tradition of local ingredients, I have tweaked the classic recipe just a little and use fresh tuna instead of jarred or tinned. I do leave the pits in the traditional Niçoise olives since they're so small, but you can pit them before serving, if you like.

START OUT

3 cups (720 ml) French-Style Potato Salad (page 134)

4 Perfect Boiled Eggs (page 257)

2 cups (475 ml) French green beans, blanched (see page 260)

1¼ cups (300 ml) quartered cherry tomatoes, or substitute what looks best at the market

2 (8-ounce/225-g) sushi-grade ahi tuna steaks (see Note)

3 tablespoons (45 ml) extra-virgin olive oil

3 tablespoons (45 ml) coarsely cracked black pepper

WHISK

2 tablespoons (30 ml) fresh lemon juice

1 tablespoon (15 ml) white wine vinegar

2 teaspoons (10 ml) finely chopped fresh dill

2 teaspoons (10 ml) finely chopped fresh basil

2 teaspoons (10 ml) finely chopped fresh chives

1 teaspoon (5 ml) finely chopped fresh flat-leaf parsley

1 teaspoon (5 ml) Dijon mustard

1 teaspoon (5 ml) anchovy paste, or puréed oil-packed anchovies

Flaky sea salt and freshly cracked black pepper

¼ cup plus 2 tablespoons (90 ml) extra-virgin olive oil

TOSS

8 cups (1,900 ml) torn butter lettuce or Boston lettuce (bite-size pieces)

1 cup (240 ml) Niçoise olives

¼ cup (60 ml) drained capers

6 to 12 oil-packed anchovy fillets, for garnish (optional)

START OUT: Give yourself enough time to let the potato salad marinate for at least an hour. Prepare the eggs and when they're cool enough to handle, quarter them. Blanch the green beans. Place the tomatoes in a colander and gently press down with a spoon to drain off excess liquid.

Rinse and pat dry tuna steaks with a paper towel, then divide 1 tablespoon (15 ml) of the oil between them and coat the outside. On a shallow plate, spread out half the cracked pepper and add the tuna. Sprinkle the other half of the pepper on top of the tuna and gently press the pepper into the steaks.

Heat a well-seasoned cast-iron or other skillet over medium heat. When the pan is hot, add the remaining 2 tablespoons (30 ml) oil, then the seasoned tuna. Sear until crispy on the outside and rare and translucent in the middle, 2 to 3 minutes on each side, depending on thickness. Transfer the tuna to a plate, and let cool for 2 minutes. Slice into ½-inch- (1.3-cm-) thick strips, then cut the strips into bite-size pieces.

WHISK: In a large salad bowl, combine the lemon juice, vinegar, dill, basil, chives, parsley, mustard, and anchovy paste and season with salt and pepper. While whisking, slowly pour in the olive oil until the dressing is emulsified. Taste and adjust the seasoning if needed.

TOSS: In the bowl with the dressing, combine the lettuce, olives, capers, potato salad, eggs, green beans, and tomatoes. Toss until all the ingredients are evenly combined and coated with dressing. Top with the tuna and anchovies (if using) and serve.

ENJOY: I'm having it with rosé or lemonade.

EXPERIMENT:
I really like fresh herbs in this recipe and you can double one type in place of another if you don't want to buy all four. I adore anchovies in my salad dressing but if anchovies are not appealing or you don't do fish, add a teaspoon of finely chopped capers to the dressing instead, and make a vegan chickpea-based "tuna" salad. Use your favorite olive or try something new if you can't get Niçoise olives.

NOTE: Because the tuna is just barely cooked, I use the highest-quality I can buy: sushi-grade. If you can't find sushi-grade fish near you, choose frozen ahi tuna over something from the case at your grocery store, which has probably been frozen and thawed at least once already.

Caesar

SERVES 4 AS A MEAL OR 6 TO 8 AS A SIDE

One night in Prohibition-era Tijuana, Mexico, Caesar Cardini was running out of food in his kitchen and created the first "celebrity salad" (it was rumored some of the clientele he needed to serve were from Hollywood) with whatever he could find—and people have been obsessed with it ever since. I do not consider myself a picky eater, but I have to admit, I like my Caesar with freshly made croutons that are crunchy on the outside, soft in the middle, and made from crusty sourdough. Anchovies, garlic, lemon zest, and egg yolk in the dressing are a must. No bland, Caesar-flavored mayonnaise "sauce" for me. Fresh, finely grated, high-quality Parmigiano-Reggiano cheese imported from Italy. Fresh crisp romaine or baby gem without any brown edges, pink ends, or big white stem hunks that someone let slip by. I make the waiter regret saying "tell me when" as I give them an arm workout cracking pepper over the top. Here is my version of the classic Caesar.

START OUT

4 cups (950 ml) Sourdough Garlic Croutons (page 235)

Caesar Dressing (page 243)

TOSS

Ice water

8 cups (1,900 ml) chopped romaine lettuce or baby gem lettuce (1-inch/2.5-cm strips), thick stems removed

1½ cups (360 ml) freshly grated Parmigiano-Reggiano (use a Microplane)

4 anchovy fillets packed in oil, for serving (optional)

Freshly cracked black pepper (use your peppermill!)

START OUT: Prepare the croutons and let them cool. Prepare the dressing.

TOSS: Fill a large bowl with ice water, add the lettuce, and soak it for 10 minutes for extra-crisp pieces. Drain and thoroughly dry.

In a large beautiful wooden salad bowl, add half the dressing, the lettuce, croutons, and ½ cup (120 ml) of the cheese. Toss until all the ingredients are evenly combined and coated with dressing. Taste and add more dressing if you like. Top with the anchovies (if using) and serve, passing a pepper mill and a bowl of the remaining 1 cup (240 ml) cheese at the table.

ENJOY: I'm having it with a buttery chardonnay and/or sparkling water.

EXPERIMENT: Pecorino Romano cheese is a good substitute for Parmigiano-Reggiano if you have it handy. Fresh lime juice and zest are also fabulous for this recipe. This is a great pantry salad. With Dijon, extra-virgin olive oil, anchovies, balsamic, and red wine vinegar in the cupboard, a loaf of sourdough, lemons, and fresh garlic on the counter, and a head of lettuce and eggs in the fridge, you're good to go anytime someone unexpectedly comes by. Pour them a drink and you can whip this up, but cut back on the garlic if you're looking for a romantic interlude.

58   THE SALAD LAB

Kale Salad

This polarizing green has become the "it" salad and is found on many restaurant menus. Kale is not just for green smoothies and low-calorie kale chips anymore. It's been consumed since Roman times. Ancient Greeks were said to boil it and use it as a cure for drunkenness (apparently, it's always been a health food). My first experience with kale was in the Netherlands, my spouse's homeland, where they boiled it (to death) with potatoes and smoked sausage. Lacinato kale, otherwise known as Tuscan or dinosaur (or dino) kale, has a deeper green color and is slightly thinner and more tender than curly kale, making it more versatile and my favorite variety.

EXPERIMENT:

As kale has become popular, more varieties are available. If you are just discovering kale or "want to like it," experiment with baby kale. It's easy to clean, requires no prepping or chopping, and is tender and lighter in flavor. Other varieties like Tuscan and curly kales are now readily available in different colors and varieties year-round nationwide. If you don't like the chewy texture, shred it or chop it into tiny pieces and let it sit in the dressing for longer. It's easy to grow: try it in your garden or in a pot on your porch, and pick some leaves after the first frost when it's sweetest.

START OUT

2 cups (475 ml) cooked quinoa (see page 264)

1 cup (240 ml) quartered cherry tomatoes, or substitute what looks best at the market

½ cup (120 ml) coarsely chopped, toasted (see page 257) pecans

Ice water

4 large eggs

WHISK

2 teaspoons (10 ml) pressed garlic

½ cup (120 ml) extra-virgin olive oil

⅓ cup (80 ml) sour cream

2 tablespoons (30 ml) fresh lemon juice or Meyer lemon juice (remember to zest first)

1 heaping tablespoon (20 ml) lightly packed grated lemon zest or Meyer lemon zest

1 tablespoon (15 ml) honey

2 teaspoons (10 ml) Dijon mustard

1 teaspoon (5 ml) flaky sea salt

½ teaspoon (2.5 ml) freshly cracked black pepper

TOSS

8 cups (1,900 ml) thinly sliced lacinato or curly kale, ribs removed

1 cup (240 ml) diced rotisserie chicken breast, skin removed (¼-inch/6-mm pieces)

1 cup (240 ml) diced seeded English or Persian cucumbers (¼-inch/6-mm pieces)

1 cup (240 ml) crumbled feta cheese (see page 43)

¼ cup (60 ml) drained small capers

START OUT: Prepare the quinoa and let it cool. Place the tomatoes in a colander and gently press down with a spoon to drain off excess liquid. Toast the nuts.

Meanwhile, fill a small pot halfway with water and bring to a boil. Fill a medium bowl with ice water. Gently lower the eggs into the boiling water. Once the pot returns to a boil, adjust the heat so the water simmers, cover, and cook for 11 minutes (10 minutes if the eggs were room temperature). Remove with a slotted spoon and transfer to the ice bath to cool before peeling and rinsing. Finely grate the eggs.

WHISK: Rinse the pressed garlic in a very fine mesh strainer and shake off any excess water. In

a large salad bowl, whisk together the garlic, oil, sour cream, lemon juice, zest, honey, mustard, salt, and pepper until well combined.

TOSS: Add the kale to the bowl with the dressing. Use clean hands (or rubber gloves) and massage the kale briefly to soften the leaves and infuse them with the dressing. Let sit for about 10 minutes.

In the bowl with the dressed kale, add the chicken, cucumber, feta, capers, quinoa, eggs, pecans, and tomatoes. Toss until all the ingredients are evenly combined and coated with dressing and serve. (Any refrigerated leftovers are even better the next day.)

ENJOY: I'm having it with a brut sparkling wine or iced black tea.

Not-So-Chinese Chicken Salad

SERVES 4 AS A MEAL OR 6 TO 8 AS A SIDE

"Chinese Chicken Salad" was probably my favorite salad in high school. It was crammed full of shredded iceberg, finely diced chicken, crispy rice noodles, and cilantro and smothered in a light dressing. We could never quite figure out what was in that dressing but it had a little kick. The restaurant I ordered it from is long gone, but the memory of that salad is forever in my brain. This is my "Adult" version, inspired by those memories.

START OUT

2 teaspoons (10 ml) Roasted Garlic Purée (page 256)

¾ cup (175 ml) avocado oil

3 ounces (85 g) rice vermicelli noodles (sometimes called rice sticks)

2 cups (475 ml) cubed Grilled Chicken Breast (½-inch/1.3-cm pieces; page 258)

¼ cup (60 ml) sliced almonds, toasted (see page 257)

2 tablespoons (30 ml) white sesame seeds, toasted (see Note) and/or black sesame seeds

WHISK

3 tablespoons (45 ml) hot water

2 tablespoons (30 ml) sugar, or substitute sweetener of choice

¼ cup (60 ml) avocado oil

3 tablespoons (45 ml) fresh tangerine juice

2 tablespoons (30 ml) rice vinegar

1 tablespoon (15 ml) plum sauce

1 tablespoon (15 ml) toasted sesame oil

1 teaspoon (5 ml) white or red miso

1 teaspoon (5 ml) grated fresh ginger

¼ teaspoon (1.5 ml) ground white pepper

Flaky sea salt

TOSS

4 cups (950 ml) thinly sliced iceberg lettuce

4 cups (950 ml) thinly sliced napa cabbage

1½ cups (360 ml) mandarin orange segments

1 cup (240 ml) peeled and shredded carrots

1 cup (240 ml) diced mixed yellow and red bell pepper (¼-inch/6-mm pieces)

½ cup (120 ml) chopped scallions (green and white parts)

½ cup (120 ml) finely chopped fresh cilantro

EXPERIMENT: If you have the cilantro "soap" gene, substitute parsley. Substitutions for dressing ingredients include orange juice for tangerine juice and black pepper for white pepper.

NOTE: You can purchase pre-toasted sesame seeds and save yourself a few minutes, but the flavor won't be as good. If you've purchased roasted nuts, I recommend toasting them again to really help their flavor shine. See page 257 for toasting instructions.

START OUT: Prepare the roasted garlic purée for the dressing (up to 3 days in advance).

Heat the oil in a small saucepan over medium-high heat until it reaches 350°F (175°C) or starts to shimmer. Line a plate with paper towels. Break apart the vermicelli into small pieces that will easily fit in the pan.

Gently place a few pieces of rice noodle into the oil. They should start to bubble and puff up almost immediately; they will quickly quadruple in size. Remove the noodles with tongs and place on the paper towels. Repeat with the remaining noodles in small batches. When they're cool enough to

handle, crumble them into 1-inch (2.5 cm) pieces. Measure 2 cups (475 ml) for the salad, and if you like, reserve any extra for garnish. Prepare the chicken. Toast the almonds and white sesame seeds (black sesame seeds don't need to be toasted).

WHISK: In a small bowl, whisk the hot water and sugar until dissolved. In a large salad bowl, add the sugar mixture, roasted garlic purée, avocado oil, tangerine juice, vinegar, plum sauce, sesame oil, miso, ginger, and pepper and season with salt. Whisk until well combined, then taste and adjust the seasoning if needed.

TOSS: In the bowl with the dressing, add the lettuce, cabbage, mandarins, carrots, bell pepper, scallions, cilantro, chicken, almonds, sesame seeds, and fried noodles. Toss until all the ingredients are evenly combined and coated with dressing. Garnish with the extra rice noodles (if using) and serve.

ENJOY: I'm having it with sparkling wine (now) or diet lemon-lime soda (in high school . . . or did I get that reversed?).

Wedge

I think iceberg lettuce gets a bad rap. If you think about it, we all use it in our hamburgers, tacos, and lettuce cups without complaint. Historically, it was the only lettuce available at your local grocery store, and it had a long shelf life (even if it turned bitter and brown). I don't know if it is due to faster delivery to market, greenhouse growing, or genetic manipulation, but today you can find crisp, flavorful, brilliantly green heads of iceberg that can compete with spring mix and romaine (maybe not my favorite baby gem lettuce). The Wedge salad made its debut in 1920s steakhouses and is popping up on menus everywhere because it still goes great with a steak. Warning: if you are looking for a low-fat or low-calorie salad, this is not it.

EXPERIMENT:
You either love blue cheese or you don't. There doesn't seem to be an in-between. Point Reyes makes a stellar blue cheese that's available nationwide. This salad (and dressing) is wonderful with Gorgonzola, feta, or grated extra-sharp cheddar. Ranch dressing is fab too; experiment! I always say, "Use any greens you like." Great substitutes for iceberg are butter (Boston) lettuce or gem lettuce. No matter how you experiment, use your knife and fork for this one.

START OUT

1 cup (240 ml) Sourdough Garlic Croutons (page 235)

1 cup (240 ml) Chopped Bacon (use thick-cut; page 258)

4 Perfect Boiled Eggs (page 257)

1 cup (240 ml) quartered cherry tomatoes, or substitute what looks best at the market

1 tablespoon (15 ml) very finely diced shallot

1 tablespoon (15 ml) red wine vinegar

WHISK

⅓ cup (80 ml) crumbled blue cheese (see page 43)

¼ cup (60 ml) buttermilk

¼ cup (60 ml) extra-virgin olive oil

3 tablespoons (45 ml) finely chopped fresh chives

2 tablespoons (30 ml) mayonnaise, or substitute nonfat Greek yogurt

1 tablespoon (15 ml) fresh lemon juice

1 tablespoon (15 ml) finely chopped fresh dill

1 tablespoon (15 ml) red wine vinegar

1 teaspoon (5 ml) hot sauce

½ teaspoon (2.5 ml) Worcestershire sauce

½ teaspoon (2.5 ml) flaky sea salt

½ teaspoon (2.5 ml) freshly cracked black pepper

TOSS

1 large head of iceberg lettuce

⅓ cup (80 ml) crumbled blue cheese

¼ cup (60 ml) finely chopped fresh chives

¼ cup (60 ml) finely chopped fresh flat-leaf parsley

START OUT: Prepare the croutons and let cool. Place them in a freezer bag, seal, and gently crush the croutons with a rolling pin or back of a skillet into ¼- to ½-inch (6-mm to 1.3-cm) pieces.

Prepare the bacon. Prepare the eggs and when they're cool, coarsely chop them.

In a small bowl, combine the cherry tomatoes, shallot, and vinegar and set aside to macerate.

WHISK: In a small glass bowl or large beaker (if using an immersion blender), combine the blue cheese, buttermilk, oil, chives, mayonnaise, lemon juice, dill, vinegar, hot sauce, Worcestershire sauce, salt, and pepper. Mix with a whisk, or use an immersion blender if you don't like the chunks of blue cheese, until well combined.

TOSS: On a large cutting board, trim the stem off the head of iceberg lettuce, keeping the core intact. Cut the head vertically into 4 to 8 wedges (depending on how many people you're serving) and gently rinse, drain, and dry with a clean dish towel or paper towel.

Drain any liquid off the tomatoes right before serving.

Pour ¼ cup (60 ml) of the dressing on the bottom of a large salad bowl. (You can also plate the salad individually by dividing the dressing equally among the serving plates.) Gently place the iceberg wedges on top and drizzle over the remaining dressing (or to taste), which helps the rest of the ingredients stick to the wedge. Next sprinkle the crushed croutons, bacon, eggs, drained tomato mixture, cheese, chives, and parsley on top, then serve.

ENJOY: I'm having it with a pinot noir or lemonade.

Chopped Salad

I didn't have my first chopped salad until my senior year of college, when my now-husband took me to my first fine French dining experience. It was also the first time I had a really good bottle of wine, but that story is for another time. This chopped salad may even be what sparked my original interest in re-creating something I had while dining out. Still one of my favorites salads to make, it will take a little wrist action. I prefer this creamy, lemony vinaigrette that pairs well with the blue cheese, but you can choose the Blue Cheese Dressing (page 245) or any other in the last chapter if you like. The key to this salad is chopping everything so fine that you could eat it with a spoon.

EXPERIMENT:
Sharpen your knife before this one because there is *a lot* of chopping. If you don't like blue cheese, you can always substitute feta or sharp cheddar. As always, add dressing to taste if you prefer a lighter touch.

START OUT

3 Perfect Boiled Eggs (page 257)

⅓ cup (80 ml) Chopped Bacon (page 258)

Ice water

⅓ cup (80 ml) finely chopped red onion (¼- to ½-inch/6-mm to 1.3-cm pieces)

1½ cups (360 ml) finely chopped Roma or beefsteak tomatoes (¼- to ½-inch/6-mm to 1.3-cm pieces)

WHISK

¼ cup (60 ml) extra-virgin olive oil

3 tablespoons (45 ml) crème fraîche or heavy whipping cream

2 tablespoons (30 ml) white wine vinegar

2 tablespoons (30 ml) finely chopped fresh flat-leaf parsley

2 teaspoons (10 ml) fresh lemon juice (remember to zest first)

2 teaspoons (10 ml) Dijon mustard

2 teaspoons (10 ml) honey

¼ teaspoon (1.5 ml) lightly packed grated lemon zest

Flaky sea salt and freshly cracked black pepper

TOSS

6 cups (1,400 ml) finely chopped romaine lettuce (¼- to ½-inch/6-mm to 1.3-cm pieces)

1½ cups (360 ml) finely chopped seeded Persian or English cucumber (¼- to ½-inch/6-mm to 1.3-cm pieces)

1 cup (240 ml) finely chopped avocado (¼- to ½-inch/6-mm to 1.3-cm pieces)

⅓ cup (80 ml) finely crumbled Roquefort, Gorgonzola, or other blue cheese (¼- to ½-inch/6-mm to 1.3-cm pieces; see page 43)

START OUT: Prepare the eggs and when they're cool enough to handle, finely chop them into ¼- to ½-inch (6-mm to 1.3-cm) pieces. Prepare the bacon and let it drain.

Fill a 500-ml beaker or a small glass bowl halfway with ice water and add the onion. Soak for 10 minutes, then drain and pat the onion dry. Meanwhile, place the tomatoes in a colander and gently press down with a spoon to drain off excess liquid.

WHISK: In a large salad bowl, combine the oil, crème fraîche, vinegar, parsley, lemon juice, mustard, honey, and lemon zest and season with salt and pepper. Whisk until well combined, then taste and adjust the seasoning if needed.

TOSS: In the bowl with the dressing, combine the lettuce, cucumber, avocado, cheese, onion, tomato, eggs, and bacon. Toss until all the ingredients are evenly combined and coated with dressing and serve.

ENJOY: I'm having it with an Haut-Médoc or mineral water.

The Original Cobb Salad

Chop up a few vegetables in the same size, throw in some bacon and blue cheese, and you've got yourself a "Cobb" salad. The original salad was from the Brown Derby chain of restaurants in Los Angeles, known for its iconic buildings that were built in the shape of an actual hat, or derby, and frequented by many Hollywood celebrities of the time (the Shirley Temple mocktail may have been invented there, too). Legend has it that in the 1930s late one night, manager Robert "Bob" Cobb opened up the refrigerator and took what he could find to make this salad for himself, the staff, and his buddy Sid Grauman. Sid, the owner of the famous Grauman Theater (now the TCL Chinese Theater) in Hollywood, loved it so much he came back the next day and demanded to have the "Cobb" salad. And the rest is history. When in doubt, if a restaurant menu only has the standard classic salads, I usually order the Cobb. With its avocado, bacon, and cheese, the Cobb contains the "holy trinity" of salad ingredients.

EXPERIMENT:
Like the original that was made with whatever Bob Cobb had on hand that evening, experiment with what's already in your refrigerator. For protein, try leftover rotisserie chicken, vegan chicken, turkey, ham, or shrimp. I have even seen it made with lobster. Only have a block of cheddar? Shred it! You get the idea.

START OUT

2 cups (475 ml) cubed Grilled Chicken Breast (½-inch/1.3-cm pieces; page 258)

¾ cup (175 ml) Chopped Bacon (use thick-cut; page 258)

4 Perfect Boiled Eggs (page 257)

1 cup (240 ml) chopped beefsteak or Roma tomatoes (½-inch/1.3-cm pieces)

WHISK

½ teaspoon (2.5 ml) pressed garlic

⅓ cup (80 ml) extra-virgin olive oil

3 tablespoons (45 ml) red wine vinegar

1 tablespoon (15 ml) fresh lemon juice

1 tablespoon (15 ml) sugar

2 teaspoons (10 ml) Dijon mustard

1 teaspoon (5 ml) Worcestershire sauce

Flaky sea salt and freshly cracked black pepper

TOSS

4 cups (950 ml) torn romaine lettuce (bite-size pieces)

4 cups (950 ml) torn iceberg lettuce (bite-size pieces)

1 cup (240 ml) cubed avocado (½-inch/1.3-cm pieces)

1 cup (240 ml) crumbled domestic blue or Roquefort cheese (see page 43)

¼ cup (60 ml) finely chopped fresh chives, for serving

2 tablespoons (30 ml) finely chopped fresh flat-leaf parsley, for serving

START OUT: Prepare the chicken and the bacon and let them cool. Cook the eggs and when they are cool enough to handle, quarter them. Meanwhile, place the tomatoes in a colander and gently press down with a spoon to drain off excess liquid.

WHISK: Rinse the pressed garlic in a very fine mesh strainer and shake off any excess water. In a large salad bowl, add the garlic, oil, vinegar, lemon juice, sugar, mustard, and Worcestershire and season with salt and pepper. Whisk until well combined, then taste and adjust the seasoning if needed.

TOSS: In the bowl with the dressing, add the romaine lettuce, iceberg lettuce, avocado, cheese, tomatoes, chicken, bacon, and eggs. Toss until all the ingredients are evenly combined and coated with dressing. Sprinkle the chives and parsley over the top and serve.

ENJOY: I'm having it with a glass of red table wine or a Shirley Temple, of course.

First Lady's
Spring Pea
Salad with
Asparagus
and Pea
Shoots
(page 74)

Celebrity-
Inspired
Favorites

Supermodel's Arugula Salad

We *love* our celebrity salads—they are the most frequently requested. Once in a while I'm lucky and a celebrity will post their favorite, an agent will answer my email, or a salad will appear in a "what I eat in a day" video and I will get tagged or DMed. When one comes across my feed, I rush off to the market to quickly hop on the viral tsunami. Unfortunately, I discover most of them in the evening, sometimes pretty late into the night. So there I am with an armful of produce in the checkout line surrounded by people with cartons of ice cream or bottles of alcohol. I love what I do. This recipe inspired by Bella Hadid is one of my most-viewed videos and she even follows me now. Crazy. Her salad is simply impressive; I love it.

EXPERIMENT:
I love to say "Experiment with what you have," especially if it will save you a last-minute trip to the market. If you already have something similar, especially if it is not of a wildly different flavor profile, use it. Limes for lemon in a dressing, Romano or Mexican Cotija for Parmigiano-Reggiano.

WHISK	TOSS	
½ cup (120 ml) extra-virgin olive oil	8 cups (1,900 ml) lightly packed arugula	1 cup (240 ml) crumbled Parmigiano-Reggiano (pea-size pieces; see Note)
¼ cup (60 ml) balsamic glaze	2 cups (475 ml) diced red bell pepper (¼-inch/6-mm pieces)	
3 tablespoons (45 ml) fresh lemon juice	2 cups (475 ml) cubed Persian cucumber (½-inch/1.3-cm pieces)	
½ teaspoon (2.5 ml) flaky sea salt	1 cup (240 ml) cubed avocado (½-inch/1.3-cm pieces)	
½ teaspoon (2.5 ml) freshly cracked black pepper		

WHISK: In a beautiful extra-large salad bowl, whisk together the oil, balsamic glaze, lemon juice, salt, and pepper until well combined.

TOSS: In the bowl with the dressing, add the arugula, bell pepper, cucumber, avocado, and cheese. Toss until all the ingredients are evenly combined and coated with dressing and serve.

ENJOY: I'm having it with one of Bella's Kin Euphorics spritzers.

NOTE: Just like wines, both "Parmigiano-Reggiano" and "Pecorino Romano" are protected designations of origin (PDO) for cheeses produced in the Italian provinces under Italian and European law. Outside the European Union, the name Parmesan can legally be used for the cheese you often see at U.S. grocery stores or pizza parlors. I usually say buy local, but for this salad—and every salad you're able to—I recommend the real Parmigiano-Reggiano from Italy. Buy a wedge and crumble/grate/shave it yourself. You lose a lot of flavor when you buy pre-shredded or shaved cheeses.

First Lady's Spring Pea Salad with Asparagus and Pea Shoots

SERVES 6 TO 8 AS A SIDE

This recipe is inspired by one from Michelle Obama's cookbook *American Grown*, dedicated to cooking fresh and healthy food, most of which was grown in the White House gardens during the Obamas' two terms there. I love experimenting with a vegetable and emulsifying it into the dressing. It gives the same flavor profile in a different texture. With fresh peas right in the dressing, this salad tastes like spring! It's got the season's all-stars like leeks, pea shoots, and—my addition—asparagus, in a bright green salad that's a perfect side for an April dinner. It's springtime on a plate, and it comes together in minutes.

START OUT

10 cups (2,400 ml) water

1 teaspoon (5 ml) granulated sea salt

Ice water

5½ cups (1,320 ml) fresh shelled green peas, or substitute frozen petite peas

1 cup (240 ml) chopped asparagus (1-inch/2.5-cm pieces), woody ends removed

1 cup (240 ml) shaved leek, white part only (see Note; a food processor is helpful)

2 tablespoons (30 ml) very finely diced shallot

WHISK

¼ cup (60 ml) extra-virgin olive oil

3 tablespoons (45 ml) fresh lemon juice or Meyer lemon juice (remember to zest first)

1 teaspoon (5 ml) lightly packed grated lemon zest or Meyer lemon zest

½ teaspoon (2.5 ml) flaky sea salt

½ teaspoon (2.5 ml) freshly cracked black pepper

TOSS

½ cup (120 ml) finely chopped fresh mint

1 cup (240 ml) lightly packed pea shoots (optional)

Flaky sea salt, for serving

Lemon wedges, for serving

EXPERIMENT: This salad is best with fresh peas in the spring but frozen petite peas are great the rest of the year. Experiment with snow peas in place of asparagus for a refreshingly sweeter version or fresh dill or parsley in place of the mint. Mint, depending on the variety and season, can vary in flavor. Try to taste all your ingredients before adding them to a salad, especially herbs. When substituting fresh herbs with dried, use only a third of the amount called for and prepare the dressing at least half an hour ahead of time and up to overnight so that the flavors can develop.

START OUT: In a large pot, combine the water and granulated sea salt and bring to a boil. Meanwhile, fill 1 large bowl and 1 small bowl three-quarters full with ice water.

When the water boils, add the peas and blanch, stirring occasionally, until the peas turn bright green, about 90 seconds. Immediately remove the peas with a slotted spoon and drop them into the large bowl of ice water. In the same pot of boiling water, add the asparagus and blanch, stirring occasionally, until bright green, about 3 minutes. Quickly remove the asparagus with the slotted spoon and drop them into the small bowl of ice water. When the vegetables are cool, strain them separately.

Refill the small bowl halfway with ice water and add the leek and shallot. Soak for 10 minutes, then drain and pat the leek and shallot dry.

WHISK: In a blender or beaker (if using an immersion blender), add ½ cup (120 ml) of the blanched peas, the oil, lemon juice, lemon zest, flaky sea salt, and pepper. Purée until smooth.

TOSS: In a large salad bowl, add the remaining blanched peas, the asparagus, leek, shallot, mint, and pea shoots (if using) and drizzle with dressing to taste. Toss until all the ingredients are evenly combined and coated with dressing. The salad can be refrigerated for up to 3 days, which gives the vegetables a chance to marinate. Before serving, garnish with a sprinkle of flaky sea salt and lemon wedges on the side.

ENJOY: I'm having it with a big glass of water, in honor of Mrs. Obama's Drink Up efforts to get children to drink more water.

NOTE: Leeks are an underrated vegetable with a fresh light onion flavor, but they are notorious for being full of hard-to-remove sand and dirt. If you cut them lengthwise almost to the root and submerge them in water for a few minutes and then run them under water while rubbing each layer where the green meets the white, you can usually remove all the grit. It's worth the effort.

Controversial
Fake Cobb Salad

SERVES 4 TO 6 AS A MEAL OR 8 AS A SIDE

This salad went viral when hundreds were inspired by what we all thought was the salad the female cast of *Friends* ate every day for ten years. It all started in a *Los Angeles Times* interview in 2010 when Courtney Cox reported it was a "Cobb salad doctored up by Jennifer Aniston with turkey bacon and chickpeas." The problem was that when the gossip and fashion magazine articles ran with the news, they took liberties with the mysterious salad's ingredients. In 2021, HBO Max broadcasted a *Friends* reunion, and the salad had a resurgence on social media. I felt like it had been done, but when my friends asked me to make it for a girls' weekend, I filmed and posted it. Six months later, when *Allure* magazine asked if they could use one of my videos in an article, I said sure and didn't think anything of it. I could never have imagined that Ms. Aniston, my long-time favorite actress, would be reviewing it, calling it "gorgeous"—but it was not the salad she had eaten on set for a decade. Despite the fact that a generic canteen Cobb was the real salad, everyone loved this one, including Ms. Aniston herself—just no chickpeas for Jen.

EXPERIMENT:
I used basil in place of mint for the video and it was fab. Other grains or pastas this recipe works well with are quinoa, farro, orzo, and pearl couscous. If chickpeas bother your tummy, like they do Jen's, skip them, or experiment with cannellini beans instead.

START OUT

4 cups (950 ml) water

2 cups (475 ml) bulgur wheat (I use Bob's Red Mill)

Ice water

¾ cup (175 ml) diced red onion (¼-inch/6-mm pieces)

½ cup (120 ml) coarsely chopped, toasted (see page 257) pistachios

WHISK

⅓ cup (80 ml) extra-virgin olive oil

¼ cup (60 ml) fresh lemon juice

½ teaspoon (2.5 ml) flaky sea salt

½ teaspoon (2.5 ml) freshly cracked black pepper

TOSS

2 cups (475 ml) seeded, halved lengthwise, and sliced English cucumber

1 cup (240 ml) cooked or rinsed and drained canned chickpeas

1 cup (240 ml) crumbled feta cheese (see page 43)

¾ cup (175 ml) finely chopped fresh flat-leaf parsley

½ cup (120 ml) finely chopped fresh mint

START OUT: In a small pot, combine the water and bulgur. Bring to a boil, cover, and adjust the heat so the water simmers. Cook until the bulgur is tender, about 12 minutes. Drain off any excess liquid and fluff the bulgur with a fork. (Alternatively, follow the package cooking directions.) Let cool.

Fill a 500-ml beaker or a small glass bowl halfway with ice water and add the onion. Soak for 10 minutes, then drain and pat the onion dry. Toast the nuts.

WHISK: In a large salad bowl, whisk together the oil, lemon juice, salt, and pepper until well combined.

TOSS: In the bowl with the dressing, combine the bulgur wheat, onion, pistachios, cucumber, chickpeas, cheese, parsley, and mint. Toss until all the ingredients are evenly combined and coated with dressing and serve.

ENJOY: I'm having it with chardonnay or water.

Famous Sisters-with-a-K's Favorite

SERVES 4 AS A MEAL OR 6 TO 8 AS A SIDE

This is the salad that put me on the map. When I started my "30 days of famous salads" on TikTok, this was *the* most requested salad. Soon I discovered "How to make the Kardashian famous salad" was the most googled thing about them that year. Looking back, my video was a little rough and I didn't even show how to make the dressing. I've come so far! And now I get invited to their media events and have worked with Health Nut (the maker of the original salad I was inspired by). Reality really is better than fiction sometimes. I think they have moved on from this salad, but it is still a light, simple, easy one to make.

EXPERIMENT: The original recipe uses soy oil (not a favorite in some circles), granulated dried spices, and dried herbs. I spoke to Health Nut's marketing people, and they are working with laboratories to switch to a different oil but are struggling to find one that works and will make everyone happy. Maybe it is too hard to preserve fresh herbs in bottles with other ingredients or it is not economically viable? If you're making the dressing at home, I find avocado oil and fresh spices do not change the flavor of the dressing much and you don't have to compromise on quality ingredients.

START OUT

1 gallon (3,800 ml) water

2 boneless skinless chicken breasts (about 1¼ pounds/565 g)

¼ cup (60 ml) halved and sliced yellow onion

1 tablespoon (15 ml) sliced ginger

1 tablespoon (15 ml) pressed garlic

1 teaspoon (5 ml) granulated sea salt

2 tablespoons (30 ml) avocado oil

1 cup (240 ml) store-bought dry chow mein noodles

1 tablespoon (15 ml) sesame seeds, toasted (see page 257)

WHISK

1 teaspoon (5 ml) pressed garlic

¼ cup (60 ml) avocado oil

¼ cup (60 ml) water

3 tablespoons (45 ml) apple cider vinegar

2 tablespoons (30 ml) sugar

1 tablespoon (15 ml) low-sodium soy sauce

2 teaspoons (10 ml) toasted sesame oil

1 teaspoon (5 ml) grated fresh ginger

1 teaspoon (5 ml) onion powder

1 teaspoon (5 ml) flaky sea salt

TOSS

4 cups (950 ml) torn romaine lettuce (bite-size pieces)

4 cups (950 ml) torn iceberg lettuce (bite-size pieces)

2 cups (475 ml) peeled and shredded carrots

1½ cups (360 ml) thinly sliced English cucumber (optional)

⅓ cup (80 ml) julienned pickled ginger

START OUT: In a medium pot, bring the water to a boil on high heat. Add the chicken breast, onion, ginger, garlic, and granulated sea salt. Adjust the heat so the water is at a slow sim-

mer and cover. Cook until the chicken reaches an internal temperature of 165°F (75°C) on an instant-read thermometer, 15 to 20 minutes. Transfer the chicken to a plate to cool completely, then shred into 2-inch- (5-cm-) long pieces with a fork.

Heat the oil in a small skillet over medium heat. Line a plate with paper towels. When the oil is hot, add the noodles and fry, stirring occasionally, until they're a deeper shade of golden brown, 1 to 2 minutes. Transfer to the plate with a slotted spoon and let drain. Toast the sesame seeds for the dressing.

WHISK: Rinse the pressed garlic in a very fine mesh strainer and shake off any excess water. In a large salad bowl, whisk together the garlic, toasted sesame seeds, avocado oil, water, vinegar, sugar, soy sauce, sesame oil, ginger, onion powder, and flaky sea salt until well combined and the sugar is dissolved.

TOSS: In the bowl with the dressing, combine the romaine lettuce, iceberg lettuce, carrots, cucumber (if using), pickled ginger, shredded chicken, and noodles. Toss until all the ingredients are evenly combined and coated with dressing and serve.

ENJOY: I'm having it with strawberry lemonade or water.

My First Celebrity's Creamy, Lemony Cobb

SERVES 4 AS A MEAL OR 6 TO 8 AS A SIDE

This is one of my favorite salads and a fan favorite; everyone loves the creamy, lemony dressing. One day I was scrolling and happened across a clip of an interview with Elle Fanning in which she mentioned her secret TikTok account. Being a huge fan, I went to follow her and discovered I was one of only twenty-eight people she followed! I DMed her and she responded right away with her favorite restaurant order (sadly, the restaurant is no longer in business, so I had to get my inspiration from her description). The power of social media!

EXPERIMENT: Meyer lemon is a citrus hybrid that's not as tart as a regular lemon; it's a little sweeter and richer. Meyer lemons are becoming more popular, and you can find them at your local grocery stores periodically, especially during the winter. I highly recommend making this dressing with Meyer lemon juice. If you can find no-nitrate applewood smoked bacon, give it a try. Don't be afraid to step outside the box, you never know where it will take you. Ms. Fanning is not a fan of tomatoes, but if you are, go for it and add some.

START OUT

1½ cups (360 ml) cubed or sliced Grilled Chicken Breast (½-inch/1.3-cm pieces; page 258)

¾ cup (175 ml) Chopped Bacon (use applewood bacon if possible; page 258)

4 Perfect Boiled Eggs (page 257)

WHISK

2 teaspoons (10 ml) pressed garlic

½ cup (120 ml) extra-virgin olive oil

⅓ cup (80 ml) sour cream

2 tablespoons (30 ml) fresh Meyer lemon juice (remember to zest first)

1 heaping tablespoon (20 ml) lightly packed grated Meyer lemon zest

1 tablespoon (15 ml) honey

2 teaspoons (10 ml) Dijon mustard

½ teaspoon (2.5 ml) flaky sea salt

½ teaspoon (2.5 ml) freshly cracked black pepper

TOSS

8 cups (1,900 ml) sliced romaine lettuce, gem lettuce, or a mix (bite-size pieces)

1 cup (240 ml) cubed avocado (½-inch/1.3-cm pieces)

½ cup (120 ml) crumbled blue cheese (see page 43)

¼ cup (60 ml) finely chopped fresh chives

START OUT: Prepare the chicken and bacon and let them cool slightly. Prepare the eggs, and when they're cool enough to handle, chop them.

WHISK: Rinse the pressed garlic in a very fine mesh strainer and shake off any excess water. In a large salad bowl, whisk together the garlic, oil, sour cream, lemon juice, lemon zest, honey, mustard, salt, and pepper until well combined.

TOSS: In the bowl with the dressing, add the lettuce, avocado, blue cheese, chives, chicken, bacon, and eggs. Toss until all the ingredients are evenly combined and coated with dressing and serve.

ENJOY: I'm having it with Elle's favorite drink, Sofia Rosé from Francis Ford Coppola Winery.

Viral Sesame Chicken

SERVES 4 AS A LIGHT MEAL OR 6 TO 8 AS A SIDE

This is my most popular salad posted to date. I was scrolling through TikTok one day, as I do, and Kylie Jenner posted a "What I eat in a day" video that included a salad. I screenshot it, went to the market, let my inspiration run wild, and the rest is history. If it had a different title, I think people would still love it. Looking back at the rave reviews of this salad, it makes me giggle: "This dressing is so good, you could put it on a flip-flop and it would still be delicious." Yes, what they said. The dressing in this salad is a staple and one of my go-tos.

EXPERIMENT: If you can't find black sesame seeds, double the white seeds. Substitute thinly sliced curly kale for the lettuce and peanuts for almonds and you have another fab combination. Have some extra tangerines? Add them. This one is easy to experiment with.

START OUT

2 cups (475 ml) cubed Grilled Chicken Breast (½-inch/1.3-cm pieces; page 258)

½ cup (120 ml) slivered almonds, toasted (see page 257)

2 tablespoons (30 ml) white sesame seeds, toasted (see page 257)

WHISK

⅓ cup (80 ml) tahini

¼ cup (60 ml) rice vinegar

2 tablespoons (30 ml) tamari, or low-sodium soy sauce

1 tablespoon plus 1 teaspoon (20 ml) light or dark brown sugar

2 teaspoons (10 ml) toasted sesame oil

½ teaspoon (2.5 ml) flaky sea salt

½ teaspoon (2.5 ml) ground white pepper

TOSS

4 cups (950 ml) torn butter lettuce (bite-size pieces)

4 cups (950 ml) torn romaine lettuce or baby gem lettuce (bite-size pieces)

2 cups (475 ml) thinly sliced red cabbage

¾ cup (175 ml) chopped scallions (green and white parts)

¾ cup (175 ml) torn fresh cilantro

2 tablespoons (30 ml) black sesame seeds

START OUT: Prepare the chicken. Toast the almonds and the white sesame seeds (no need to toast the black sesame seeds) and let them cool.

WHISK: In a large salad bowl, whisk together the tahini, vinegar, tamari, sugar, sesame oil, salt, and pepper until smooth and well combined.

TOSS: In the bowl with the dressing, add the butter lettuce, romaine lettuce, cabbage, scallions, cilantro, black sesame seeds, chicken, almonds, and white sesame seeds. Toss until all the ingredients are evenly combined and coated with dressing and serve.

ENJOY: I'm having it with fresh coconut water.

Cowboy Caviar
(page 116)

Let's Travel: Destination-Inspired Recipes

Chicken and Avocado with Honey Hot Sauce Vinaigrette

SERVES 4 AS A MEAL OR 6 TO 8 AS A SIDE

Sonoma County, California

I always get asked about my favorite salad. Although mine changes with my mood, this is my daughter's favorite and the one that she never got tired of when she was eating salads every day. There's something about the walnuts and feta with the hint of spice and sweet in the dressing that makes it the perfect combination. It is inspired by a fun little bistro in Santa Rosa, California, called Franchetti's. You feel like family when you're there, and we have spent many hours at Franchetti's celebrating birthdays, graduations, successes, and friendships. Always supporting the community, they gave away meals to many displaced families during the fires of 2017.

EXPERIMENT:
Rotisserie chickens can be extremely salty. I try to find the no-salt or low-sodium ones when I can. If the only ones available are too salty, substitute homemade grilled chicken breast (see page 258). Always taste the chicken before adding salt to the salad or dressing. People often ask for a substitute for feta—experiment with a fresh goat cheese or plain Boursin.

START OUT

½ cup (120 ml) coarsely chopped, toasted (see page 257) walnuts

WHISK

½ cup (120 ml) extra-virgin olive oil or avocado oil

⅓ cup (80 ml) fresh lemon juice

2 tablespoons plus 1½ teaspoons (35 ml) honey

2 teaspoons (10 ml) Dijon mustard

1 teaspoon (5 ml) Tabasco sauce

Flaky sea salt and freshly cracked black pepper

TOSS

4 cups (950 ml) chopped romaine lettuce (bite-size pieces)

4 cups (950 ml) thinly sliced lacinato kale, ribs removed

2 cups (475 ml) cubed rotisserie chicken breast, skin removed (1-inch/2.5-cm pieces)

2 cups (475 ml) cubed avocado (½-inch/1.3-cm pieces)

½ cup (120 ml) crumbled feta cheese (see page 43)

¼ cup (60 ml) very coarsely chopped fresh dill (½-inch/1.3-cm pieces)

START OUT: Toast the nuts.

WHISK: In a large salad bowl, combine the olive oil, lemon juice, honey, mustard, and Tabasco and season with salt and pepper. Whisk until emulsified, then taste and adjust the seasoning.

TOSS: In the salad bowl with the dressing, combine the romaine lettuce, kale, chicken, avocado, feta, dill, and walnuts. Toss until all the ingredients are evenly combined and coated with dressing and serve.

ENJOY: I'm having it with a blanc de blanc sparkling wine or Sonoma County pinot noir.

Beverly Hills McCarthy Salad

SERVES 4 AS A MEAL OR 6 TO 8 AS A SIDE

Los Angeles

Want to eat like a Hollywood celebrity? Before the Beverly Hills Hotel was a historic landmark, Neil McCarthy, famed polo captain from the 1940s, would frequently hang out at the Polo Lounge there. Legend has it that he requested these exact ingredients be made into a salad, and they have been serving it ever since. This outrageously expensive salad is one of the most historic and popular salads in Los Angeles—and my version, inspired by the original, is one of the most viral salads I have ever made. I replaced the canola oil and brown sugar in the dressing with extra-virgin olive oil and honey, and I didn't bother to separate the egg yolks from the whites before adding them both to the salad. Use your fine china and table linens when serving this salad to make you feel like the celebrity that you are.

EXPERIMENT: Get out the rubber gloves because beets stain everything, including your hands. If you are using your wooden bowl to serve this salad, treat it with a food-safe beeswax and/or mineral oil beforehand (see page 27), and make the dressing in the bottom to protect the bowl from turning pink. You can also toss the salad and sprinkle the beets on top after plating or serve them on the side. Even better: transport yourself to Beverly Hills and serve it without tossing, dressing on the side. Clean the bowl right after dining. Worst-case scenario, you can use a very fine grain sandpaper to remove any stain.

START OUT

1 teaspoon (5 ml) Roasted Garlic Purée (page 256)

2 medium beets, boiled (see page 260) or substitute 1½ cups (360 ml) cubed store-bought cooked peeled beets

2 cups (475 ml) cubed Grilled Chicken Breast (½-inch/1.3-cm pieces; page 258)

4 Perfect Boiled Eggs (page 257)

Ice water

2 tablespoons (30 ml) very finely diced shallot

1½ cups (360 ml) cubed tomatoes (whatever looks best at the market; ½-inch/1.3-cm pieces)

WHISK

⅓ cup (80 ml) extra-virgin olive oil

3 tablespoons (45 ml) balsamic vinegar

2 tablespoons (30 ml) honey

1 tablespoon (15 ml) Dijon mustard

½ teaspoon (2.5 ml) flaky sea salt

½ teaspoon (2.5 ml)

freshly cracked black pepper

TOSS

6 cups (1,400 ml) chopped romaine lettuce (½-inch/1.3-cm pieces)

2 cups (475 ml) chopped iceberg lettuce (½-inch/1.3-cm pieces)

1 cup (240 ml) cubed avocado (½-inch/1.3-cm pieces)

1 cup (240 ml) diced extra-sharp cheddar cheese (¼-inch/6-mm pieces)

START OUT: Prepare the roasted garlic purée for the dressing (up to 3 days in advance if you like). Prepare the boiled beets (if not using store-bought), and, when cool, peel and cut into ½-inch (1.3-cm) cubes.

Meanwhile, prepare the chicken. Prepare the eggs and when they're cool enough to handle, finely chop them. Fill a 250-ml beaker or a small glass bowl halfway with ice water and add the

shallot. Soak for 10 minutes, then drain and pat the shallot dry. Place the tomatoes in a colander and gently press down with a spoon to drain off excess liquid.

WHISK: In a large salad bowl, whisk together the roasted garlic purée, shallot, olive oil, vinegar, honey, mustard, salt, and pepper until emulsified.

TOSS: In the bowl with the dressing, add the romaine lettuce, iceberg lettuce, avocado, cheese, tomatoes, beets, chicken, and eggs. Toss until all the ingredients are evenly combined and coated with dressing and serve.

ENJOY: I'm having it with a sparkling rosé or iced black tea with fresh mint.

Fancy Italian Caesar

New York City

This Caesar is all about the croutons. They are almost the size of a stick of butter and have eight tablespoons of the melted goodness in the recipe. The croutons are crispy and crunchy on the outside, soft and chewy on the inside. The gigantic hunks of bread are a fun tomatoey surprise, creating a nice contrast to the rich, salty, cheesy dressing. Using only the best-quality ingredients, this one is inspired by one of the most popular Italian American restaurants in New York City, Carbone. Now's the time to break out the real Italian Parmigiano-Reggiano cheese, the imported olive oil, and the best Spanish anchovies you can find. Bonus: your house will smell like an old-school pizzeria by the time you're done.

EXPERIMENT:
I like to use a Microplane to grate Parmigiano-Reggiano cheese, but you can also use a food processor or hand grater. If you are nowhere near an Italian grocery store or bakery and cannot find fancy Italian bread, a loaf of French bread works well. Two teaspoons (10 ml) of anchovy paste can be substituted for the imported anchovies.

START OUT

1 tablespoon (15 ml) Roasted Garlic Purée (page 256)

1 loaf Italian semolina country bread, or 6 to 8 large semolina rolls, unsliced

½ cup (120 ml) unsalted butter, melted

1 tablespoon (15 ml) tomato paste

1 teaspoon (5 ml) dried oregano

¼ teaspoon (1.5 ml) red pepper flakes

¼ teaspoon (1.5 ml) flaky sea salt

1 coddled egg yolk (see page 243)

WHISK

1 tablespoon (15 ml) pressed garlic

¾ cup (175 ml) freshly grated Parmigiano-Reggiano (use a Microplane)

3 white Spanish anchovies, or substitute any whole oil-packed anchovies

1 tablespoon (15 ml) red wine vinegar

1 tablespoon (15 ml) fresh lemon juice

1 tablespoon (15 ml) whole-grain mustard

1 teaspoon (5 ml) Worcestershire sauce

¼ cup (60 ml) extra-virgin

olive oil (preferably Italian olive oil)

Freshly cracked black pepper

TOSS

8 cups (1,900 ml) lightly packed baby gem lettuce leaves (about 4 small heads), or substitute romaine torn into roughly 1-inch by 2-inch (2.5-cm by 5-cm) strips

⅔ cup (160 ml) freshly grated Parmigiano-Reggiano (use a Microplane)

6 white Spanish anchovies (optional), for serving

START OUT: Prepare the roasted garlic purée (up to 3 days in advance if you like). Preheat the oven to 375°F (190°C) and use convection mode if that's an option. Line a baking sheet with a wire rack, or if you don't have one, parchment paper or a silicone baking mat.

Remove the crust from the bread and cut into 12 to 16 1-inch- (2.5-cm-) thick, 1-inch by 2-inch (2.5-cm by 5-cm) rectangular pieces (depending on how many you'd like per serving; save any

extra bread for another use). In a large bowl, whisk the roasted garlic purée, melted butter, tomato paste, dried oregano, red pepper flakes, and salt. Add the bread and toss to coat evenly. Place on the prepared baking sheet and bake, stirring halfway through, until the croutons begin to turn golden and are still soft inside (I like to call them "medium-rare"), 10 to 12 minutes (longer for regular ovens).

Prepare the coddled egg yolk.

WHISK: Rinse the pressed garlic in a very fine mesh strainer and shake off any excess water. In an extra-large, preferably wooden, salad bowl, combine the garlic, coddled egg yolk, Parmigiano-Reggiano, anchovies, vinegar, lemon juice, mustard, and Worcestershire sauce. With a fork or the back of a salad tosser, smash the ingredients until they form a paste. Slowly drizzle the olive oil into the paste while whisking until everything is incorporated and emulsified. Season with pepper.

TOSS: In the bowl with the dressing, add the baby gem lettuce leaves and toss until the lettuce is evenly coated with dressing. Garnish with the croutons and sprinkle the Parmigiano-Reggiano over everything, then top with the anchovies (if using) and serve.

ENJOY: I'm having it with an Italian montepulciano or Italian sparkling water.

Arizona Chopped Salad

SERVES 4 AS A MEAL OR 6 TO 8 AS A SIDE

Phoenix

Did you know the Grand Canyon State is famous for its original chopped salad? With ingredients like smoked salmon, freeze-dried corn, and pearl couscous, it's definitely not your standard chopped. I love all the textures and crunch in this one. You can find it at the Phoenix airport if you are traveling through, although like a lot of premade airport salads, the freshness is questionable. It's much tastier made to order at many of the restaurants in Phoenix or, even better, at home. Try not to skip the freeze-dried corn—it's crucial to the flavor and texture! You can usually find it in the dried fruit section of your local store, or online if necessary.

EXPERIMENT: If you are taking this salad to an event and serving the dressing on the side, the ingredients are typically placed in rows or stripes to make it look like an Arizona sunset. Other variations or substitutions include grilled chicken for the salmon, roasted salted sunflower seeds for the pepitas, feta for the Asiago, and dried currants for the cranberries. You can always use fresh or frozen corn as a substitute if you cannot find the freeze-dried corn.

START OUT

1 cup (240 ml) pearl couscous

4 cups (950 ml) water, or as needed

½ teaspoon (2.5 ml) flaky sea salt, or as needed

½ cup (120 ml) pepitas, toasted (see page 257)

WHISK

½ teaspoon (2.5 ml) pressed garlic

⅔ cup (160 ml) coarsely chopped fresh basil

¼ cup (60 ml) extra-virgin olive oil

¼ cup (60 ml) mayonnaise

3 tablespoons (45 ml) buttermilk

2 tablespoons (30 ml) freshly grated Pecorino Romano cheese (use a Microplane)

1 tablespoon (15 ml) red wine vinegar

1 tablespoon (15 ml) fresh lemon juice

1 tablespoon (15 ml) honey

¼ teaspoon (1.5 ml) freshly cracked black pepper

¼ teaspoon (1.5 ml) flaky sea salt

TOSS

8 cups (1,900 ml) lightly packed arugula

2 cups (475 ml) diced red bell pepper (¼-inch/6mm pieces)

1 cup (240 ml) chopped smoked salmon (not lox; 1-inch/2.5cm pieces)

1 cup (240 ml) freeze-dried corn

1 cup (240 ml) freshly shaved Asiago cheese

⅓ cup (80 ml) dried cranberries

START OUT: If your couscous has cooking directions on the package, follow those. If not, put the water and salt in a small pot and bring to a boil, then add the pearl couscous. Cook until tender and not chewy in the center, about 7 minutes. Drain, rinse, and set aside to cool completely.

Toast the pepitas.

WHISK: Rinse the pressed garlic in a very fine mesh strainer and shake off any excess water. In a beaker or medium bowl, combine the garlic, basil, oil, mayonnaise, buttermilk, cheese, vinegar, lemon juice, honey, black pepper, and salt. Emulsify with an immersion blender.

TOSS: In a large salad bowl, arrange the arugula on the bottom and top with the couscous, pepitas, red bell pepper, smoked salmon, corn, cheese, and cranberries and drizzle with dressing to taste. Toss until all the ingredients are evenly combined and coated with dressing and serve.

ENJOY: I'm having it with chilled rosé or sparkling water with lemon.

Smoked Jalapeño Mexican Grill

SERVES 4 AS A MEAL

Colorado

This "salad" is inspired by a well-known restaurant chain that started out next to the University of Colorado to feed hungry college students, then took over the country and never looked back. I think I bought this style of salad once a week until I figured out the dressing recipe. Chipotle (which means "smoked chile") peppers in adobo sauce elevate any dish, but *especially* chicken and salad dressings. The restaurant has since released their recipe for the dressing but they do not reveal what is in their "chipotle purée paste." Here is my interpretation of their famous dressing and my favorite order.

MARINATE

⅓ cup (80 ml) water

2 canned chipotle peppers in adobo sauce plus 3 tablespoons (45 ml) adobo sauce (from a 7-ounce/200-g can)

1 tablespoon (15 ml) avocado oil

1½ teaspoons (7.5 ml) chili powder

1 teaspoon (5 ml) pressed garlic

1 teaspoon (5 ml) granulated sea salt

½ teaspoon (2.5 ml) freshly cracked black pepper

½ teaspoon (2.5 ml) ground cumin

½ teaspoon (2.5 ml) dried oregano

1 pound (450 g) boneless skinless chicken thighs

START OUT

1½ cups (360 ml) cooked medium-grain rice (see page 264)

Flaky sea salt

1 tablespoon (15 ml) avocado oil

2 cups (475 ml) sliced mixed yellow and red bell peppers (¼-inch/6-mm strips)

1 cup (240 ml) halved and sliced yellow onion (¼-inch/6-mm strips)

WHISK

¼ cup (60 ml) avocado oil

2 tablespoons (30 ml) red wine vinegar

2 tablespoons (30 ml) water

1 tablespoon plus 2 teaspoons (25 ml) honey

1 canned chipotle pepper in adobo sauce plus ½ teaspoon (2.5 ml) adobo sauce (from a 7-ounce/200-g can)

½ teaspoon (2.5 ml) dried oregano

½ teaspoon (2.5 ml) flaky sea salt

½ teaspoon (2.5 ml) freshly cracked black pepper

TOSS

3 cups (720 ml) diced Roma or beefsteak tomatoes (¼-inch/6-mm pieces)

¾ cup (175 ml) diced red onion (¼-inch/6-mm pieces)

¾ cup (175 ml) finely chopped fresh cilantro

5 tablespoons (75 ml) fresh lime juice

1 teaspoon (5 ml) flaky sea salt

3 medium ripe avocados, halved and pitted

2 tablespoons (30 ml) very finely diced seeded and deveined fresh jalapeño

8 cups (1,900 ml) chopped romaine lettuce (1-inch/2.5-cm strips)

1½ cups (360 ml) cooked or rinsed and drained canned black beans

½ cup (120 ml) grated cheddar cheese

½ cup (120 ml) grated Monterey Jack cheese

94   THE SALAD LAB

MARINATE: In a small blender, small food processor, or large beaker, combine the water, chipotles, adobo sauce, oil, chili powder, garlic, granulated sea salt, black pepper, cumin, and oregano. Blend until smooth. In a large bowl, combine the marinade with the chicken, cover, and marinate for at least 8 hours in the refrigerator.

START OUT: Remove the chicken from the refrigerator and set it out on the counter for at least 1 hour to get to room temperature. Meanwhile, prepare the rice.

Heat a griddle pan or cast-iron skillet on high heat. Remove the chicken from the marinade and season with a pinch of flaky sea salt. When the pan is hot, sear the chicken until char marks are visible or the chicken is golden brown, about 1 minute per side. Turn the heat down to medium high and cook until the internal temperature reads 165°F (75°C) on an instant-read thermometer, 4 to 5 minutes per side. Set the chicken aside on a plate to rest for 5 minutes before cutting into ½-inch (1.3-cm) cubes.

In the same pan over medium high, heat the oil until hot. Add the bell peppers and yellow onion and cook, stirring often, until the onion begins to look translucent, 5 to 6 minutes. Transfer to a plate and set aside.

WHISK: In a small blender, small food processor, or large beaker, combine the oil, vinegar, water, honey, chipotle, adobo sauce, oregano, flaky sea salt, and black pepper. Blend until smooth.

TOSS: In a medium bowl, mix the diced tomatoes, ½ cup (120 ml) of the red onion, ¼ cup (60 ml) of the cilantro, 2 tablespoons (30 ml) of the lime juice, and ½ teaspoon (2.5 ml) of the flaky sea salt. Stir to evenly combine the ingredients and set the pico de gallo aside.

Scoop the avocado out of the skin and add it to another medium bowl. Mash it with a fork until slightly smooth with small chunks, then add the remaining ½ cup (120 ml) cilantro, ¼ cup (60 ml) red onion, and 3 tablespoons (45 ml) lime juice; the jalapeño; and the remaining ½ teaspoon (2.5 ml) flaky sea salt and gently stir until combined.

In a large salad bowl, combine the lettuce, beans, cheddar and jack cheeses, rice, chicken, sautéed vegetables, pico de gallo, and guacamole and drizzle with dressing to taste. Toss until all the ingredients are evenly combined and coated with dressing and serve.

ENJOY: I'm having it with sparkling water or chardonnay.

EXPERIMENT:
For a vegan option, the marinade is fabulous to use for Roasted Tofu (page 258). You can easily skip a few steps by using 1 cup (240 ml) each of premade fresh pico de gallo and guacamole—but I am told the guacamole is very close to the original! I like to toss it all together, but try serving everything buffet-style or top the tossed salad with the pico and guacamole.

Fisherman's Wharf Shrimp Louie

SERVES 4 AS A MEAL OR 6 TO 8 AS A SIDE

San Francisco

Having dinner at Fisherman's Wharf in San Francisco was always a treat for me, so this salad holds a special place in my heart. I am the fourth generation in my family to live in the San Francisco Bay Area. The Wharf started out as a docking area for commercial fishermen, and my great-grandmother would walk over and buy fresh seafood right off the boat. Now it is more of a tourist attraction, but you can still find fresh shrimp, crab, and the famous sourdough bread used to make the croutons in this salad—the perfect combination.

EXPERIMENT:
This original recipe has fresh mushrooms and black olives, which I omit when I make this for myself. Always experiment with things you love and skip what you don't.

START OUT

2 cups (475 ml) Sourdough Garlic Croutons (page 235)

4 Perfect Boiled Eggs (page 257)

Ice water

½ cup (120 ml) halved and sliced red onion

1½ cups (360 ml) quartered cherry tomatoes, or substitute what looks best at the market

WHISK

½ cup (120 ml) mayonnaise

3 tablespoons (45 ml) ketchup

2 tablespoons (30 ml) fresh lemon juice (remember to zest first)

2 tablespoons (30 ml) dill pickle relish

1 teaspoon (5 ml) Tabasco

½ teaspoon (2.5 ml) celery salt

½ teaspoon (2.5 ml) lightly packed grated lemon zest

Flaky sea salt and freshly cracked black pepper

TOSS

8 cups (1,900 ml) chopped romaine lettuce (1-inch strips)

1 cup (240 ml) prepared bay shrimp (see Notes)

1 cup (240 ml) fresh Dungeness crab meat, shell fragments removed (see Notes)

1 cup (240 ml) peeled and shredded carrots

1 cup (240 ml) shredded red cabbage

½ cup (120 ml) thinly sliced button mushrooms

¼ cup (60 ml) drained and sliced canned pitted black olives

Lemon wedges, for serving (optional)

START OUT: Prepare the croutons and eggs. When the eggs are cool enough to handle, slice them.

Meanwhile, fill a 500-ml beaker or a small glass bowl halfway with ice water then add the onion. Soak for 10 minutes, then drain and pat the onion dry. Place the tomatoes in a colander and gently press down with a spoon to drain off excess liquid.

WHISK: In a large salad bowl, combine the mayonnaise, ketchup, lemon juice, relish, Tabasco, celery salt, and lemon zest and season with flaky sea salt and pepper. Whisk until emulsified, then taste and adjust the seasoning as needed.

TOSS: In the bowl with the dressing, add the romaine lettuce, shrimp, crab, carrots, cabbage, mushrooms, olives, croutons, eggs, onions, and tomatoes. Toss until all the ingredients are evenly combined and coated with dressing and serve with lemon wedges (if you like).

ENJOY: I'm having it with fumé blanc (sauvignon blanc) or iced black tea.

NOTES: Bay shrimp are tiny shrimp sold shelled and precooked. If you can't find them, use prawns or regular shrimp and chop them after cooking.

Fresh Dungeness crab can be hard to come by, depending on the season, fishing regulations, and shortages. You can find good-quality canned crab, which I usually pick through for shells and rinse before adding to any salad. There is always imitation crab which is wallet-friendly, or you can use all shrimp. It's not quite the same, but it's still delicious.

Maurice Salad

Detroit

I had the pleasure of re-creating the Maurice salad with the Hudson's Grill chefs during lunch hour in their bustling kitchen. It was so much fun and lots of laughs. The manager had spent a lot of time meeting with former J. L. Hudson Department Store chefs and other local historians to get this nearly one-hundred-year-old recipe as close to the original as possible. This salad holds wonderful memories for the people of Detroit. After I debuted my version inspired by the original on The Salad Lab, one of my followers said it reminded her of "a day out shopping with Grandma at Hudson's department store and having a fancy lunch." Unfortunately, the department store is long gone, but the salad is served in many of the restaurants in Detroit to this day.

START OUT

1 Perfect Boiled Egg
(page 257)

WHISK

¾ cup (175 ml)
mayonnaise

2 tablespoons (30 ml)
finely chopped fresh flat-
leaf parsley

2 tablespoons (30 ml)
very finely diced white or
yellow onion

1 tablespoon (15 ml)
whole-grain mustard

1 tablespoon (15 ml) sugar

1 tablespoon (15 ml)
very finely diced pickled
gherkin

1 teaspoon (5 ml) white
wine vinegar

1 teaspoon (5 ml) onion
juice (see Experiment)

½ teaspoon (2.5 ml)
table salt

TOSS

8 cups (1,900 ml) thinly
sliced romaine lettuce
hearts, or iceberg lettuce

1½ cups (360 ml) cubed
thick-sliced roasted turkey
(½-inch/1.3-cm pieces)

1½ cups (360 ml)
cubed thick-sliced ham
(½-inch/1.3-cm pieces)

1½ cups (360 ml) julienned
thick-sliced Swiss cheese
(⅛- to ¼-inch/3- to 6-mm
thick)

¾ cup (175 ml) pimento-
stuffed green olives

½ cup (120 ml) diced
pickled gherkin
(¼-inch/6-mm pieces;
optional)

START OUT: Prepare the egg for the dressing and when it's cool enough to handle, finely dice it.

WHISK: In a large salad bowl, whisk together the mayonnaise, parsley, onion, mustard, sugar, gherkin, vinegar, onion juice, salt, and chopped egg until well combined. Remove about half the dressing and set aside in a small bowl.

TOSS: In the large bowl with half the dressing, add the lettuce, turkey, ham, cheese, olives, and gherkin (if using). Toss until all the ingredients are evenly combined and coated with dressing. Taste and add more dressing if desired, then serve.

ENJOY: I am having it with a mimosa or a ginger ale.

EXPERIMENT: Bottled onion juice can usually be found in the condiment section or cocktail mixing section of your market; when in doubt, ask. You can also juice or finely grate a white or yellow onion. The valley of Emmental in Switzerland is where the first recorded instance of "Swiss" cheese production took place in the fourteenth century. The bacteria used to make the cheese give off carbon dioxide, which creates air bubbles—making the famous holes. You can find domestic and imported versions of "Swiss" cheese at any market today, but real Swiss Emmentaler is my favorite.

French Fry Salad

Pittsburgh

I had so many requests to make this salad and I put off making it for so long. I had a cold French fry mental block. Finally, I gave in and to my surprise, I loved it. The trick is to take the "fries" right out of the oven and onto the salad. Legend has it that someone in a well-frequented Pittsburgh restaurant ordered a steak sandwich without the bun and poured an order of French fries on top, and that was the beginning of salads automatically coming with French fries on top throughout the Northeast. This salad takes a little planning in the execution: you ideally want the fries to be warm when you add them to the salad, so try to have the steak cooked and everything chopped by the time they come out of the oven.

EXPERIMENT:
Some people are very passionate about their French fries and insist on having them fried in oil, while others don't mind them cold in the salad. You can always pick some up from a restaurant or use frozen fries (you'll need 2 cups/475 ml total)—try it!

START OUT

1 pound (450 g) sirloin steak, about 1 inch (2.5 cm) thick

Ice water

⅓ cup (80 ml) diced red onion (¼-inch/6-mm pieces)

1½ cups (360 ml) chopped tomatoes (use what looks best at the market; ½-inch/1.3-cm pieces)

2 large russet potatoes, cut into ½-inch- (1.3-cm-) thick fries

3 tablespoons (45 ml) extra-virgin olive oil

1 teaspoon (5 ml) granulated sea salt, plus more as needed

1 teaspoon (5 ml) freshly cracked black pepper

WHISK

1 teaspoon (5 ml) pressed garlic

½ cup (120 ml) mayonnaise

½ cup (120 ml) sour cream

½ cup (120 ml) buttermilk

3 tablespoons (45 ml) finely chopped fresh flat-leaf parsley

3 tablespoons (45 ml) finely chopped fresh chives

3 tablespoons (45 ml) finely chopped fresh dill

¼ teaspoon (1.5 ml) sweet paprika

¼ teaspoon (1.5 ml) onion powder

Flaky sea salt and freshly cracked black pepper

TOSS

4 cups (950 ml) thinly sliced iceberg lettuce

4 cups (950 ml) thinly sliced romaine lettuce

1½ cups (360 ml) thinly sliced peeled cucumber

1 cup (240 ml) grated sharp cheddar, or substitute crumbled blue cheese (see page 43)

¾ cup (175 ml) thinly sliced red and/or yellow bell pepper

START OUT: Remove the steak from the refrigerator and set out on the counter for at least an hour to get to room temperature. Preheat the oven to 450°F (230°C) and use convection mode if that's an option. Line a baking sheet with parchment paper or a silicone baking mat.

Fill a 500-ml beaker or a small glass bowl halfway with ice water and add the onion. Soak for 10 minutes, then drain and pat the onion dry. Place the tomatoes in a colander and gently press down with a spoon to drain off excess liquid.

In a large bowl, toss the potatoes, 2 tablespoons (30 ml) of the oil, and ½ teaspoon (2.5 ml) of the granulated sea salt. Spread the potatoes out on the prepared baking sheet. Bake, stirring halfway through, until golden and crisp, about 30 minutes (longer for a regular oven). Season with another pinch of salt. Keep warm.

Meanwhile, heat a large cast-iron skillet over medium-high heat (if your pan can't easily fit all the steak, work in batches). Season the steak with the remaining ½ teaspoon (2.5 ml) granulated sea salt and the black pepper on both sides. Gently pour the remaining 1 tablespoon (15 ml) of oil into the pan and when the oil begins to smoke, add the steak. Cook until browned on each side, about 1 minute, then turn down the heat to medium and continue cooking, flipping once more, to your desired doneness: when the temperature reads 135°F (57°C) on an instant-read thermometer for medium-rare, or 145°F (63°C) for medium. Transfer the steak to a cutting board and let it rest for 5 minutes. Cut the steak into ½-inch (1.3-cm) cubes.

WHISK: Rinse the pressed garlic in a very fine mesh strainer and shake off any excess water. In a small bowl, combine the garlic, mayonnaise, sour cream, buttermilk, parsley, chives, dill, paprika, and onion powder and season with flaky sea salt and black pepper. Whisk until emulsified, then taste and adjust the seasoning if needed.

TOSS: In a large salad bowl, add the iceberg lettuce, romaine lettuce, cucumber, cheese, bell pepper, onion, tomatoes, and steak and drizzle with dressing to taste. Toss until all the ingredients are evenly combined and coated with dressing. Top with the hot French fries, and serve.

ENJOY: I'm having it with pinot noir or "pop."

Tropical Salad with Fruit and Creole Chicken

SERVES 4 AS A MEAL OR 6 TO 8 AS A SIDE

Florida

When I think of Florida, I have visions of a seafood salad, but this one made with chicken instead is a hit! I kept getting daily requests for it from the same few followers. It is inspired by the popular Florida-based restaurant chain Bahama Breeze. Traditionally salads don't have a lot of fruit in them, but this one has four different varieties, plus chicken coated with spicy creole seasoning for a little extra kick. I think it's the creamy fresh goat cheese that ties it all together. I could have never guessed this salad would be so popular with my community and the video would eventually have over four million views—but after making it, I get it.

EXPERIMENT: If you can't find good pineapple, try using mango. Bon Jovi fan? John Bon Jovi sells his own Creole seasoning online; proceeds go to feed the underserved.

START OUT	WHISK	TOSS
1 pound (450 g) boneless skinless chicken breast	½ teaspoon (2.5 ml) pressed garlic	8 cups (1,900 ml) lightly packed spring mix (baby lettuce blend)
½ cup (120 ml) Honey-Roasted Sliced Almonds (page 257), or store-bought	⅔ cup (160 ml) rice vinegar	1 cup (240 ml) chopped fresh pineapple (1-inch/2.5-cm triangles; see Note, page 107)
Ice water	⅓ cup (80 ml) fresh orange juice	1 cup (240 ml) red seedless grapes, halved
1 tablespoon (15 ml) very finely diced shallot	2 tablespoons (30 ml) extra-virgin olive oil	1 cup (240 ml) peeled fresh mandarin orange or tangerine segments
1 teaspoon (5 ml) Creole seasoning	2 tablespoons (30 ml) finely chopped fresh cilantro	1 cup (240 ml) sliced strawberries
1 tablespoon (15 ml) avocado oil	1 tablespoon (15 ml) honey	⅔ cup (160 ml) crumbled fresh goat cheese (see page 43)
Flaky sea salt	1 teaspoon (5 ml) Dijon mustard	
	½ teaspoon (2.5 ml) Creole seasoning	
	Flaky sea salt and freshly cracked black pepper	

START OUT: Remove the chicken from the fridge and let it come to room temperature. Meanwhile, prepare the almonds if necessary. Fill a 250-ml beaker or a small glass bowl halfway with ice water and add the shallot. Soak for 10 minutes, then drain and pat the shallot dry.

In a large bowl, combine the chicken and Creole seasoning and toss until the chicken is evenly coated. Heat the oil in a griddle pan or cast-iron skillet on high heat. Season the chicken with a pinch of salt. Once the oil is hot, place the chicken in the pan and sear until char marks are visible or the chicken is golden brown, about 1 minute per side. Turn the heat down to medium high and cook until the internal temperature reads 165°F (75°C) on an instant-read thermometer, 4 to 5 minutes per side. Set the chicken aside on a plate to rest for 5 minutes before cutting into ½-inch (1.3-cm) cubes.

WHISK: Rinse the pressed garlic in a very fine mesh strainer and shake off any excess water. In a large salad bowl, combine the garlic, shallot, vinegar, orange juice, oil, cilantro, honey, mustard, and Creole seasoning and season with salt and pepper. Whisk until well combined, then taste and adjust the seasoning if needed.

TOSS: In the bowl with the dressing, add the spring mix, pineapple, grapes, oranges, strawberries, goat cheese, almonds, and chicken. Toss until all the ingredients are evenly distributed and coated with dressing and serve.

ENJOY: I'm having it with sparkling brut rosé or iced black tea.

NOTE: There are a few ways I like to pick perfectly ripe fresh pineapple: I like one that smells like a sweet pineapple, has bright green leaves, and is turning from green to yellow, especially at the bottom. Next, look for larger "buttons" covering the sides; they should give a little when you push them. Finally, I pull out one of the center fronds; it should come out without too much resistance.

Poke Bowl Salad

Hawaii

Poke originates from the Hawaiian Islands and is one of my favorite things to eat. Most definitely family-approved, a poke bowl is a must when visiting. When I'm not in Hawaii, making one always takes me back to my happy place. It's relatively easy to make, always such a treat, refreshing and satisfying on a hot day, and spreads a little aloha whenever it is served. I purchase frozen sushi-grade ahi tuna for this salad. Most display-case seafood has been frozen and thawed before it gets put out for sale, exposing it to temperature changes and bacteria, and it's not as fresh as fish that has remained frozen, in my opinion. If you can find it freshly caught, freeze it for 10 minutes to firm up so it is easier to cut.

EXPERIMENT:
Yellowtail tuna and salmon, preferably fresh and wild-caught, are both excellent substitutions for ahi tuna. It's also fun to experiment with Roasted Tofu (page 258) for a vegan option. Prepare the tofu as directed, then toss it in the marinade just like you would the fish. Speaking of the marinade, double the wasabi if you like the burn. Skip the flowers and sprouts if they are not easy to find.

MARINATE

½ cup (120 ml) halved and thinly sliced yellow onion

½ cup (120 ml) finely chopped scallions (green and white parts)

5 tablespoons (75 ml) low-sodium soy sauce

2 tablespoons (30 ml) avocado oil

2 tablespoons (30 ml) very finely diced seeded and deveined fresh red chile, such as Anaheim or serrano

2 tablespoons (30 ml) furikake or sesame seeds

4 teaspoons (20 ml) toasted sesame oil

2 teaspoons (10 ml) grated fresh ginger

2 teaspoons (10 ml) pressed garlic

1 teaspoon (5 ml) wasabi (optional)

½ teaspoon (2.5 ml) red pepper flakes (optional)

1 pound (450 g) frozen sushi-grade ahi tuna, slightly thawed

START OUT

2 cups (475 ml) sushi rice

3 cups (720 ml) water

1 cup (240 ml) frozen edamame

TOSS

1 cup (240 ml) cubed avocado (½-inch/1.3-cm pieces)

1 cup (240 ml) cubed seeded English cucumber (½-inch/1.3-cm pieces)

1 cup (240 ml) peeled and cubed carrots (½-inch/1.3cm-pieces)

1 cup (240 ml) cubed, peeled, and pitted (see page 119) mango (½-inch/1.3-cm pieces)

¼ cup (60 ml) broccoli or alfalfa sprouts (optional)

¼ cup (60 ml) edible flowers (optional)

2 tablespoons (30 ml) julienned pickled ginger

Kewpie mayo, for serving

Sriracha, for serving

MARINATE: In a medium bowl, whisk together the yellow onion, scallions, soy sauce, avocado oil, red chile, furikake, sesame oil, ginger, garlic, wasabi (if using), and red pepper flakes (if using) until well combined.

Cut the cold tuna into ½-inch (1.3-cm) cubes. Place the cubed tuna in the bowl with the marinade and toss to coat. Cover, transfer to the refrigerator, and marinate for 30 minutes.

START OUT: Meanwhile, rinse the sushi rice in a strainer until the water runs clear. In a medium saucepan, combine the water and rice. Bring to a soft boil, then reduce the heat to low. Cover and cook until all the liquid is absorbed, about 20 minutes. Uncover and let the rice cool to room temperature. (To cool the rice more quickly, empty the hot rice onto parchment paper or a silicone baking mat and spread out evenly into a thin layer.) Thaw the edamame.

TOSS: In a large salad bowl, combine the sushi rice, edamame, avocado, cucumber, carrots, mango, sprouts (if using), edible flowers (if using), and pickled ginger. Use a slotted spoon to remove the tuna from the marinade, leaving any extra in the bowl, and add the tuna to the salad. Toss until all the ingredients are evenly combined and serve drizzled with Kewpie mayo and sriracha.

ENJOY: I'm having it with POG (a Hawaiian combination of passionfruit, orange, and guava juices) or a Hawaiian beer, such as Big Island Lager.

Poke Bowl Salad

BBQ Salad

BBQ Salad

North Carolina

Customerized, a small PR firm from North Carolina, was the first to reach out to me and help The Salad Lab get started. This salad was a special request from my team and we tried to adhere to North Carolina traditions of smoky-savory barbecue, coleslaw, and their beloved hush puppies. North Carolina barbeque sauces are usually heavy on the vinegar and so they make a great salad ingredient. This salad is packed with flavor and spice and is perfect for meal prep, as it's even better the next day. Just store the croutons separately in an airtight container until you're ready to serve. (Save the extras for snacking—they're great with honey—or freeze them.)

EXPERIMENT:
In a hurry? Replace the dressing recipe with ¼ cup (60 ml) mayonnaise and ½ cup (120 ml) North Carolina–style bottled barbeque sauce whisked together. Cheerwine is a cherry soda that originated in North Carolina and its manufacturer is said to be the longest-running family-owned soda company in the United States. If you can't find it, Pepsi is also from North Carolina and is a favorite among the locals.

START OUT

1 pound (450 g) Grilled Chicken Breast (page 258), left whole

¼ cup (60 ml) store-bought North Carolina–style barbeque sauce

Ice water

1 cup (240 ml) diced red onion (¼-inch/6-mm pieces)

½ cup (120 ml) coarsely chopped, toasted (see page 257) salted pecans

WHISK

¼ cup (60 ml) apple cider vinegar

¼ cup (60 ml) mayonnaise

¼ cup (60 ml) distilled white vinegar

2 teaspoons (10 ml) red pepper flakes

½ teaspoon (2.5 ml) Tabasco

¼ teaspoon (1.5 ml) cayenne pepper

Flaky sea salt

TOSS

4 cups (950 ml) shredded green cabbage

4 cups (950 ml) shredded red cabbage

2 cups (475 ml) cubed cored Granny Smith apples (½-inch/1.3cm pieces)

1½ cups (360 ml) thinly sliced celery

3 cups (720 ml) neutral vegetable oil or avocado oil

1 cup (240 ml) yellow cornmeal

⅓ cup (80 ml) all-purpose flour

¼ cup (60 ml) sugar

1 teaspoon (5 ml) baking powder

½ teaspoon (2.5 ml) granulated sea salt

½ teaspoon (2.5 ml) baking soda

½ teaspoon (2.5 ml) garlic powder

½ teaspoon (2.5 ml) onion powder

Pinch of cayenne

1 cup (240 ml) buttermilk

¼ cup (60 ml) finely grated yellow or white onion

1 large egg, beaten

2 tablespoons (30 ml) melted butter

START OUT: Prepare the chicken, then coat each side liberally with the barbecue sauce and cut into ½-inch (1.3-cm) cubes. Fill a 500-ml beaker or a small glass bowl halfway with ice water and add the onion. Soak for 10 minutes, then drain and pat the onion dry. Toast the pecans.

WHISK: In a large salad bowl, combine the apple cider vinegar, mayonnaise, white vinegar, red pepper flakes, Tabasco, and cayenne pepper and season with flaky sea salt. Whisk until well combined, then taste and adjust the seasoning if needed.

TOSS: In the bowl with the dressing, add the green cabbage, red cabbage, apples, celery, pecans, chicken, and onion. Toss until all the ingredients are evenly combined and coated with dressing and refrigerate while preparing the hush puppy croutons.

In a deep skillet or medium pot, heat the neutral oil over medium heat to 350°F (175°C). Use a thermometer to prevent overly oily, or burned, hush puppies. Line a plate with paper towels.

In a large bowl, combine the cornmeal, flour, sugar, baking powder, granulated sea salt, baking soda, garlic powder, onion powder, and cayenne. In a separate medium bowl, whisk together the buttermilk, onion, egg, and melted butter. Add the wet ingredients to the dry and mix until evenly combined and no lumps remain.

When the oil is ready, gently drop 1 teaspoon (5 ml) of batter into the hot oil (be very careful at this step), frying 6 to 8 at a time and checking the oil temperature to make sure it isn't getting too hot or cool. Cook, flipping once, until the hush puppy croutons are golden brown on the outside, about 1 minute per side. Use a slotted spoon to remove the croutons and place on the prepared plate to drain. Repeat with the remaining batter.

Top the salad with half the warm hush puppies and serve. (You can freeze the rest of the hush puppies, or serve them on the side.)

ENJOY: I'm having it with merlot or Cheerwine.

Windy City–Style Chopped

Chicago

The Second City isn't known only for its hot dogs. The famous chopped salad from local restaurant chain Portillo's has been the number-one Chicago favorite salad for more than thirty years. The creamy house dressing has classic Italian roots and even includes the local favorite ingredient celery seed (hot dog lovers know). The original salad has fans from all over the world, so you do not need to be from Chicago to love my version inspired by it.

START OUT

Flaky sea salt

1 cup (240 ml) ditalini pasta

1 cup (240 ml) cubed Grilled Chicken Breast (½-inch/1.3-cm pieces; page 258)

¾ cup (160 ml) Chopped Bacon (use applewood bacon if possible; page 258)

1 cup (240 ml) chopped Roma tomatoes (½-inch/1.3-cm pieces) or quartered cherry tomatoes

WHISK

1 teaspoon (5 ml) pressed garlic

¼ cup (60 ml) mayonnaise

3 tablespoons (45 ml) extra-virgin olive oil

3 tablespoons (30 ml) red wine vinegar

2 tablespoons (30 ml) water

1 tablespoon (15 ml) sugar

1 tablespoon (15 ml) freshly grated Parmigiano-Reggiano (use a Microplane)

1 teaspoon (5 ml) celery seed

1 teaspoon (5 ml) dried oregano

1 teaspoon (5 ml) Dijon mustard

½ teaspoon (2.5 ml) flaky sea salt

½ teaspoon (2.5 ml) freshly cracked black pepper

TOSS

4 cups (950 ml) thinly sliced romaine lettuce

3 cups (720 ml) thinly sliced iceberg lettuce

1 cup (240 ml) finely chopped red cabbage (¼-inch/6mm pieces)

½ cup (120 ml) chopped scallions (green and white parts)

4 ounces (115 g) crumbled Gorgonzola cheese (see page 43)

Freshly grated Parmigiano-Reggiano (use a Microplane), for serving

Red pepper flakes, for serving

EXPERIMENT: My viewers have recently reported that (depending on location and supply) Portillo's has "modernized" the salad and swapped out the iceberg for spring mix. Unless you live in an area where there are Italian markets, ditalini pasta can be hard to find. Try experimenting with orzo, macaroni, or another small pasta shape if you can't find it.

START OUT: Fill a large pot with water and salt it generously. Bring to a boil, then add the pasta, gently stir, and cook according to the package directions until al dente. Strain the pasta, then rinse and drain.

Prepare the chicken and bacon. Meanwhile, place the tomatoes in a colander and gently press down with a spoon to drain off excess liquid.

WHISK: Rinse the pressed garlic in a very fine mesh strainer and shake off any excess water. In a large salad bowl, whisk together the garlic, mayonnaise, oil, vinegar, water, sugar, Parmigiano-Reggiano, celery seed, dried oregano, mustard, salt, and pepper until emulsified.

TOSS: In the bowl with the dressing, add the romaine lettuce, iceberg lettuce, cabbage, scallions, Gorgonzola cheese, pasta, chicken, bacon, and tomatoes. Toss until all the ingredients are evenly combined and coated with dressing and serve, passing the grated Parmigiano-Reggiano cheese and red pepper flakes at the table.

ENJOY: I'm having it with pinot noir or a Green River soda.

Cowboy Caviar

SERVES 4 TO 6 AS A MEAL OR 8 TO 12 AS A SIDE

Texas

Who knew Texas's Cowboy Caviar was such a hot topic! Some say it's a type of Mexican salsa or pico de gallo while others claim that it was Helen Corbitt who invented it. She was a New Yorker who had moved to Texas in the 1940s—and was later Neiman Marcus's food service director. She made the dish for a New Year's party, using black-eyed peas (symbolizing good luck for the new year) in a red wine vinaigrette, and served it with tortilla chips, jokingly calling it "Texas caviar." It has since evolved on the internet to become a free-for-all, adding any kind of beans, pineapple, mango, sliced black olives, sweet pickled jalapeños . . . the list goes on and on. Whatever you call it, it's a definite crowd pleaser even if people have gone wild with the ingredients. Here is my latest take inspired by the original salad.

EXPERIMENT:
Taste your jalapeños and Anaheim chiles and adjust measurements to your preferred level of heat (you can always add some of the veins and seeds back in if you like it really spicy). If you can't find red Anaheim chiles, use ripe (red) jalapeño or red serrano. Many people have the gene that makes cilantro taste like soap and are very passionate about the herb. You can always serve the cilantro on the side, or I like to experiment with flat-leaf parsley as a substitute. For a creamier, richer version, try doubling the avocado or topping with crema or sour cream.

START OUT

Ice water

¾ cup (175 ml) diced red onion (¼-inch/6-mm pieces)

1 cup (240 ml) diced Roma tomatoes, or substitute what looks best at the market (¼-inch/6-mm pieces)

WHISK

1 tablespoon (15 ml) pressed garlic

¼ cup (60 ml) avocado oil

3 tablespoons (45 ml) red wine vinegar

1 tablespoon (15 ml) agave syrup

1 teaspoon (5 ml) fresh lime juice

1 teaspoon (5 ml) chili powder

Flaky sea salt and freshly cracked black pepper

TOSS

2 cups (475 ml) cooked or rinsed and drained canned black-eyed peas

2 cups (475 ml) cooked or rinsed and drained canned black beans

2 cups (475 ml) raw sweet or thawed frozen corn kernels

1 cup (240 ml) peeled and diced jicama (¼-inch/6-mm pieces)

1 cup (240 ml) finely chopped fresh cilantro

1 cup (240 ml) diced avocado (¼-inch/6 mm pieces)

¾ cup (175 ml) finely crumbled Cotija cheese

½ cup (120 ml) diced red bell pepper (¼-inch/6-mm pieces)

½ cup (120 ml) diced yellow or orange bell pepper (¼-inch/6-mm pieces)

½ cup (120 ml) diced green bell pepper (¼-inch/6-mm pieces)

½ cup (120 ml) chopped scallions (green parts only)

3 tablespoons (45 ml) very finely diced seeded and deveined fresh jalapeño

3 tablespoons (45 ml) very finely diced seeded and deveined fresh red Anaheim chile

8 cups (1,900 ml) thick tortilla chips, for serving

START OUT: Fill a 500-ml beaker or a small glass bowl halfway with ice water and add the onion. Soak for 10 minutes, then drain and pat the onion dry. Place the tomatoes in a colander and gently press down with a spoon to drain off excess liquid.

WHISK: Rinse the pressed garlic in a very fine mesh strainer and shake off any excess water. In a huge salad bowl (at least 17 inches/43 cm in diameter if possible), combine the garlic, oil, vinegar, agave, lime juice, and chili powder and season with salt and pepper. Whisk until well combined, then taste and adjust the seasoning if needed.

TOSS: In the bowl with the dressing, add the black-eyed peas, black beans, corn, jicama, cilantro, avocado, cheese, red bell peppers, yellow peppers, green peppers, scallions, jalapeño, Anaheim chile, tomatoes, and onions. Toss until all the ingredients are evenly combined and coated with dressing. The salad can sit for up to a couple hours (and the flavor will get even better); just remember to stir it occasionally. Serve with the chips on the side.

ENJOY: I'm having it with a rosé, agua fresca, or a giant glass of water.

Jamaican Coleslaw

SERVES 8 TO 12 AS A SIDE

Caribbean

The spicy-sweet and creamy crunch is a favorite—and a fun surprise—at picnics. Serve with jerk chicken and fried plantains for dinner and you can't go wrong. You can almost hear the crystal-clear blue ocean gently rolling up onto the sand as you take your first bite.

WHISK

1 teaspoon (5 ml) pressed garlic

¼ cup (60 ml) mayonnaise

¼ cup (60 ml) sour cream

2 tablespoons (30 ml) sugar

2 tablespoons (30 ml) fresh lime juice

1 tablespoon (15 ml) malt vinegar

1 teaspoon (5 ml) Dijon mustard

1 teaspoon (5 ml) Jamaican hot sauce (a Scotch bonnet or habanero hot sauce), or to taste

Flaky sea salt and freshly cracked black pepper

TOSS

6 cups (1,400 ml) shredded green cabbage

2 cups (475 ml) shredded red cabbage

2 cups (475 ml) julienned fresh mango (see How to Prep a Mango, opposite)

2 cups (475 ml) peeled and shredded carrots

½ cup (120 ml) diced yellow onion (¼-inch/6-mm pieces)

½ cup (120 ml) finely chopped fresh cilantro

¼ cup (60 ml) very finely diced seeded and deveined fresh jalapeño

WHISK: Rinse the pressed garlic in a very fine mesh strainer and shake off any excess water. In a large, deep bowl combine the garlic, mayonnaise, sour cream, sugar, lime juice, vinegar, mustard, and hot sauce and season with salt and pepper. Whisk until emulsified, then taste and adjust the seasoning if needed.

TOSS: In the bowl with the dressing, add the green cabbage, red cabbage, mango, carrots, onion, cilantro, and jalapeño. Toss until all the ingredients are evenly combined and coated with dressing. Store covered in the refrigerator until ready to serve. (The coleslaw is best prepared at least an hour ahead of time and is even better the next day. If storing and serving later, strain off excess liquid each time before plating up.)

ENJOY: I'm having it with Jamaican lager or ginger beer.

EXPERIMENT:
I like to shred cabbage really thin with a food processor's slicing blade, especially if it doesn't have time to marinate in the dressing. If you're using pre-shredded cabbage, which can sometimes have large chunks and thick pieces, make sure to give the slaw plenty of time to sit. Try Anaheim or Scotch bonnet peppers if you like your food hot. I have made this with avocado oil instead of sour cream for those that are dairy free and it was fab. Play some steel-drum music while chopping to put you in the mood.

HOW TO PREP A MANGO: Use a sharp paring knife to cut the layer of skin off the base of the mango where the stem was connected. This will give you a flat surface so the fruit doesn't slide or roll around. Gently cut the skin off from top to bottom in long strips, trying to preserve as much of the fruit as possible until all the skin is removed. Run your knife down lengthwise through the fruit parallel to the pit and about half an inch from the center; you should be able to feel the tough fibers near the pit but adjust if you hit the pit. Repeat on the other side and the fruit is ready to chop.

Steak and Chimichurri

Argentina

This herby sauce is to Argentinians what barbeque sauce or hot sauce is to Americans: they put that stuff on everything. According to Argentinian historian Daniel Balmaceda, *chimichurri* was a generic term to describe strong sauces used to conserve and accompany different meats by the Quechua, an indigenous population that has lived in the Andean region of north Argentina for millennia. Different folklore about this specific herby-garlicky sauce's origins include an Irish immigrant named Jimmy McCurry (who became "Chimichurri") inventing the version we know today. Twentieth-century Basque migrants also lay claim, or maybe it was captive British soldiers in the 1800s saying "Give me curry." I'm leaning toward the local version of history. No matter who invented it, this sauce is a favorite of Argentinians—and it makes one outstanding salad dressing.

EXPERIMENT:
Try grass-fed beef: it's getting easier to find these days and I find it tastes, smells, and digests so much better than beef raised with corn. It's a little more expensive but well worth it in my opinion.

START OUT

1½ pounds (680 g) rib-eye steak

4 tablespoons (60 ml) extra-virgin olive oil

1 tablespoon (15 ml) pressed garlic

2 teaspoons (10 ml) freshly cracked black pepper

1½ teaspoons (7.5 ml) granulated sea salt

1 pound (450 g) asparagus

2 large portobello mushroom caps

1 teaspoon (5 ml) fresh lemon juice

1 cup (240 ml) quartered cherry tomatoes

WHISK

2 tablespoons (30 ml) pressed garlic

2 cups (475 ml) finely chopped fresh flat-leaf parsley

1 cup (240 ml) extra-virgin olive oil

3 tablespoons (45 ml) red wine vinegar

2 tablespoons (30 ml) dried oregano

1 tablespoon (15 ml) very finely diced seeded and deveined fresh red Anaheim chile, or substitute jalapeño

1 teaspoon (5 ml) flaky sea salt

½ teaspoon (2.5 ml) freshly cracked black pepper

½ teaspoon (2.5 ml) red pepper flakes

TOSS

6 cups (1,400 ml) lightly packed spring mix (baby lettuce blend)

2 cups (475 ml) lightly packed arugula

1 cup (240 ml) cubed avocado (½-inch/1.3-cm pieces)

START OUT: Take the steak out of the refrigerator and set it on the counter for at least an hour to allow it to come to room temperature. Mix 2 tablespoons (30 ml) of the oil and the garlic and rub it all over the steak. Generously season the steak with the black pepper and 1 teaspoon (5 ml) of the granulated sea salt. Preheat the grill to 450°F (230°C) or for high-heat grilling, or heat a grill pan over medium high (when you're ready to grill).

Remove the tough ends of the asparagus and in a large bowl, toss with 1 tablespoon (15 ml) of the olive oil and ¼ teaspoon (1.5 ml) of the granulated sea salt.

Wipe any dirt off the mushrooms and rub with the remaining 1 tablespoon (15 ml) olive oil and season with the remaining ¼ teaspoon (1.5 ml) salt.

Place the steak on the grill and cook for 6 minutes, rotating halfway through for crosshatched grill marks. Flip the steak and cook for another 6 minutes, rotating after 3 minutes again. Continue cooking and remove the steak from the grill when the internal temperature reaches 140 to 145°F (60 to 63°C) on an instant-read thermometer (for medium). Transfer to a plate and let it rest for 10 minutes before cutting it into 1-inch- (2.5-cm-) thick strips.

Put the asparagus on the grill and cook until grill marks begin to appear and the asparagus is tender but not soft, turning once, 3 to 5 minutes per side depending on the thickness. Transfer to a plate and let cool. Chop into 1-inch (2.5-cm) pieces then toss with the lemon juice.

Put the portobellos on the grill and cook, flipping once, until grill marks appear, 5 to 7 minutes per side. Set aside to cool. Chop into 1-inch (2.5-cm) pieces.

While the steak rests, place the tomatoes in a colander and gently press down with a spoon to drain off excess liquid.

WHISK: Rinse the pressed garlic in a very fine mesh strainer and shake off any excess water. In a blender or food processor, combine the garlic, parsley, oil, vinegar, oregano, Anaheim chile, flaky sea salt, black pepper, and red pepper flakes. Blend until smooth.

TOSS: In a large salad bowl, add the spring mix, arugula, avocado, tomatoes, steak, asparagus, and mushrooms and drizzle with about half the dressing, or to taste. Toss until all the ingredients are evenly combined and coated with dressing, then taste and add more dressing if you like (or pass the extra dressing on the side) before serving.

ENJOY: I'm having it with cabernet sauvignon or iced tea with mango and orange juice.

Ceviche

Peru

There are so many great Peruvian restaurants popping up these days. It's reported that ceviche, Peru's signature dish, dates back to the 1500s when explorers from Spain introduced the technique of marinating raw fish in vinegar, citrus juice, and spices and added the aji amarillo chile, a spicy, fruity, vibrant orange-yellow pepper grown in Peru. The fish appears to be "cooked" by the citrus, which really just coagulates the proteins. Because the fish isn't actually cooked, use the highest-quality, freshest fish available: sushi-grade. I like my ceviche spicy, but add less chile if you're sensitive to spice. This fish-based salad is sometimes served with fried plantains and sweet potato chips (which you can also use), but I prefer to make dehydrated chips.

EXPERIMENT:
Fresh is best, but if you can't find fresh-off-the-boat or sushi-grade frozen mahimahi, experiment with sea bass, tilapia, and halibut. They are the best fish for absorbing the citrus juices. Vegetarians and vegans can use sliced hearts of palm in place of the fish. Save yourself a few hours and use store-bought sweet potato chips instead of making the dehydrated chips. Fun fact: leftover dehydrated chips make great dog treats.

START OUT

2 medium sweet potatoes (peel if you like)

2 tablespoons plus 1 teaspoon (35 ml) extra-virgin olive oil

1½ teaspoons (7.5 ml) granulated sea salt

Flaky sea salt and freshly cracked black pepper

Ice water

1 cup (240 ml) halved and thinly sliced red onion

WHISK

2 tablespoons (30 ml) pressed garlic

1⅓ cups (315 ml) fresh lime juice

¼ cup (60 ml) finely chopped fresh cilantro

2 tablespoons (30 ml) very finely diced seeded and deveined fresh aji amarillo chile, or substitute 1 tablespoon (15 ml) fresh yellow habanero or Scotch bonnet

2 tablespoons (30 ml) fresh orange juice (remember to zest first)

2 teaspoons (10 ml) flaky sea salt

2 teaspoons (10 ml) lightly packed grated orange zest

1 teaspoon (5 ml) grated fresh ginger

TOSS

2 pounds (900 g) fresh, or frozen and slightly thawed, sushi-grade mahimahi, cut into ½-inch (1.3-cm) cubes

¼ cup (60 ml) fresh raw white corn kernels

START OUT: Line two baking sheets with parchment paper, silicone baking mats, or metal racks.

Using a sharp knife, food processor slicing attachment, or mandoline (please wear a protective glove if using a mandoline), slice enough of the sweet potato into ⅛-inch (3-mm) or thinner slices to completely cover the two baking sheets so the slices are touching but not overlapping. Dice enough of the remaining potato into ¼-inch (6-mm) cubes to measure ½ cup (120 ml) and set aside (save any extra sweet potato for another use).

In a medium bowl, soak the sweet potato slices in water for 1 hour. Drain and pat completely dry. Meanwhile, preheat the oven to 250°F (120°C), and use convection mode if that's an option.

Spread the slices out on the prepared baking sheets and lightly brush 2 tablespoons (30 ml) of the olive oil over both sides of the potatoes. Bake, checking every half hour or so, until they appear dehydrated, crisp, and brittle, 1 to 3 hours, depending on your oven. Remove from the oven, cool completely, then sprinkle the chips with the granulated sea salt. (The chips can be made ahead of time and stored in an airtight container for up to 1 week.)

Raise the oven temperature to 425°F (220°C) and use convection mode if that's an option. Line a baking sheet with parchment paper or a silicone baking mat.

In a small bowl, mix the reserved diced sweet potatoes and the remaining 1 teaspoon (5ml) oil, season with flaky sea salt and pepper, then toss to coat. Spread the mixture evenly on the prepared baking sheet. Bake until the edges start to brown, stirring halfway through, about 10 minutes (longer for a regular oven). Transfer the parchment with the sweet potatoes to the counter to cool.

Fill a 500-ml beaker or glass bowl halfway with ice water and add the onion. Soak for 10 minutes, then drain and pat the onion dry.

WHISK: Rinse the pressed garlic in a very fine mesh strainer and shake off any excess water. In a medium ceramic or glass bowl, whisk together the garlic, lime juice, cilantro, chile, orange juice, flaky sea salt, orange zest, and ginger and until well combined.

TOSS: In the bowl with the dressing, stir in the fish, toss to coat, and place in the refrigerator for 1 hour (for "medium-rare") or up to 4 hours (for "well-done"), stirring occasionally to evenly distribute the dressing.

In a medium salad bowl, combine the fish and as much of the dressing as you like with the corn, onions, and sweet potatoes cubes. Toss until all the ingredients are evenly combined and coated with dressing and serve with the dehydrated sweet potato chips on the side for scooping.

ENJOY: I'm having it with a chardonnay or yerba maté.

Esquites Salad

Mexico

There is a Mexican-influenced restaurant in Sausalito, California, owned by a famous chef who had her own show on PBS for years. I went there one year for my birthday and had the most amazing "street corn" and margaritas. During the summer corn season, I thought it would be fun to turn it into a salad. I originally called this Street Corn Salad and later changed to Esquites Salad after I was quickly educated on the Mexican and Mexican American name for it. I'm forever on the learning curve; there's nothing like a social media account to humble you! This salad is delicious and holds its freshness well for parties, and it's excellent with carne asada and refried beans for dinner.

EXPERIMENT:

Try grating some zest from the lime before juicing it and adding a pinch to the dressing. I love zesting citrus and adding it whenever I am using its juice in a recipe. It adds a depth to the flavor, but a little bit goes a long way; sometimes just a pinch is all you need. If you are looking to get more greens in, experiment with serving on a bed of lettuce or finely shredded kale. It's also fun to eat as a dip with thin plantain chips. For more heat, add diced, seeded, and deveined jalapeño.

START OUT

2 tablespoons (30 ml) unsalted butter

8 cups (1,900 ml) fresh corn kernels (from about 8 ears)

Flaky sea salt and freshly cracked black pepper

Ice water

½ cup (120 ml) very finely diced red onion

WHISK

1 tablespoon (15 ml) pressed garlic

½ cup (120 ml) avocado oil

¼ cup (60 ml) mayonnaise

¼ cup (60 ml) Mexican crema, or substitute sour cream

2 tablespoons (30 ml) fresh lime juice

1 tablespoon (15 ml) puréed chipotle in adobo sauce (see Note)

¼ teaspoon (1.5 ml) ancho chile powder

½ teaspoon (2.5 ml) granulated sea salt

½ teaspoon (2.5 ml) freshly cracked black pepper

TOSS

1 cup (240 ml) crumbled Cotija cheese, plus more for serving

¼ cup (60 ml) finely chopped fresh cilantro, plus a few sprigs for serving

START OUT: In a large cast-iron or other heavy skillet, melt the butter over medium-high heat. Add the corn, season with flaky sea salt and pepper, and cook, stirring occasionally, until the corn is slightly charred and softened, 8 to 10 minutes. Turn off the heat and let it stand for 2 minutes. Remove from the skillet and set aside.

Meanwhile, fill a 500-ml beaker or glass bowl halfway with ice water and add the onion. Soak for 10 minutes, then drain and pat the onion dry.

WHISK: Rinse the pressed garlic in a very fine mesh strainer and shake off any excess water. In a large salad bowl, whisk together the garlic, oil, mayonnaise, crema, lime juice, chipotle purée, ancho chile powder, granulated sea salt, and pepper until emulsified.

NOTE: To make puréed chipotle in adobo sauce, put an entire 7-ounce (200-g) can of chipotle peppers in adobo sauce in a blender and blend until smooth. Portion any leftover purée into an ice cube tray and freeze for up to three months for future use.

TOSS: In the bowl with the dressing, combine the corn, onion, cheese, and cilantro. Toss until all the ingredients are evenly combined and coated with dressing. Top with a sprinkle of cheese and a few sprigs of cilantro and serve.

ENJOY: I'm having it with a margarita or iced horchata.

Across-the-Pond Irish Salad

SERVES 4 TO 6 AS A MEAL OR 8 TO 12 AS A SIDE

Ireland

This salad is inspired by a chef I discovered from Ireland, and to me represents the very exciting food scene there currently. If it is possible to taste the personality of a chef in a dish, I want to make him my best friend! It's full of flavor from herbs and spices and is perfectly salty. I can say without reservation that this pizza-inspired salad with all the roasted vegetables is one of my all-time favorites and reminds me of my favorite childhood pizza parlor, Old Cal Pizza, with an Irish twist. I have started preparing it at my cooking demos, and everyone loves it and asks for seconds. It takes a little time to prepare, so put some music on and have fun roasting and chopping.

EXPERIMENT:
I often say, use what you have. That is especially true with more pricey ingredients like nuts and cheese. You can easily substitute pistachios for almonds and feta for goat cheese. I made this salad with both, and it was still fabulous. If you like, use a coddled egg yolk (see page 243) in the dressing.

START OUT

2 tablespoons (30 ml) Roasted Garlic Purée (page 256)

Extra-virgin olive oil

1 tablespoon (15 ml) pressed garlic

1 tablespoon (15 ml) Italian seasoning

1 teaspoon (5 ml) dried oregano

Flaky sea salt and freshly cracked black pepper

3 cups (720 ml) cubed sourdough bread (1-inch/2.5-cm pieces)

⅔ cup (160 ml) almonds

2 teaspoons (10 ml) ground fennel seed

2 cups (475 ml) grape tomatoes

1 tablespoon (15 ml) honey

¼ cup (60 ml) fresh oregano

3 cups (720 ml) cubed Italian eggplant (1-inch/2.5-cm pieces)

Ice water

⅔ cup (160 ml) halved and thinly sliced red onion

WHISK

2 tablespoons (30 ml) fresh lemon juice

2 tablespoons (30 ml) sherry vinegar

2 tablespoons (30 ml) honey

2 tablespoons (30 ml) finely chopped fresh oregano

1 tablespoon (15 ml) miso paste

1 tablespoon (15 ml) Dijon mustard

1 large egg yolk

½ teaspoon (2.5 ml) red pepper flakes

¼ cup (60 ml) extra-virgin olive oil

TOSS

8 cups (1,900 ml) thinly sliced lacinato kale, ribs removed

½ cup (120 ml) finely chopped fresh flat-leaf parsley

¼ cup (60 ml) drained capers

¾ cup (175 ml) crumbled fresh goat cheese (Irish goat cheese if you want to be authentic; see page 43)

START OUT: Prepare the roasted garlic purée for the dressing (up to 3 days in advance if you like, or make it at the same time as the croutons and roasted vegetables).

Preheat the oven to 425°F (220°C) and use convection mode if that's an option. Line a baking sheet with parchment paper or a silicone baking mat.

Prepare the croutons. In a medium bowl, whisk together 3 tablespoons (45 ml) oil, the pressed garlic, Italian seasoning, dried oregano, ½ teaspoon (2.5 ml) salt, and ½ teaspoon (2.5 ml) pepper. Add the sourdough bread cubes and toss until evenly coated. Place the bread on the prepared baking sheet and spread out evenly so the cubes can brown on all sides. Bake until golden brown and crispy on the outside, stirring halfway through, 12 to 15 minutes (longer for a regular oven). Lift the parchment with the croutons off the baking sheet to cool.

Next, make the almonds. Keep the oven at 425°F (220°C) and line the pan with parchment again. Pour the almonds, 2 tablespoons (30 ml) oil, the ground fennel, and ¼ teaspoon (1.5 ml) salt onto the parchment and toss until the almonds are coated. Bake until the almonds are shiny and toasted, stirring halfway through, 8 to 10 minutes (longer for a regular oven). Let cool for 5 minutes, then coarsely chop and set aside.

Then, prepare the roasted vegetables. Line two baking sheets with parchment. On one, add the tomatoes, 2 tablespoons (30 ml) olive oil, the honey, fresh oregano, and ½ teaspoon (2.5 ml) salt. Toss to coat.

In a medium bowl, combine the eggplant, 3 tablespoons (45 ml) olive oil, ½ teaspoon (2.5 ml) salt, and ½ teaspoon (2.5 ml) pepper and mix until evenly distributed. Spread the eggplant out on the second baking sheet.

Transfer both pans to the oven. Roast the tomatoes, flipping halfway through, until they are blistered and beginning to burst, 20 to 25 minutes (longer for a regular oven). Roast the eggplant, stirring halfway through, until it is nicely golden and caramelized, 20 to 30 minutes (longer for a regular oven). Lift the parchment off the baking sheets and let the vegetables cool.

Meanwhile, fill a 500-ml beaker or a small glass bowl halfway with ice water and add the onion. Soak for 10 minutes, then drain and pat the onion dry.

WHISK: In a beaker (if using an immersion blender) or blender, combine the roasted garlic purée, lemon juice, vinegar, honey, chopped oregano, miso, mustard, egg yolk, and red pepper flakes. Start to blend and slowly pour in the oil. Blend until the dressing is emulsified.

TOSS: In a large salad bowl, add the kale, parsley, capers, croutons, almonds, tomatoes, eggplant, and onion and drizzle with dressing to taste. Toss until all the ingredients are evenly combined and coated with dressing, then sprinkle the goat cheese on top and serve.

ENJOY: I'm having it with old-vine zinfandel or iced Irish breakfast tea.

Panzanella

Italy

Come late summer, you can't do much better than a panzanella salad. Originating in Italy, it started with stale crusty bread soaked in water (then squeezed out), heirloom tomatoes, fresh basil, and high-quality olive oil to create the *combinazione perfetta*. I prefer to use homemade sourdough croutons that absorb the dressing and all that delicious tomato juice. Going to a farmers' market for the ingredients for this one is worth the trip: the flavor and smell of a vine-ripened tomato is unbeatable.

EXPERIMENT:
Don't worry, if you can only find regular Roma tomatoes, it will probably still be one of your favorites. Experiment with adding avocado, cucumber, or red pepper flakes if you like. Play some classic Italian music while preparing this salad to get the full effect.

START OUT

6 cups (1,400 ml) Sourdough Garlic Croutons (page 235)

Ice water

1¼ cups (300 ml) halved and thinly sliced red onion

WHISK

3 tablespoons (45 ml) red wine vinegar

1 teaspoon (5 ml) flaky sea salt

½ teaspoon (2.5 ml) freshly cracked black pepper

⅓ cup (80 ml) extra-virgin olive oil

TOSS

2 cups (475 ml) chopped red heirloom or other seasonal red tomatoes (bite-size wedges; see Note)

2 cups (475 ml) chopped

mixed yellow, orange, green, and/or black heirloom tomatoes (bite-size wedges)

2 cups (475 ml) quartered cherry tomatoes

2 cups (475 ml) lightly packed torn fresh basil (torn into quarters or so)

Flaky sea salt and freshly cracked black pepper

START OUT: Prepare the croutons. Meanwhile, fill a 500-ml beaker or a small glass bowl halfway with ice water and add the onion. Soak for 10 minutes, then drain and pat the onion dry.

WHISK: In a large salad bowl, combine the vinegar, salt, and pepper. While whisking, slowly add the oil until well combined.

TOSS: In the bowl with the dressing, add the red tomatoes, mixed tomatoes, cherry tomatoes, basil, croutons, and onion. Toss until all the ingredients are evenly combined and coated with dressing. Taste and season with more salt and pepper if necessary. Let stand for 5 minutes to give the croutons a chance to absorb the tomato juices and dressing, then serve.

ENJOY: I'm having it with a nice rosé or *acqua minerale gassata*.

NOTE: To pick out the best tomatoes (wherever and whenever you're shopping), use your nose. I love their smell! Give the tomatoes a sniff: you should be able to smell them at room temperature. Look for ones with a deep red color and try to avoid hard ones that look faded or green and don't have a smell as they were most likely picked too early.

French-Style Potato Salad

France

Everyone loves potato salad, and it seems every continent and country has its own spin. I never knew the French had their own style until I made a Niçoise (page 56). This simple potato salad is great for a summer picnic or barbeque with its fresh-tasting light, herby, mayonnaise-free dressing.

START OUT

Flaky sea salt

2 pounds (900 g) medium Yukon gold or red potatoes

Ice water

2 tablespoons (30 ml) very finely diced shallot

WHISK

2 tablespoons (30 ml) finely chopped fresh flat-leaf parsley

1 tablespoon (15 ml) white wine vinegar

1 tablespoon (15 ml) fresh lemon juice

1 teaspoon (5 ml) Dijon mustard

1 teaspoon (5 ml) finely chopped fresh tarragon or ½ teaspoon (2.5 ml) dried (optional)

Flaky sea salt and freshly cracked black pepper

¼ cup plus 2 tablespoons (90 ml) extra-virgin olive oil

TOSS

¼ cup (60 ml) sauvignon blanc or pinot gris

Flaky sea salt and freshly cracked black pepper

EXPERIMENT: There are many varieties of potatoes including purple or "blue" baby ones. Experiment with Yukon golds, red, and blue ones for the Fourth of July and Bastille Day on July 14 (the French flag is red, white, and blue, too), or try the Red, White, and Blue Potato Salad (page 168). Everyone's independence should be celebrated. I often throw more fresh herbs like chives and dill in this salad if I have them sitting on the counter.

START OUT: Fill a large pot with water, lightly salt it, and bring to a boil. Add the potatoes and bring back to a soft boil, adjusting the heat to medium low. Cook the potatoes until fork-tender, 15 to 25 minutes, depending on size. Drain the potatoes into a colander and let them stand until they are cool enough to handle. Peel the potatoes if you like. Slice them ¼-inch (6-mm) thick.

Meanwhile, fill a 250-ml beaker or a small glass bowl halfway with ice water and add the shallot. Soak for 10 minutes, then drain and pat the shallot dry.

WHISK: In a small bowl, combine the shallot, parsley, vinegar, lemon juice, mustard, and tarragon (if using) and season with salt and pepper. While whisking, slowly pour in the oil until the dressing is emulsified. Taste and adjust the seasoning if needed.

TOSS: In a large bowl, combine the potatoes and wine and gently toss to combine. Let sit for a few minutes for the potatoes to absorb some of the wine. Drizzle the dressing over the potatoes and gently toss to coat. Taste and adjust the seasoning if needed. Let sit for at least an hour at room temperature (or, even better, overnight in the refrigerator) before serving.

ENJOY: I'm having it with a sauvignon blanc.

Tapas Salad

Spain

If you've ever been to Spain, you've probably had tapas. They are usually small plates of freshly prepared dishes that are served in cafés and bars and they vary dramatically from region to region in Spain. Those dishes of herbaceous olives, salty and oily tuna, and creamy Manchego are the inspiration for this salad. When you first visit Spain, you'll be surprised at how similar it is to California. The one difference I found was the long siestas and late dinners (they may be on to something). Most Spanish salad dressings, like this one, are on the lighter and refreshing side, which lets the fresh produce shine.

EXPERIMENT:
Love tinned fish? Experiment with sardines or Spanish anchovies. Prefer fresh fish over canned? Try using a grilled or steamed fresh white fish like cod, halibut, snapper, or salmon. Vegan? Skip the cheese, fish, and eggs and add hearts of palm, grilled mushrooms, and some roasted or marinated vegetables. There are many types of Spanish olives; if you find a variety at an olive bar, try a few. I recently discovered there is a chain of salad restaurants in Spain that uses cubed Emmentaler cheese in their salads; experiment with it here instead of Manchego if you like.

START OUT

4 Perfect Boiled Eggs (page 257)

Ice water

½ cup (120 ml) halved and sliced red onion

1 cup (240 ml) quartered cherry tomatoes

WHISK

1 teaspoon (5 ml) pressed garlic

½ cup (120 ml) extra-virgin olive oil

3 tablespoons (45 ml) finely chopped fresh flat-leaf parsley

2 tablespoons (30 ml) red wine vinegar

Flaky sea salt and freshly cracked black pepper

TOSS

1 cup (240 ml) canned oil-packed Spanish tuna

6 cups (1,400 ml) chopped romaine lettuce (1-inch/2.5-cm strips)

⅔ cup (160 ml) cubed Manchego cheese (½-inch/1.3-cm pieces), or substitute another mild, hard sheep or goat cheese

⅓ cup (80 ml) pimento-stuffed green olives

⅓ cup (80 ml) pitted black Spanish olives, or substitute oil-cured olives

Freshly cracked black pepper, for serving

START OUT: Prepare the eggs and when they're cool enough to handle, quarter them. Meanwhile, fill a 500-ml beaker or a small glass bowl halfway with ice water and add the onion. Soak for 10 minutes, then drain and pat the onion dry. Place the tomatoes in a colander and gently press down with a spoon to drain off excess liquid.

WHISK: Rinse the pressed garlic in a very fine mesh strainer and shake off any excess water. In a large salad bowl, combine the garlic, oil, parsley, and vinegar and season with salt and pepper. Whisk until well combined, then taste and adjust the seasoning if needed.

TOSS: Strain the tuna and break apart with a fork into ½-inch (1.3-cm) chunks. In the bowl with

the dressing, combine the lettuce, cheese, green olives, black olives, eggs, tomatoes, onion, and tuna. Toss until all the ingredients are evenly combined and coated with dressing and serve, passing extra freshly cracked black pepper at the table.

ENJOY: I'm having it with a rosé or sparkling water.

Fattoush

Lebanon

The name of this famous salad derives from the Arabic word *fatteh*, which means "crumbs." It's served in many parts of the Middle East, but I was originally introduced to it by a Lebanese follower who was determined I should make this salad. She was right, it is among the top favorites of our salad community, with good reason: the pita croutons are really delicious. This is like a chopped salad given that everything (except the pita croutons) is about the same size. I love the contrasting flavors of the dried and fresh mint, but if you can't find fresh mint, it is still just as good with dried.

EXPERIMENT:
Try adding any or all of the following: za'atar seasoning, pomegranate seeds, diced red or orange bell peppers, chopped dates, watermelon radish, white onion or scallions (instead of red onion), a sprinkling of Aleppo pepper for a little kick, or a drizzling of extra pomegranate molasses over the top (so good!). If you're in a hurry, crumbled pita chips work just fine; but they can be salty, so taste them before making the dressing and adjust the seasoning accordingly.

START OUT

2 cups (475 ml) Pita Croutons (page 233)

2 cups (475 ml) diced Roma, hothouse, or Campari tomatoes (¼-inch/6-mm pieces)

Ice water

¾ cup (175 ml) diced red onion (¼-inch/6-mm pieces)

WHISK

1½ teaspoons (7.5 ml) pressed garlic

¾ cup (175 ml) extra-virgin olive oil

¼ cup (60 ml) fresh lemon juice

3 tablespoons (45 ml) pomegranate molasses

4 teaspoons (20 ml) dried mint

1½ teaspoons (7.5 ml) dried sumac

Heaping ¼ teaspoon (2 ml) ground cinnamon

Heaping ¼ teaspoon (2 ml) ground allspice

Flaky sea salt and freshly cracked black pepper

TOSS

8 cups (1,900 ml) chopped romaine lettuce (bite-size pieces)

2 cups (475 ml) finely chopped fresh flat-leaf parsley

2 cups (475 ml) diced seeded Persian cucumber (¼-inch/6-mm pieces)

½ cup (120 ml) finely diced radish (¼-inch/6-mm pieces)

⅓ cup (80 ml) finely chopped fresh mint

Dried sumac, for serving (optional)

START OUT: Prepare the croutons. Meanwhile, place the tomatoes in a colander and gently press down with a spoon to drain off excess liquid. Fill a 500-ml beaker or a small glass bowl halfway with ice water and add the onion. Soak for 10 minutes, then drain and pat the onion dry.

WHISK: Rinse the pressed garlic in a very fine mesh strainer and shake off any excess water. In a large salad bowl, combine the garlic, oil, lemon juice, molasses, dried mint, sumac, cinnamon, and allspice and season with salt and pepper. Whisk until well combined and taste and adjust the seasoning if needed.

TOSS: In the bowl with the dressing, add the romaine lettuce, parsley, cucumber, radish, fresh mint, onion, and tomatoes. Toss until all the ingredients are evenly combined and coated with dressing. Right before serving, add the pita croutons, toss again, and, if you like an extra-tart taste, garnish with more sumac. Serve while the croutons are still crunchy. (If you have extra pita croutons, serve them alongside in a separate bowl; they always seem to disappear.)

ENJOY: I'm having it with a sauvignon blanc or a "Shirley Temple" with sparkling water and 1 tablespoon (15 ml) pomegranate molasses.

West African Avocado and Citrus Salad

Senegal

This salad has some of my favorite things: mango, avocado, and citrus. There are so many wonderful, delicious, colorful salads from every corner of the world, but I love that they often have these flavorful ingredients in common. The minute I found this refreshing combo from Senegal, I knew I had to share. I add my own California twist by using whatever beautiful citrus is in season beyond navel oranges, like kumquats and blood oranges. This salad is a perfect side dish; try serving it alongside fresh grilled fish or chicken yassa (a braised chicken dish from Senegal) and rice.

START OUT

¼ cup (60ml) dried coconut flakes

WHISK

½ cup (120 ml) finely chopped fresh flat-leaf parsley

¼ cup (60 ml) avocado oil

¼ cup (60 ml) fresh lime juice (remember to zest first)

2 tablespoons (30 ml) fresh orange juice

2 tablespoons (30 ml) very finely diced seeded and deveined fresh jalapeño, or more if you like heat

1 teaspoon (5 ml) lightly packed grated lime zest

Flaky sea salt and freshly cracked black pepper

TOSS

2 cups (480 ml) peeled and pitted (see page 119) mango wedges (1½ inches/4 cm thick)

2 cups (480 ml) sliced avocado (½ inch/1.3 cm thick)

1 cup (240 ml) supremed (see page 195) orange segments (about 2 navel oranges), or substitute any seasonal citrus

START OUT: Preheat the oven to 375°F (190°C) and position a rack in the middle. Line a baking sheet with parchment paper or a silicone baking mat. Add the coconut in an even layer. Bake until the shavings start to look toasty brown on the edges, about 3 minutes. Gently lift the parchment with the coconut off the baking sheet to cool.

WHISK: In a large salad bowl, add the parsley, oil, lime juice, orange juice, jalapeño, and lime zest and season with salt and pepper. Whisk until well combined, then taste and adjust the seasoning if needed.

TOSS: In the bowl with the dressing, add the mango, avocado, oranges, and toasted coconut. Gently toss until all the ingredients are evenly combined and coated with dressing and serve.

ENJOY: I'm having it with bissap (see below) or ginger beer.

 EXPERIMENT: Some versions of this salad have quartered cherry tomatoes; add them if you'd like another colorful element. Use peanut oil in place of the avocado oil for a more classic flavor profile. Bissap is a popular beverage in Senegal. It is a purplish-red juice made from hibiscus flowers, water, and sugar. Fresh mint leaves and orange blossom water can be added.

Kani (Kanikama) Salad

Japan

This salad is a popular home-cooked dish in Japan and is also available in most Japanese restaurants outside of the country. *Kani* means "crab" in Japanese and it is often made with kanikama, a seafood-based imitation snow crab or Japanese spider crab meat. The salad contains Kewpie mayonnaise, a rich, flavorful mayonnaise made with more egg than American varieties. Japanese-style mayonnaise has become very popular lately and is easier to find in grocery stores, but when in doubt, stop by your local Asian market if one is nearby. Break out your sharpest knife and brush up on your cutting skills; everything should be cut into matchsticks of about the same size. Serve the salad with avocado and steamed sushi rice and eat it in nori, and you almost have a California roll. I also like to serve it on large butter lettuce leaves.

WHISK

½ cup (120 ml) Kewpie mayonnaise, or substitute another mayonnaise

¼ cup (60 ml) ponzu sauce, or substitute low-sodium soy sauce

2 tablespoons (30 ml) rice vinegar

2 tablespoons (30 ml) fresh lemon juice

2 tablespoons (30 ml) black sesame seeds, or substitute white sesame seeds, toasted (see page 257)

¼ teaspoon (1.5 ml) ground white pepper

TOSS

2 cups (475 ml) shredded imitation crab meat (kanikama; see Note)

2 cups (475 ml) peeled and julienned carrots (see How to Julienne, opposite)

2 cups (475 ml) seeded and julienned English or Persian cucumber

1½ cups (360 ml) peeled (see page 119) julienned fresh mango

¼ cup (60 ml) very finely diced seeded and deveined fresh red Anaheim chile (optional)

3 tablespoons (45 ml) julienned pickled ginger

WHISK: In a large salad bowl, whisk together the mayonnaise, ponzu, vinegar, lemon juice, sesame seeds, and pepper until well combined.

TOSS: In the bowl with the dressing, combine the imitation crab, carrots, cucumber, mango, chile (if using), and ginger. Toss until all the ingredients are evenly combined and coated with dressing and serve, or refrigerate in a sealed container for up to 2 days.

ENJOY: I'm having it with cold sake or hot green tea.

NOTE: The imitation crab has a "grain" and is easier to cut into short lengths first (about 2½ inches/6.5 cm) and then shred it with a fork or by hand rather than trying to cut it lengthwise.

EXPERIMENT: When it's fresh crab season and you are feeling bougie, fresh crab is always a fabulous addition. Kent mangoes are the best variety you can get. They may be a little more expensive but the flavor is worth the splurge. Fresh red Anaheim chiles are common in my region, but if you can't find them, substitute red or green jalapeños, or 2 tablespoons (30ml) finely diced seeded and deveined red serrano chile.

HOW TO JULIENNE

Julienne is essentially the fancy-sounding French word for "short, thin strips," and vegetables can be easily julienned (it's also a verb) with a special julienne peeler or (very carefully) with the julienne attachment on a mandoline. If you don't have either of those tools, cut the vegetable (or whatever else you may be julienning) into 2-inch (5-cm) pieces, then cut those pieces lengthwise into thin slices, called planks. Stack a few of the planks on top of each other and slice them lengthwise again into thin matchsticks.

Bibimbap Salad

Korea

I can understand why this Korean classic is trending in the United States. It's easy to adapt to any way of eating, and the rich combinations of flavors with salty, sweet, spicy, and umami ingredients make this "salad" a hit. When I was shopping for this recipe, I went to a Korean market that had presliced beef, as well as preserved flowering fern, which the owner of the market said was traditional for the dish. While the salad will still taste great without it, flowering fern has a fascinating "forest floor" flavor and a chewy texture that I really enjoy. Use it if you can find it.

MARINATE	START OUT	WHISK	TOSS
1 tablespoon plus 2 teaspoons (25 ml) sesame seeds, toasted (see page 257)	4 cups (950 ml) cooked short-grain rice (see page 264)	1 teaspoon (5 ml) pressed garlic	1 tablespoon (15 ml) unsalted butter
3 tablespoons (45 ml) low-sodium soy sauce	3 teaspoons (15 ml) extra-virgin olive oil	3 tablespoons (45 ml) gochujang	4 large eggs
2 tablespoons (30 ml) toasted sesame oil	½ cup (120 ml) thinly sliced stemmed shiitake mushrooms	2 tablespoons (30 ml) water	Granulated sea salt and freshly cracked black pepper
1 tablespoon (15 ml) pressed garlic	1 cup (240 ml) peeled and julienned (see page 143) carrots	2 tablespoons (30 ml) avocado oil	3 cups (720 ml) lightly packed baby spinach
1 tablespoon (15 ml) light or dark brown sugar	2 cups (475 ml) halved lengthwise and sliced zucchini	1 tablespoon (15 ml) toasted sesame oil	⅓ cup (80 ml) cabbage kimchi or daikon kimchi
8 ounces (225 g) rib-eye steak or filet mignon, thinly sliced	1 cup (240 ml) bean sprouts	1 tablespoon (15 ml) light or dark brown sugar	¼ cup (60 ml) flowering fern (optional)
		2 teaspoons (10 ml) rice vinegar	
		½ teaspoon (2.5 ml) flaky sea salt	

MARINATE: Toast the sesame seeds. In a small bowl, whisk together 2 teaspoons (10 ml) of the sesame seeds (reserve the rest for the dressing), the soy sauce, sesame oil, garlic, and sugar. Add the beef to the marinade, cover, and refrigerate for 30 minutes or up to 1 hour.

START OUT: Prepare the rice.

Meanwhile, heat a cast-iron skillet or wok over high heat. When it begins to smoke, pour the extra marinade off and add the steak. Cook, stirring often, until the beef is just cooked through, 3 to 4 minutes. Remove from the pan and set aside on a large plate.

Heat 2 teaspoons (10 ml) of the olive oil in the same pan over medium-high heat. When the oil is hot, add the mushrooms and cook, stirring often, until soft, about 3 minutes. Add to the plate with the steak.

Add the remaining 1 teaspoon (5 ml) oil to the pan, then the carrots, and cook, stirring often, until just tender, about 5 minutes. Remove and add to the same plate.

Add the zucchini to the hot skillet and cook, stirring often, until it begins to brown, about 5 minutes. Add to the plate.

Finally, add the bean sprouts to the hot skillet and cook, stirring often, until they start to look translucent, 2 to 3 minutes. Add to the plate. (The vegetables can cool; they are meant to be at room temperature or only slightly warm.)

WHISK: Rinse the pressed garlic in a very fine mesh strainer and shake off any excess water. In a small bowl, whisk together the garlic, the remaining 1 tablespoon (15 ml) toasted sesame seeds, and the gochujang, water, avocado oil, sesame oil, sugar, vinegar, and flaky sea salt until well combined.

TOSS: Heat a well-seasoned cast-iron skillet over medium heat and melt the butter. Brush it around the pan and when the butter stops foaming, carefully crack the eggs into the pan. Season with a pinch of granulated sea salt and a grind of pepper and cook, covered, until the whites are fully opaque and set and the yolks are runny, 2 to 3 minutes. Remove from the pan onto a separate plate.

To assemble, in a large salad bowl, add the rice, layer the spinach on top, then arrange the beef, mushrooms, carrots, zucchini, bean sprouts, kimchi, and flowering fern (if using) on top and drizzle with dressing to taste. Toss until all the ingredients are evenly combined and coated with dressing and serve with the fried eggs on top.

ENJOY: I'm having it with gewürztraminer or hot green tea.

EXPERIMENT: If you can't find presliced beef, place the steak in the freezer for 20 to 30 minutes before prepping: this will make it much easier to cut. If you don't eat meat, use Roasted Tofu (see baking directions on page 258) and toss it in the marinade from this recipe. Invest in a wok if you like to prepare Asian dishes. It's the pan that, once seasoned, will be invaluable and last you the rest of your life.

Southern Hemisphere Sweet Potato Salad

Australia

On Australia Day, everyone down under celebrates outside with barbecues. This fun salad is perfect for any celebration—indoor or outdoor. It is prepared with golden sweet potatoes to celebrate their national colors of green and gold, seasoned with Cajun spices that were introduced via trade to Australia. They speak English in Australia, but it seems like vegetables have their own special language there. They love arugula, but you'd better call it "rocket" or they won't know what you're talking about. Bell peppers are called "capsicum," cilantro is "coriander," and if you remove the pit from the avocado, it's "stoned." Who knew?

EXPERIMENT:
Serve with grilled fresh seafood (a little shrimp on the barbie), lamb, or portobello mushroom caps. Taste everything before measuring and adding to any salad. Depending on the time of year, herbs can be strong, or water-logged.

START OUT

2 large golden or regular sweet potatoes

1 tablespoon plus 1 teaspoon (20 ml) extra-virgin olive oil

1 tablespoon (15 ml) Cajun spice mix

½ teaspoon (2.5 ml) flaky sea salt

¼ teaspoon (1.5 ml) freshly cracked black pepper

1 ear fresh sweet corn, husk and silk removed, or 1 cup (240 ml) frozen corn

Ice water

½ cup (120 ml) halved and thinly sliced red onion

WHISK

½ cup (120 ml) buttermilk

¼ cup (60 ml) mayonnaise

¼ cup (60 ml) finely chopped fresh cilantro

2 tablespoons (30 ml) fresh lime juice (remember to zest first)

¼ teaspoon (1.5 ml) lightly packed grated lime zest

Flaky sea salt and freshly cracked black pepper

TOSS

6 cups (1,400 ml) lightly packed arugula

2 cups (475 ml) sliced red bell pepper

1 cup (240 ml) sliced avocado (sliced horizontally)

½ cup (120 ml) coarsely chopped fresh cilantro

¼ cup (60 ml) torn fresh mint

START OUT: Preheat the oven to 425°F (220°C) and use convection mode if that's an option. Line a baking sheet with parchment paper or a silicone baking mat.

Cut each sweet potato in half and then into ½-inch- (1.3-cm-) thick wedges or sticks. (You need 4 cups/950 ml for the salad. Save any extra for another meal.) Add to a large bowl and toss with 1 tablespoon (15 ml) of the olive oil, the Cajun spice, ¼ teaspoon (1.5 ml) of the salt, and the pepper. Spread the fries out onto the prepared baking sheet, trying not to crowd them. Bake, turning

once about halfway through, until the edges are lightly browned, the centers are tender, and the surface looks dry and a little puffed up, 20 to 25 minutes (longer for a regular oven). Transfer the parchment paper with the potatoes to the counter to cool.

Meanwhile, preheat the barbecue or grill pan to medium-high heat. Coat the corn with the remaining 1 teaspoon (10 ml) oil and ¼ teaspoon (1.5 ml) salt. Place the corn on the grill and cook, turning about every 2 minutes, until char marks appear on each side, 12 to 15 minutes total. Remove from the grill and set aside until cool enough to handle. Hold the pointed end and place the bottom of the corn on a stable cutting board or in a medium bowl, then slowly cut downward along the cob with a sharp knife to remove the kernels. (If using frozen corn, cook with the oil and salt in the skillet, stirring occasionally, until browned in spots, 12 to 15 minutes total.)

Fill a 500-ml beaker or a small glass bowl halfway with ice water and add the onion. Soak for 10 minutes, then drain and pat the onion dry.

WHISK: In a small bowl, add the buttermilk, mayonnaise, cilantro, lime juice, and lime zest and season with salt and pepper. Whisk until well combined and taste and adjust the seasoning if needed.

TOSS: In a large salad bowl, arrange the arugula, sweet potatoes, corn, bell pepper, avocado, cilantro, mint, and onion. Drizzle with dressing to taste and serve, without tossing.

ENJOY: I'm having it with an Australian chardonnay or ginger beer.

Strawberry
Jicama Salad
(page 156)

Seasonal
and
Holiday
Favorites

Pea Salad

This simple salad was introduced to me in my teenage era. I am still besties with the ride-or-die group I went to high school with, and they all tell me I was the one to introduce it to them. They ask me for the recipe to this day. The version here is a new and improved version of the rich, mayonnaise-filled classic. Mine is lightly dressed with a bright citrus dressing so you can really taste the peas. There is something a little magical about onions, cheese, and bacon along with the sweet pop of green peas that makes a perfect side for a spring brunch or picnic.

EXPERIMENT: Try shaved Parmigiano-Reggiano instead of cheddar. You can always go old-school and use mayonnaise and red wine vinegar instead of oil and lemon juice. If you're serving it with barbecue, enjoy with a pinot noir or cabernet.

START OUT

½ cup (120 ml) Chopped Bacon (use applewood bacon if possible; page 258)

6 Perfect Boiled Eggs (page 257)

8 cups (1,900 ml) fresh peas, blanched (see page 260), or substitute defrosted frozen petite peas (about 2 pounds/900g)

WHISK

½ cup (120 ml) extra-virgin olive oil

2 tablespoons (30 ml) fresh lemon juice (remember to zest first)

1 tablespoon (15 ml) Dijon mustard

1 teaspoon (5 ml) lightly packed grated lemon zest

Flaky sea salt and freshly cracked black pepper

TOSS

1½ cups (360 ml) diced extra-sharp aged cheddar cheese (white cheddar if available; ¼-inch/6-mm pieces)

1 cup (240 ml) chopped scallions (green and white parts)

½ cup (120 ml) pea shoots (optional)

3 tablespoons (45 ml) finely chopped fresh flat-leaf parsley

START OUT: Prepare the bacon and let it drain, then finely dice it. Prepare the eggs, and when they're cool enough to handle, finely dice them. Blanch the peas and drain.

WHISK: In a large salad bowl, combine the oil, lemon juice, mustard, and zest, and season with salt and pepper. Whisk until emulsified, then taste and adjust the seasoning if needed.

TOSS: In the bowl with the dressing, add the bacon, eggs, peas, cheese, scallions, pea shoots (if using), and parsley. Toss until all the ingredients are evenly combined and coated with dressing and serve, or refrigerate in an airtight container overnight.

ENJOY: I'm having it with rosé or iced black tea with lemon.

Lemon Basil Pasta Salad

SERVES 4 TO 6 AS A MEAL OR 8 TO 10 AS A SIDE

There is a new pasta in town. It's called cascatelli, and it's designed to resemble a waterfall. It holds the perfect amount of sauce, or dressing in this case. This salad comes together in twenty minutes and is my go-to for a quick spring (or anytime) pasta salad. Always have a bag of pasta, a block of Parmigiano-Reggiano, tomatoes, basil, and lemons on hand and you'll be prepared to whip up something fantastic when the unexpected knocks at your door.

EXPERIMENT:
This is great as a base for several more meals and will last for days. Change up leftovers by adding shrimp, chicken, or a grilled Italian sausage, and throw it on a bed of baby spinach or kale. Keep it vegetarian by adding asparagus (see page 261), and vegans switch to vegan Parmesan, and everyone has a quick midweek meal. Swap hemp seeds, sunflower seeds, or macadamia nuts for the pine nuts.

START OUT

Flaky sea salt

1 pound (450 g) cascatelli pasta, or substitute any other bite-size pasta

1½ cups (360 ml) diced plum tomatoes, or substitute what looks best at the market (¼-inch/6-mm pieces)

¼ cup (60 ml) pine nuts, toasted (see page 257)

WHISK

1 teaspoon (5 ml) pressed garlic

⅓ cup (80 ml) extra-virgin olive oil

3 tablespoons (45 ml) fresh lemon juice (remember to zest first)

2 tablespoons (30 ml) white balsamic vinegar, or substitute wine vinegar

1 tablespoon (15 ml) drained and finely chopped capers

1 teaspoon (5 ml) lightly packed grated lemon zest

1 teaspoon (5 ml) honey

¼ teaspoon (1.5 ml) flaky sea salt

¼ teaspoon (1.5 ml) red pepper flakes

TOSS

1 cup (240 ml) lightly packed fresh basil

½ cup (120 ml) freshly grated Parmigiano-Reggiano (use a Microplane)

START OUT: Fill a large pot halfway with water and generously salt the water. Bring to a boil, then add the pasta. Cook according to the package directions until al dente. Drain, lightly rinse in cold water to stop the cooking, and let drain. Meanwhile, place the tomatoes in a colander and gently press down with a spoon to drain off excess liquid. Toast the pine nuts.

WHISK: Rinse the pressed garlic in a very fine mesh strainer and shake off any excess water. In a large salad bowl, whisk together the garlic, oil, lemon juice, vinegar, capers, zest, honey, salt, and red pepper flakes until well combined.

TOSS: Put a few basil leaves in a pile, roll them tightly, then slice across the roll to make long, thin strips (called a chiffonade cut). Repeat with all of the basil.

In the bowl with the dressing, add the pasta, pine nuts, tomatoes, basil, and Parmigiano-Reggiano. Toss until all the ingredients are evenly combined and coated with dressing and serve.

ENJOY: I'm having it with a chardonnay or sparkling water.

Strawberry Jicama Salad

When you need something delicious for a special occasion—say, Valentine's Day—this easy salad is crunchy, refreshing, and fast to make. The sweet strawberries add balance to the tart lime dressing and mildly spicy jalapeño. Jicama is a fabulous, underrated root vegetable. Its papery brownish-yellow exterior masks a creamy white interior that has a crisp, fibrous texture resembling raw potato or unripe pear, with a lightly sweet and starchy flavor. Jicama can be found in most markets today, though if you're having trouble finding it, the vegetable originates in Central America and can be found at Mexican or Central American markets.

EXPERIMENT:

If good strawberries are not available, experiment with red apples or red bell peppers. If you want to get festive for Valentine's Day (or any holiday), cut the jicama into ½-inch (1.3-cm) slices, and then cut into desired shapes like hearts or flowers with 1-inch (2.5-cm) vegetable cutters. Taste your jalapeños first, and if you like spice but yours are on the milder side, use more or add some of the seeds back in.

WHISK

½ cup (120 ml) fresh lime juice (remember to zest first)

¼ cup (60 ml) extra-virgin olive oil

¼ cup (60 ml) sugar, or substitute sweetener of choice

2 tablespoons (30 ml) poppy seeds

1 teaspoon (5 ml) lightly packed grated lime zest

½ teaspoon (2.5 ml) flaky sea salt

TOSS

4 cups (950 ml) cubed peeled jicama (½-inch/1.3-cm pieces)

4 cups (950ml) cubed English cucumber (½-inch/1.3-cm pieces)

2 cups (475 ml) sliced strawberries (¼ inch/6 mm thick)

¼ cup (60 ml) very finely diced seeded and deveined fresh jalapeño, or more if you like heat

2 tablespoons (30 ml) finely chopped fresh cilantro

WHISK: In a large salad bowl, whisk the lime juice, oil, sugar, poppy seeds, zest, and salt together until well combined.

TOSS: In the bowl with the dressing, add the jicama, cucumber, strawberries, jalapeño, and cilantro. Toss until all the ingredients are evenly combined and coated with dressing and serve (or refrigerate for up to a few hours).

ENJOY: I'm having it with a glass of rosé or an iced green tea.

Pub Salad

I love a good Irish American pub. Always a warm, cozy "welcome in, have a drink and some comfort food" vibe. According to my Irish friends, pubs in Ireland are adapting their menus to changing trends, with more focus on quality and locally available produce these days. This Irish American pub salad is simply delicious, easy to prepare, and a good one to make for St. Patrick's Day. But if you are in Dublin, you may not find it on the menu. You always have the option to make the dressing separately and add it to taste, but anytime there are beets in your salad, make the dressing in the bowl. The oil in the dressing prevents the beets from staining it!

EXPERIMENT:
Let's start a pickled green bean trend. Look for them at your local farmers' market or grocery store and give them a try in this salad in place of the blanched green beans. If you've never tried pickled green beans you are in for a treat. When I was little my grandmother would sit me on her kitchen countertop and open up a jar of them for me to snack on while she made dinner.

START OUT
4 Perfect Boiled Eggs (page 257)

½ cup (120 ml) green beans, blanched (see page 260)

Ice water

½ cup (120 ml) halved and thinly sliced yellow onion

1 cup (240 ml) quartered cherry tomatoes

WHISK
⅓ cup (80 ml) extra-virgin olive oil

3 tablespoons (45 ml) white wine vinegar

2 teaspoons (10 ml) Dijon mustard

1 teaspoon (5 ml) finely chopped fresh tarragon or ½ teaspoon (2.5 ml) dried tarragon

Flaky sea salt and freshly cracked black pepper

TOSS
8 cups (1,900 ml) torn butter lettuce (bite-size pieces)

1½ cups (360 ml) halved lengthwise and sliced English cucumber

1 cup (240 ml) sliced pickled beets

¾ cup (175 ml) diced white sharp cheddar (¼-inch/6-mm pieces)

START OUT: Prepare the eggs, and when they're cool enough to handle, slice them. Blanch the green beans.

Meanwhile, fill a 500-ml beaker or a small glass bowl halfway with ice water and add the onion. Soak for 10 minutes, then drain and pat the onion dry. Place the tomatoes in a colander and gently press down with a spoon to drain off excess liquid.

WHISK: In a large salad bowl, combine the oil, vinegar, mustard, and tarragon and season with salt and pepper. Whisk until emulsified, then taste and adjust the seasoning if needed.

TOSS: In the large salad bowl with the dressing, combine the lettuce, cucumber, beets, cheese, eggs, green beans, tomatoes, and onion. Toss until all the ingredients are evenly combined and coated with dressing and serve.

ENJOY: I'm having it with an Irish beer or iced Irish breakfast tea.

Brunch Salad

SERVES 4 AS A MEAL OR 6 TO 8 AS A SIDE

A wonderful local bakery and café in Petaluma, California, called Della Fattoria inspired this salad. It's one of my favorites of all time. What makes it special is the citrus dressing and local farm-fresh ingredients, especially the eggs. It doesn't hurt that Petaluma used to be called the "egg capital of the world" until the 1960s and still has an annual Egg and Butter Parade in the spring. Come April, around every corner you turn it seems like someone is selling their farm-fresh eggs. What a difference a good egg makes.

EXPERIMENT:
Add a third egg and/or seasonal grilled or roasted vegetables like asparagus, red or orange bell peppers, and zucchini (see page 261); or add some grilled salmon or Grilled Chicken Breast (page 258) if you're the high-protein type to make it a hearty "breakfast for dinner" meal.

START OUT

½ cup (120 ml) Chopped Bacon (use applewood bacon if possible; page 258)

Ice water

¼ cup (60 ml) diced red onion (¼-inch/6-mm pieces)

2 tablespoons (30 ml) very finely diced shallot

1¼ cups (300 ml) quartered heirloom cherry tomatoes or other heirloom tomatoes, chopped

WHISK

⅓ cup (80 ml) extra-virgin olive oil

¼ cup (60 ml) fresh orange juice (remember to zest first)

2 tablespoons (30 ml) fresh lemon juice (remember to zest first)

2 teaspoons (10 ml) Dijon mustard

1 teaspoon (5 ml) lightly packed grated orange zest

½ teaspoon (2.5 ml) lightly packed grated lemon zest

½ teaspoon (2.5 ml) flaky sea salt

¼ teaspoon (1.5 ml) freshly cracked black pepper

TOSS

6 cups (1,400 ml) lightly packed spring mix (baby lettuce blend)

2 cups (475 ml) lightly packed arugula

1½ cups (360 ml) cubed avocado (½-inch/1.3-cm pieces)

¼ cup (60 ml) finely chopped fresh flat-leaf parsley

8 large eggs

START OUT: Prepare the bacon and let it drain. Fill two 250-ml beakers or small glass bowls halfway with ice water and add the onion to one and the shallot to the other. Soak for 10 minutes, then drain and pat the onion and shallot dry, keeping them separate. Place the tomatoes in a colander and gently press down with a spoon to drain off excess liquid. Meanwhile, fill a medium saucepan with cold water and bring to a soft boil. Line a plate with paper towels.

WHISK: In a large salad bowl, whisk together the shallot, oil, orange juice, lemon juice, mustard, orange zest, lemon zest, salt, and pepper until emulsified.

TOSS: In the bowl with the dressing, add the spring mix, arugula, avocado, parsley, bacon, onion, and tomatoes, but do not toss yet.

Just before serving, crack 4 eggs into individual small bowls, making sure no shells have fallen in. Stir the boiling water with a whisk until swirling and gently pour each egg into the swirling water. Cook the eggs for 2 minutes and check to see if the whites are set. If so, remove from the pan with a slotted spoon onto the plate to drain, or cook for another 30 seconds if you like the yolk slightly thick. Repeat the process with the 4 remaining eggs.

Toss the salad until all the ingredients are evenly combined and coated with dressing. Plate the salads individually and top with the warm eggs, or top the large bowl with the eggs and serve.

ENJOY: I'm having it with mimosas or orange juice.

Grilled Peach Salad

Presenting one of my top-requested summer salads. I am always amazed at how grilling intensifies the flavor of the peaches and adds caramelized sweetness. It's better to use firmer seasonal peaches or substitute nectarines over too-soft ripe fruit for this recipe. Great to take to barbecues, it embodies the light taste of late spring/early summer, and you won't have to worry about taking any leftovers home.

EXPERIMENT:
Substitute regular grated mozzarella if you cannot find fresh. If you're vegetarian or vegan, replace the prosciutto with thinly sliced grilled portobello mushrooms (see page 261), and replace the mozzarella with chopped avocado; even if you aren't vegan, both substitutions work beautifully in this salad. If you don't want to make the almonds, use store-bought.

START OUT

½ cup (120 ml) Quick Pickled Onions (page 256)

½ cup (120 ml) Honey-Roasted Sliced Almonds (page 257), or store-bought

5 firm peaches (freestone if you can find them), halved and pitted

1 tablespoon (15 ml) extra-virgin olive oil

½ teaspoon (2.5 ml) granulated sea salt

½ teaspoon (2.5 ml) ground cinnamon

WHISK

¾ cup (175 ml) coarsely chopped fresh basil

½ cup (120 ml) extra-virgin olive oil

¼ cup (60 ml) freshly grated Parmigiano-Reggiano (use a Microplane)

2 tablespoons (30 ml) balsamic vinegar

2 tablespoons (30 ml) fresh orange juice (remember to zest first)

1 tablespoon (15 ml) honey

2 teaspoons (10 ml) Dijon mustard

½ teaspoon (2.5 ml) lightly packed grated orange zest

Flaky sea salt and freshly cracked black pepper

TOSS

4 cups (950 ml) lightly packed spring mix (baby lettuce blend)

4 cups (950 ml) lightly packed arugula

1 cup (240 ml) blueberries

1 cup (240 ml) mini or small mozzarella balls, halved

4 ounces (115 g) chopped prosciutto (2-inch/5-cm squares; optional)

START OUT: Prepare the pickled onions 30 minutes or up to 1 day in advance. Prepare the almonds if necessary. Preheat the grill to medium heat or a cast-iron skillet over medium heat.

In a large bowl, combine the peaches, oil, granulated sea salt, and cinnamon and toss until the peaches are coated. Place the peaches cut side down on the grill and cook, undisturbed, until grill marks appear, 4 to 5 minutes. Flip and grill until the skin begins to char and the peaches soften a little, another 4 to 5 minutes. Remove and set aside to cool for 5 minutes. Cut each half into 4 wedges.

WHISK: In a food processor, blender, or large beaker (if using an immersion blender), combine the basil, oil, cheese, vinegar, orange juice, honey, mustard, and zest and season with flaky sea salt and pepper. Blend until emulsified and well combined, then taste and adjust the seasoning if needed.

TOSS: In a large salad bowl, add the spring mix, arugula, blueberries, mozzarella, pickled onions, almonds, and peaches and drizzle with dressing to taste. Toss until all the ingredients are evenly combined and coated with dressing. If using, the prosciutto is very sticky, so lay it on top after tossing (otherwise it will all stick together in a big clump) and serve.

ENJOY: I'm having it with petite sirah or lemonade.

Watermelon Feta Salad

As a kid I would get in trouble for sneaking the center of the watermelon and leaving the butchered remains in the fridge (I still sometimes do it). Watermelon is my favorite summer fruit. On a hot summer day a few years ago, someone served me watermelon with torn mint, salt, and pepper. With some encouragement from the host, I skeptically tried it. I was hooked! This is one of my all-time most popular salads; it's so fresh and easy to make. It's surprisingly fabulous in every way, blending sweet, salty, spicy, and savory in one delicious bite. (Hot tip: play a little Harry Styles in the background while you prep it.)

EXPERIMENT:
Recently I found yellow and orange watermelons at the market. Try a multicolored watermelon salad or replace a quarter of the melon with honeydew and cantaloupe for fun. Some versions of this classic combination call for red onion, another way to experiment.

START OUT

Ice water

1 tablespoon (15 ml) very finely diced shallot

WHISK

¼ cup (60 ml) fresh lemon juice (remember to zest first)

2 tablespoons (30 ml) extra-virgin olive oil

2 tablespoons (30 ml) finely chopped fresh basil

2 teaspoons (10 ml) lightly packed grated lemon zest

Flaky sea salt and freshly cracked black pepper

TOSS

8 cups (1,900ml) cubed seedless watermelon (1-inch/2.5-cm pieces; about 1 large watermelon)

1½ cups (360 ml) cubed seeded English cucumber (½-inch/1.3-cm pieces)

1½ cups (360 ml) crumbled feta cheese (see page 43)

½ cup (120 ml) coarsely chopped fresh mint

3 tablespoons (45 ml) very finely diced seeded and deveined fresh jalapeño

¼ cup (60 ml) fresh mint sprigs, for serving (optional)

START OUT: Fill a 250-ml beaker or a small glass bowl halfway with ice water and add the shallot. Soak for 10 minutes, then drain and pat the shallot dry.

WHISK: In an extra-large salad bowl, combine the shallot, lemon juice, oil, basil, and zest and season with salt and pepper. Whisk until well combined, then taste and adjust the seasoning if needed.

TOSS: In the bowl with the dressing, add the watermelon, cucumber, feta, chopped mint, and jalapeño. Toss until all the ingredients are evenly combined and coated with dressing, top with the mint sprigs (if using), and serve.

ENJOY: I'm having it with a rosé or iced mint tea.

Hot Girl Salad

Demonstrating and re-creating trending salads is what I do. This viral salad was inspired by Megan Thee Stallion's hit song "Hot Girl Summer" and Jayria, an influencer on TikTok (@herdresscode) that posted a similar salad recipe. Jayria reported that she ate it to get her "hot girl summer" body back after Covid. She used a bottled supermarket dressing that was in short supply at the time, so I tried to re-create it at home as well as I could. I don't promise my recipe will give you that idealistic IG body or help you lose twenty pounds, but I will say it is light, delicious, and easy to prepare, and will make you feel like the fabulously hot girl you are in every season!

EXPERIMENT:
Try swapping in one of the dressings in this book (pages 242–55). This one is already vegetarian, but replace the eggs with Roasted Tofu (page 258) or roasted portobellos (see page 263) and you have a nice vegan option.

START OUT

6 Perfect Boiled Eggs (page 257)

½ cup (120 ml) sunflower seeds, toasted (see page 257)

Ice water

⅔ cup (160 ml) diced red onion (¼-inch/6-mm pieces)

WHISK

½ teaspoon (2.5 ml) pressed garlic

¼ cup (60 ml) extra-virgin olive oil

2 tablespoon (30 ml) red wine vinegar

1 tablespoon (15 ml) fresh lemon juice

1 teaspoon (5 ml) maple syrup

1 teaspoon (5 ml) sweet paprika

1 teaspoon (5 ml) Italian seasoning

½ teaspoon (2.5 ml) red pepper flakes

Flaky sea salt and freshly cracked black pepper

TOSS

6 cups (1,400 ml) chopped cucumber, partially peeled in strips first (½-inch/1.3-cm pieces)

2 cups (475 ml) chopped green bell pepper (½-inch/1.3-cm pieces)

⅔ cup (160 ml) chopped pepperoncini

START OUT: Prepare the eggs and when they're cool enough to handle, dice them. Toast the sunflower seeds. Meanwhile, fill a 500-ml beaker or a small glass bowl halfway with ice water and add the onion. Soak for 10 minutes, then drain and pat the onion dry.

WHISK: Rinse the pressed garlic in a very fine mesh strainer and shake off any excess water. In a large salad bowl, combine the garlic, oil, vinegar, lemon juice, maple syrup, paprika, Italian seasoning, and red pepper flakes and season with salt and pepper. Whisk until well combined, then taste and adjust the seasoning if needed.

TOSS: In the bowl with the dressing, add the cucumber, bell pepper, pepperoncini, eggs, sunflower seeds, and onion. Toss until all the ingredients are evenly combined and coated with dressing (some may pool on the bottom, so toss well) and serve. This salad will keep for a few days in the refrigerator with the dressing stored separately if you'd like to meal prep, but it is best served the day it's prepared.

ENJOY: I'm having it with a wheatgrass shot or ice water with lemon.

Summer Wedding Salad

SERVES 6 TO 8 AS A SIDE

Weddings can be one of the biggest celebrations in your life, filled with traditions, expectations, and excitement. With such a melting pot of cultures and dietary restrictions, it's challenging to create something that satisfies everyone. I propose you celebrate wedding season with a plate full of delicious, farm-fresh roasted vegetables. This salad is a welcome shift away from a traditional iceberg, shredded carrots, and ranch—and it will look stunning in pictures. Another bonus? It would be a beautiful addition to any summer celebration, and anyone can enjoy it regardless of dietary restrictions. Something old, something new, something borrowed, something blue . . .

EXPERIMENT: If you have an adjustable blade on your food processor, try shaving radishes on the lowest/thinnest setting. You don't have to be hosting a wedding to prepare this salad: it is nice to serve when entertaining as a first course or light lunch, or add chicken or seafood for a snazzy light dinner. Can't find broccoli microgreens? Use any sprouts or microgreens you like, or you can skip them.

START OUT

1½ cups (360 ml) peeled, halved lengthwise, and chopped petite carrots (3-inch/7.5-cm pieces)

1 cup (240 ml) chopped asparagus (1-inch/2.5-cm pieces), woody ends removed

1 cup (240 ml) halved lengthwise and sliced yellow squash

3 tablespoons (45 ml) extra-virgin olive oil

Flaky sea salt and freshly cracked black pepper

WHISK

½ teaspoon (2.5 ml) pressed garlic

⅓ cup (80 ml) extra-virgin olive oil

3 tablespoons (45 ml) fresh lemon juice (remember to zest first)

1 tablespoon (15 ml) champagne vinegar

1 tablespoon (15 ml) maple syrup, or substitute honey

½ teaspoon (2.5 ml) lightly packed grated lemon zest

Flaky sea salt and freshly cracked black pepper

TOSS

1 cup (240 ml) sliced avocado (about 1 medium)

Fresh lemon juice

7 cups (1,680ml) lightly packed spring mix (baby lettuce blend) or other baby greens

1 cup (240 ml) broccoli microgreens

1 cup (240 ml) thinly sliced English cucumber

1 cup (240 ml) blueberries

¼ cup (60 ml) shaved watermelon radish

¼ cup (60 ml) torn fresh basil

2 tablespoons (30 ml) finely chopped fresh flat-leaf parsley

2 tablespoons (30 ml) coarsely chopped fresh dill

½ cup (120 ml) edible flowers such as nasturtium, borage, chamomile, or flowering chives (optional)

START OUT: Preheat the oven to 425°F (220°C) and use convection mode if that's an option. Line a baking sheet with parchment paper or a silicone baking mat.

Add the carrots, asparagus, squash, and oil to the pan, season with salt and pepper, and toss. Spread out evenly so the vegetables brown on all sides. Bake until golden brown and crispy on the outside, stirring or flipping halfway through, 15 to 20 minutes (longer in a regular oven). Gently lift the parchment with the vegetables off the baking sheet to cool.

WHISK: Rinse the pressed garlic in a very fine mesh strainer and shake off any excess water. In a large salad bowl, combine the garlic, oil, lemon juice, vinegar, maple syrup, and lemon zest and season with salt and pepper. Whisk until well combined, then taste and adjust the seasoning if needed.

TOSS: In a small bowl, gently mix the avocado and a squeeze of lemon juice, to prevent the avocado from browning.

In the bowl with the dressing, add the spring mix, microgreens, cucumber, blueberries, radish, basil, parsley, dill, and roasted vegetables. Toss until all the ingredients are evenly combined and coated with dressing, top with the sliced avocado and the flowers (if using), and serve.

ENJOY: I'm having it with a California sparkling brut or sparkling cider.

Red, White, and Blue Potato Salad

Everyone loves potatoes. The average American eats 120 pounds of potatoes each year. That's double the amount of the next largest consumed vegetable, lettuce. Hey, that's a lot of salads; maybe I should make more potato salads? This one is for all the potato lovers out there looking for a great alternative to the classic mayonnaise-based potato salad (find my version on page 48). I love the rich buttery texture of the mixed potatoes paired with the Meyer lemon, dill, and chive dressing. It's one of my favorites to accompany a meal on a hot summer day.

START OUT

Flaky sea salt

3 pounds (1.4 kg) mixed baby red, Yukon gold, and purple potatoes

Ice water

½ cup (120 ml) diced shallot (¼-inch/6-mm pieces)

WHISK

½ cup (120 ml) extra-virgin olive oil

¼ cup (60 ml) fresh Meyer lemon or regular lemon juice (remember to zest first)

¼ cup (60 ml) finely chopped fresh chives

3 tablespoons (45 ml) finely chopped fresh dill

2 tablespoons (30 ml) finely chopped fresh flat-leaf parsley

1 teaspoon (5 ml) white wine vinegar

1 teaspoon (5 ml) lightly packed grated Meyer lemon zest or regular lemon zest

Flaky sea salt and freshly cracked black pepper

TOSS

Flaky sea salt, for serving (optional)

START OUT: Fill a large pot half full of water and lightly salt the water. Over high heat, bring to a boil, add the potatoes, then cover and lower the heat to medium low or a soft boil. Cook until you can easily pierce the potatoes with a fork all the way to the center, 15 to 20 minutes. Remove the potatoes from the pot, drain, and let cool. Cut into quarters or ¾-inch (2-cm) pieces.

Meanwhile, fill a 250-ml beaker or a small glass bowl halfway with ice water and add the shallot. Soak for 10 minutes, then drain and pat the shallot dry.

WHISK: In a large salad bowl, combine the oil, lemon juice, chives, dill, parsley, vinegar, and zest and season with salt and pepper. Whisk until well combined, then taste and adjust the seasoning if needed.

TOSS: In the bowl with the dressing, add the potatoes and shallot. Gently toss until all the ingredients are evenly combined and coated with dressing. Let sit covered at room temperature for 20 minutes, or refrigerate overnight, so the potatoes can absorb the dressing (this salad can be kept in the refrigerator for up to 5 days). Serve cold or at room temperature, garnished with flaky sea salt, if you like.

ENJOY: I'm having it with sparkling wine or lemonade.

EXPERIMENT:
Head to your local farmers' market and try the many varieties of potatoes available there, as they often have the best flavor. I have made this many times with all baby red potatoes. You can also substitute sweet yellow or red onions if shallots are not available. Don't forget this one for Independence Day!

Chicken Pesto Pasta Salad

Sometimes the best meals are the ones made with simple, fresh ingredients. With only eight in this one (okay, I'm considering the dressing one—but there will be extra you can use throughout the week), this salad packs an incredible amount of flavor and textures. A kid-friendly salad and a family favorite, it is perfect for a warm day at the beach or lake—though it's so good you'll wanna make it all year long!

EXPERIMENT:
There are approximately 349 types of pasta besides bow tie pasta. Experiment with a different and fun bite-size shape that holds lots of dressing. Make this one vegetarian by replacing the chicken with roasted mushrooms (see page 263) or add them just for fun. Hemp hearts and sunflower seeds are affordable substitutes for macadamia nuts and pine nuts.

START OUT

Flaky sea salt

1 pound (450 g) campanelle, cascatelli, or orecchiette pasta

2 cups (475 ml) cubed Grilled Chicken Breast (½-inch/1.3-cm pieces; page 258)

Ice water

½ cup (120 ml) halved and thinly sliced red onion

2 cups (475 ml) quartered cherry tomatoes

WHISK

1 tablespoon (15 ml) pressed garlic, or more to taste

2 cups (475 ml) fresh basil

¼ cup (60 ml) macadamia nuts, or substitute pine nuts

¾ cup (175 ml) freshly grated Parmigiano-Reggiano (use a Microplane)

½ cup (120 ml) extra-virgin olive oil

3 tablespoons (45 ml) water, plus more as needed

1 tablespoon (15 ml) fresh lemon juice

¼ teaspoon (1.5 ml) red pepper flakes

Flaky sea salt and freshly cracked black pepper

TOSS

2 cups (475 ml) drained and chopped water-packed canned artichoke hearts (½-inch/1.3-cm pieces)

1½ cups (360 ml) fresh mini mozzarella balls, quartered (8-ounce/225-g package)

1 cup (240 ml) chopped orange bell pepper, or substitute yellow, red, or a combination (½-inch/1.3-cm pieces; optional)

START OUT: Fill a large pot with water and generously salt it. Bring to a rolling boil, then add the pasta. Return to a boil and cook according to the package directions until al dente. Strain, lightly rinse the pasta in cold water to stop the cooking, and let cool.

Meanwhile, prepare the chicken. Fill a 500-ml beaker or a small glass bowl halfway with ice water and add the onion. Soak for 10 minutes, then drain and pat the onion dry. Place the tomatoes in a colander and gently press down with a spoon to drain off excess liquid.

NOTE: Ever made pesto and it turns out bitter? What is that? Extra-virgin olive oil contains bitter-tasting (good for you) polyphenols that are coated with fatty acids. If the oil is emulsified in a food processor for a long time, the polyphenols get squeezed out and your pesto can turn very bitter. Ideally you want to use a mortar and pestle. I find if you chop the basil and nuts prior to adding them to the food processor or immersion blender and give it a few pulses, it turns out fab!

WHISK: Rinse the pressed garlic in a very fine mesh strainer and shake off any excess water. Finely chop the basil and nuts (see Note on page 171).

In a mortar and pestle, small food processor, or large beaker (if using an immersion blender), add the garlic, basil, nuts, cheese, oil, water, lemon juice, and red pepper flakes and season with salt and pepper. Smash or pulse into a slightly chunky paste. Add more water 1 tablespoon (15 ml) at a time if you want a thinner dressing. Taste and adjust the seasoning if needed.

TOSS: In a large salad bowl, add the pasta, chicken, tomatoes, onion, artichokes, mozzarella, and bell pepper (if using) and drizzle with about half the dressing (or to taste). Toss until all the ingredients are evenly combined and coated with dressing. Taste and add more dressing if you'd like. Cover the surface with plastic wrap or parchment paper (to prevent oxidizing) and refrigerate until ready to serve, ideally for an hour or two to let flavors commingle.

ENJOY: I'm having it with a pinot gris or Italian flavored sparkling water.

Roasted Vegetable Salad

SERVES 4 TO 6 AS A MEAL OR 8 TO 10 AS A SIDE

This Mediterranean-style vegetable salad is sensational served warm or cold any time of the year. Turn on the oven, break out your parchment paper, baking sheets, cutting board, and a good knife (don't forget the fun music for dancing around the kitchen), and it comes together in no time. I like to cut the eggplant in small cubes and roast them with the skin on so the salad has body and doesn't turn into a dip similar to baba ghanoush. The sweetness from the roasted tomatoes and onions paired with the simple dressing of roasted puréed garlic, oil, parsley, and lemon juice creates a classic Mediterranean combination. No matter how you serve it, this roasted vegetable salad is always a hit.

EXPERIMENT:
This salad is so diverse, it can be lightened up by serving it on a bed of greens like baby gem lettuce or spring mix. Top with grilled seafood, chicken, or steak and serve on lavash or pita bread. Make into a vegetarian sandwich with roasted portobello mushrooms (see page 263). Drizzle a little pomegranate molasses and/or sprinkle some sumac on top for an extra pop of flavor. Yum!

START OUT

2 tablespoons (30 ml) Roasted Garlic Purée (page 256)

10 cups (2,400 ml) cubed eggplant (½-inch/1.3-cm pieces; about 2 large)

4 tablespoons (60 ml) extra-virgin olive oil

½ teaspoon (2.5 ml) granulated sea salt

2½ cups (590 ml) grape or cherry tomatoes

2 yellow and/or red bell peppers, halved, stemmed, and seeded

2 small red onions, unpeeled

WHISK

¼ cup (60 ml) extra-virgin olive oil

¼ cup (60 ml) fresh lemon juice

¼ cup (60 ml) finely chopped fresh flat-leaf parsley

¼ teaspoon (1.5 ml) flaky sea salt

¼ teaspoon (1.5 ml) red pepper flakes

TOSS

⅔ cup (160 ml) crumbled feta cheese (see page 43)

START OUT: Prepare the roasted garlic purée for the dressing up to 3 days ahead of time (or stick it in the oven while you make the roasted vegetables). Preheat the oven to 425°F (220°C) and use convection mode if that's an option. Line two baking sheets with parchment paper or silicone baking mats.

On one baking sheet, combine the eggplant, 3 tablespoons (45 ml) of the oil, and ¼ teaspoon (1.5 ml) of the granulated sea salt and toss. On the other, combine the grape tomatoes, halved peppers, remaining 1 tablespoon (15 ml) oil, and remaining ¼ teaspoon (1.5 ml) granulated sea salt. Wrap the onions in aluminum foil.

Put the baking sheets in the oven and the onions directly on a rack. Roast the eggplant, stirring

or flipping halfway through, until tender and golden, 20 to 25 minutes (longer for a regular oven). Roast the tomatoes and peppers until they start to blister and brown on top, 15 to 20 minutes (longer for a regular oven), and the onions until they soften and begin to look translucent, 20 to 25 minutes (longer for a regular oven). Gently lift the parchment with the vegetables off the baking sheet to cool, being careful to reserve the tomato juices. Once cool, peel the onions and chop the peppers and onions into ½-inch (1.3-cm) cubes.

WHISK: In a large salad bowl, whisk together the roasted garlic purée, oil, lemon juice, parsley, flaky sea salt, and red pepper flakes until emulsified.

TOSS: In the bowl with the dressing, add all of the roasted vegetables, including the tomato juices. Toss until all the ingredients are evenly combined and coated with dressing. Top with crumbled feta and serve warm or cold. (It will keep well in the refrigerator for a few days, but is best freshly prepared.)

ENJOY: I'm having it with a syrah or Turkish coffee.

Autumn Fruit Salad

Fruit salads are a hit at most gatherings and this one is exceptional. I find fall and winter fruits more dense and able to hold their distinct flavors better in salads than summer fruit like melon, which starts to taste the same after a few bites. This salad has lots of colors, crunch, and texture, plus a ton of flavor from the deliciously spiced dressing; it reminds me of apple pie. It makes a fabulous dessert too (see Experiment, below).

START OUT

3 tablespoons (45 ml) light or dark brown sugar

1 tablespoon (15 ml) plus 8 cups (1,900 ml) water

1 teaspoon (5 ml) ground cinnamon

½ teaspoon (2.5 ml) granulated sea salt

½ teaspoon (2.5 ml) vanilla extract

1 cup (240 ml) pecan halves

1 teaspoon (5 ml) citric acid or ½ cup (120 ml) fresh lemon juice

2 cups (475 ml) cubed cored Honeycrisp apples or other flavorful in-season red apples (½-inch/1.3-cm pieces)

2 cups (475 ml) cubed cored Granny Smith apples or other flavorful in-season green apples (½-inch/1.3-cm pieces)

2 cups (475 ml) cubed cored Bartlett or other seasonal green pears (½-inch/1.3-cm pieces)

2 cups (475 ml) cubed cored Starkrimson or other seasonal red pear (½-inch/1.3-cm pieces)

WHISK

½ cup (120 ml) fresh tangerine juice

¼ cup (60 ml) fresh lime juice

¼ cup (60 ml) maple syrup

½ teaspoon (2.5 ml) ground cinnamon

½ teaspoon (2.5 ml) ground cardamom

½ teaspoon (2.5 ml) pumpkin pie spice

½ teaspoon (2.5 ml) flaky sea salt

TOSS

2 cups (475 ml) cubed Fuyu persimmons (½-inch/1.3-cm pieces), or substitute 1 cup (240 ml) chopped dried persimmons (1-inch/2.5-cm pieces)

1 cup (240 ml) pomegranate seeds

1 cup (240 ml) halved tangerine segments

½ cup (120 ml) dried cranberries

EXPERIMENT:

I know this is a salad book, but this is as close to a dessert salad as it gets. Serve on a thin slice of pound cake with whipped cream and you have a winter shortcake, or on top of vanilla ice cream. Skip making the pecans if you're short on time, and use ⅔ cup (160 ml) coarsely chopped store-bought candied pecans.

START OUT: Line a baking sheet with parchment paper or a silicone baking mat.

In a medium saucepan, combine the brown sugar, 1 tablespoon (15 ml) water, the cinnamon, granulated sea salt, and vanilla. Place the pan over medium heat and cook, stirring often, until the sugar melts into a bubbling sauce, about 1 minute. Stir in the pecans so that the sauce coats them. Cook, stirring the entire time, until the pecans look glossy and candied and smell nutty, 2 to 3 minutes. As the nuts heat up in the pan, the syrup will become shiny—keep an eye on it, it goes quickly. Transfer the candied pecans to the prepared baking sheet and spread into one layer. Allow the pecans to cool to room temperature, then coarsely chop them.

In a large bowl, add the remaining 8 cups (1,900 ml) water and the citric acid (or lemon juice) and stir until the acid is dissolved. Add the Honeycrisp and Granny Smith apples to the mixture and soak for 10 minutes, then use a slotted spoon to transfer them to a colander to drain. Repeat with the Bartlett and Starkrimson pears, soaking for 10 minutes, then strain. (This step will keep them from browning.)

WHISK: In a large salad bowl, whisk together the tangerine juice, lime juice, maple syrup, cinnamon, cardamom, pumpkin pie spice, and flaky sea salt until well combined.

TOSS: In the bowl with the dressing, add the persimmons, pomegranate seeds, tangerines, dried cranberries, apples, pears, and pecans. Toss until all the ingredients are evenly combined and coated with dressing and serve.

ENJOY: I'm having it with chardonnay or Irish breakfast tea.

Fall Chopped Salad

SERVES 4 TO 6 AS A MEAL OR 8 TO 10 AS A SIDE

I often order chopped salads when I go out. I am grateful for someone else doing all the prepping and chopping. I also appreciate the opportunity to eat a salad with all the ingredients in one bite, even with a spoon. This maple vinaigrette is a keeper and is full of autumn flavors. It's designed for the fall but I enjoy it year-round. It warms the soul anytime I need a bit of that.

EXPERIMENT:
Not a fan of winter squash? Experiment with roasted beets, cauliflower, or portobello mushrooms (see pages 262–63). This salad is vegetarian, but replace the cheese with a vegan variety or a little nutritional yeast and you have a vegan meal. I buy the mixed dried fruit from Trader Joe's, but any mix of dried berries and raisins is fab.

START OUT

1 medium Delicata squash, halved, seeded, and cut into ¼-inch (6-mm) slices, roasted (see page 262)

8 cups (1,900 ml) water

1 teaspoon (5 ml) citric acid or ½ cup (120 ml) fresh lemon juice

2 cups (475 ml) cubed cored Honeycrisp apples, or any seasonal apples (½-inch/1.3cm pieces)

Ice water

⅓ cup (80 ml) diced red onion (¼-inch/6-mm pieces)

½ cup (120 ml) sliced almonds, toasted (see page 257)

WHISK

½ teaspoon (2.5 ml) pressed garlic (optional)

½ cup (120 ml) unsweetened applesauce

¼ cup (60 ml) extra-virgin olive oil

2 tablespoons (30 ml) maple syrup

2 tablespoons (30 ml) apple cider vinegar

2 teaspoons (10 ml) grated fresh ginger

1 teaspoon (5 ml) ground cinnamon

½ teaspoon (2.5 ml) red pepper flakes

Flaky sea salt and freshly cracked black pepper

TOSS

8 cups (1,900 ml) thinly sliced lacinato kale, ribs removed

1½ cups (360 ml) finely chopped yellow and/or orange bell pepper (¼- to ½-inch/6-mm to 1.3-cm pieces)

¾ cup (175 ml) freshly shaved Pecorino Romano or Parmigiano-Reggiano

⅔ cup (160 ml) "Berry Blend" dried fruit (a combination of dried golden raisins, cherries, and cranberries)

START OUT: Roast the squash and let it cool. Meanwhile, in a large bowl, add the water and citric acid (or lemon juice) and stir until the acid is dissolved. Add the apples to the mixture and soak for 10 minutes, then drain and pat dry.

Fill a 500-ml beaker or a small glass bowl halfway with ice water and add the onion. Soak for 10 minutes, then drain and pat the onion dry. Toast the nuts.

WHISK: Rinse the pressed garlic (if using) in a very fine mesh strainer and shake off any excess water. In a large salad bowl, combine the garlic (if using), applesauce, oil, maple syrup, vinegar, ginger, cinnamon, and red pepper flakes and season with salt and pepper. Whisk until emulsified, then taste and adjust the seasoning if needed.

TOSS: In the bowl with the dressing, add the kale. Use clean hands (or rubber gloves) and massage the kale for 1 to 2 minutes to soften and infuse the leaves with the dressing. Let sit for about 10 minutes. Add the roasted squash, onion, apples, almonds, bell pepper, cheese, and dried fruit. Toss until all the ingredients are evenly combined and coated with dressing and serve.

ENJOY: I'm having it with chardonnay or hot chai tea.

Harvest Salad

The warm days and crisp nights make fall my favorite season in Northern California. Grape leaves in the vineyards turn beautiful shades of deep green, burgundy, and gold, and the farmers' markets are filled with their bountiful autumn harvests. Play your cooking soundtrack while chopping and prepping. This one has lots of roasting to warm up the kitchen and celebrate all the season has to offer.

START OUT

2 teaspoons (10 ml) Roasted Garlic Purée (page 256)

1½ cups (360 ml) cubed sweet potatoes (½-inch/1.3-cm pieces)

1½ cups (360 ml) cubed peeled golden beets (½-inch/1.3-cm pieces), or substitute red beets

1 large red onion, halved

4 tablespoons (60 ml) extra-virgin olive oil

Flaky sea salt and freshly cracked black pepper

1½ cups (360 ml) cubed portobello mushrooms (½-inch/1.3-cm pieces)

1½ cups (360 ml) halved Brussels sprouts

1½ cups (360 ml) Sourdough Garlic Croutons (page 235)

1 cup (240 ml) cooked quinoa (see page 264)

½ cup (120 ml) coarsely chopped, toasted (see page 257) pecans

WHISK

¼ cup (60 ml) extra-virgin olive oil

¼ cup (60 ml) jellied cranberry sauce

2 tablespoons (30 ml) apple cider vinegar

2 teaspoons (10 ml) fresh lemon juice (remember to zest first)

2 teaspoons (10 ml) Dijon mustard

1 teaspoon (5 ml) fresh thyme

1 teaspoon (5 ml) lightly packed grated lemon zest

Flaky sea salt and freshly cracked black pepper

TOSS

8 cups (1,900 ml) lightly packed Power Greens mix or a combination of baby greens like spinach, kale, chard, collard, chicory, or mustard greens

½ cup (120 ml) diced aged Gouda cheese, rinds removed (¼-inch/6 mm pieces)

½ cup (120 ml) finely chopped pitted Medjool dates (¼- to ½-inch/6-mm to 1.3-cm pieces)

START OUT: Prepare the roasted garlic purée for the dressing up to 3 days in advance (or you can make it at the same time as the vegetables). Preheat the oven to 425°F (220°C) and use convection mode if that's an option. Line two baking sheets with parchment paper or silicone baking mats.

Put the sweet potatoes, beets, onion halves, and 2 tablespoons (30 ml) of the oil in one pan, season with salt and pepper, and toss. Spread out evenly so the vegetables brown on all sides. Put the mushrooms, sprouts, and remaining 2 tablespoons (30 ml) oil on the other pan, season with salt and pepper, and toss.

Bake until the vegetables are golden brown and crispy on the outside, stirring or flipping halfway through, 20 to 30 minutes (longer for a regular oven), taking one tray out if it finishes before the other. Gently lift the parchment with the vegetables off the baking sheet to cool.

When the oven is free, bake the croutons, if you haven't already. Meanwhile, prepare the quinoa and let it cool. After the vegetables have cooled, halve the Brussels sprouts again if they're large and slice the onions. Toast the pecans.

WHISK: In a large salad bowl, combine the roasted garlic purée, oil, cranberry sauce, vinegar, lemon juice, mustard, thyme, and zest and season with salt and pepper. Whisk until emulsified, then taste and adjust the seasoning if needed.

TOSS: In the bowl with the dressing, add the greens, cheese, dates, quinoa, pecans, and all of the roasted vegetables. Toss until all the ingredients are evenly combined and coated with dressing. Top with croutons and serve.

ENJOY: I'm having it with chardonnay or warm fresh apple cider.

EXPERIMENT:
Our farmers' market carries different dried fruits in the fall. Experiment with diced dried apricots, nectarines, or apples in this salad for added texture and a pop of sweetness.

Waldorf Salad

It is said that the Waldorf salad was created by the maître d' of the Waldorf Astoria, Oscar Tschirky, in the 1890s. It was always part of the Thanksgiving menu in our family. When I was a kid, the classic apples, celery, and mayonnaise combination had little chance of taking prime real estate on my plate, but this updated version can compete with the best stuffing and mashed potatoes, or even apple pie.

EXPERIMENT:
Make it a meal by adding grilled chicken, and serve it on a bed of butter lettuce. Dress it up with a drizzle of truffle oil like the new Waldorf Astoria Hotel's version. If you can't find crème fraîche, experiment with sour cream or use all full-fat yogurt. This salad can also be served as a light dessert.

START OUT

½ cup (120 ml) Honey-Roasted Sliced Almonds (page 257), or store-bought

1 gallon (3,800 ml) water

1 tablespoon (15 ml) citric acid or 1½ cups (360 ml) fresh lemon juice

3 cups (720 ml) julienned cored Fuji or Pink Lady apples or other local red apples (1 or 2 apples)

3 cups (720 ml) julienned cored Granny Smith apples or other seasonal tart green apples (1 or 2 apples)

WHISK

½ cup (120 ml) plain yogurt

½ cup (120 ml) crème fraîche

¼ cup (60 ml) almond butter

1 tablespoon (15 ml) apple cider vinegar

1 tablespoon (15 ml) fresh lemon juice (remember to zest first)

1 tablespoon (15 ml) honey

1 teaspoon (5 ml) lightly packed grated orange zest

½ teaspoon (2.5 ml) lightly packed grated lemon zest

½ teaspoon (2.5 ml) ground cardamom

½ teaspoon (2.5 ml) flaky

sea salt

TOSS

1 cup (240 ml) diced celery (¼-inch/6-mm pieces)

1 cup (240 ml) quartered red grapes

¼ cup (60 ml) golden raisins

¼ cup (60 ml) dried coconut flakes

¼ cup (60 ml) finely chopped fresh flat-leaf parsley

¼ cup (60 ml) microgreens, for serving

START OUT: Prepare the almonds. In a large bowl, combine the water and citric acid (or lemon juice). Stir until the acid is dissolved. Add the apples and soak in the solution for 10 minutes, then drain and pat dry.

WHISK: In a large salad bowl, whisk together the yogurt, crème fraîche, almond butter, vinegar, lemon juice, honey, orange zest, lemon zest, cardamom, and salt until well combined.

TOSS: In the bowl with the dressing, combine the drained apples, almonds, celery, grapes, raisins, coconut flakes, and parsley. Toss until all the ingredients are evenly combined and coated with dressing. Sprinkle with microgreens and serve.

ENJOY: I'm having it with sauvignon blanc or Earl Grey tea.

All in One Thanksgiving Salad

I am all about making holidays easier. This is a big salad for a big meal. It's not traditional, but it makes the holiday stress-free because nothing needs to be warm when served. You may think there is not enough dressing, but you can always double the recipe. Just like a typical Thanksgiving meal, a lot of it can be prepped ahead of time, starting with the roasted vegetables. Perfect for vegetarian guests if you serve the turkey on the side, and for vegans if you swap out the cheese for nutritional yeast.

START OUT

1½ cups (360 ml) Classic Homemade Croutons (page 232)

2 teaspoons (10 ml) Roasted Garlic Purée (page 256)

2 cups (475 ml) cubed sweet potatoes (peel if you like; ½- to ¾-inch/1.3- to 2-cm pieces)

2 cups (475 ml) cubed Yukon gold potatoes (peel if you like; ½- to ¾-inch/1.3- to 2-cm pieces)

2 cups (475 ml) cubed portobello mushrooms (½- to ¾-inch/1.3- to 2-cm pieces)

2 cups (475 ml) chopped cauliflower (1-inch/2.5-cm florets)

2 cups (475 ml) halved Brussels sprouts

4 tablespoons (60 ml) extra-virgin olive oil

Flaky sea salt and freshly cracked black pepper

1 cup (240 ml) green beans, blanched (see page 260)

1 cup (240 ml) petite peas, blanched (see page 260)

Ice water

¼ cup (60 ml) diced red onion (¼-inch/6-mm pieces)

WHISK

¼ cup (60 ml) extra-virgin olive oil

2 tablespoons (30 ml) apple cider or champagne vinegar

2 tablespoons (30 ml) maple syrup

2 teaspoons (10 ml) fresh lemon juice (remember to zest first)

2 teaspoons (10 ml) Dijon mustard

1 teaspoon (5 ml) fresh thyme

1 teaspoon (5 ml) lightly packed grated lemon zest

Flaky sea salt and freshly cracked black pepper

TOSS

6 cups (1,400 ml) lightly packed mixed winter baby greens, or substitute any seasonal mixed greens

2 cups (475 ml) cubed roasted turkey meat (½-inch/1.3-cm pieces)

½ cup (120 ml) diced or grated aged Gouda cheese, rinds removed (¼-inch/6-mm pieces)

½ cup (120 ml) dried cranberries

START OUT: Prepare the croutons. Prepare the roasted garlic purée for the dressing up to 3 days in advance (or make it at the same time as the roasted vegetables). Keep the oven at 425°F (220°C) and use convection mode if that's an option. Line two baking sheets with parchment paper or silicone baking mats.

Put the sweet potatoes and Yukon gold potatoes onto one baking sheet, and put the mushrooms, cauliflower, and Brussels sprouts on the other. Drizzle 2 tablespoons (30ml) of the oil onto each baking sheet and season with salt and pepper. Toss to coat.

Put the baking sheets in the oven and roast until the vegetables are golden brown and crispy on the outside, stirring or flipping

halfway through, 25 to 30 minutes for the potatoes and 20 to 30 minutes for the others (both longer for a regular oven). Gently lift the parchment with the vegetables off the baking sheets to cool.

Meanwhile, blanch the green beans and peas. Fill a 500-ml beaker or small glass bowl halfway with ice water and add the onion. Soak for 10 minutes, then drain and pat the onion dry.

WHISK: In an extra-large salad bowl, combine the roasted garlic purée, oil, vinegar, maple syrup, lemon juice, mustard, thyme, and zest and season with salt and pepper. Whisk until emulsified, then taste and adjust the seasoning if needed.

TOSS: In the bowl with the dressing, add the leafy greens, turkey, cheese, cranberries, croutons, roasted vegetables, green beans, peas, and onion. Toss until all the ingredients are evenly combined and coated with dressing and serve.

ENJOY: I'm having it with chardonnay or sparkling cranberry juice.

EXPERIMENT:
I have a little addiction to aged Goudas, though you can sub aged cheddar, Parmigiano-Reggiano, or other hard cheese you like. Vegans, add a few tablespoons of nutritional yeast to the dressing or skip it. Don't like cranberries? Experiment with golden raisins or dried tangerine wedges.

Beet Salad

Sometimes I just crave a good beet salad. Anyone else? This terrific version may take a little time, but oh my, it's worth it. The baked goat cheese is inspired by Chez Panisse, a restaurant/landmark/culinary leader in Berkeley, California, started by Alice Waters fifty years ago as a place where friends and neighbors could gather around the table, eat good food, and exchange ideas about politics, art, and culture. Ms. Waters was literally groundbreaking: she led neighborhoods all over the country to build community gardens and educate children on where their food comes from.

EXPERIMENT:
Try replacing the fennel with shaved celery, the goat cheese with feta, the balsamic with sherry vinegar, or the chives with scallion greens. Experiment with what you have.

MARINATE

1 (8-ounce/225-g) fresh goat cheese log

¼ cup (60 ml) extra-virgin olive oil

2 tablespoons (30 ml) fresh thyme

START OUT

2 tablespoons (30 ml) extra-virgin olive oil, plus more for the pan

5 cups (1,200 ml) peeled red and/or golden beet wedges (½-inch/1.3-cm wedges, from 4 to 5 medium beets)

½ teaspoon (2.5 ml) flaky sea salt

½ cup (120 ml) fine, dry bread crumbs

WHISK

¼ cup (60 ml) extra-virgin olive oil

2 tablespoons (30 ml) fresh lemon juice (remember to zest first)

2 tablespoons (30 ml) balsamic vinegar

2 tablespoons (30 ml) honey

½ teaspoon (2.5 ml) flaky sea salt

½ teaspoon (2.5 ml) freshly cracked black pepper

¼ teaspoon (1.5 ml) lightly packed grated lemon zest

TOSS

8 cups (1,900 ml) lightly packed arugula

2 cups (475 ml) sliced blood orange, rind, pith, and seeds removed (¼-inch/6-mm crosswise slices; about 2 oranges), or substitute tangerine

½ cup (120 ml) thinly sliced fennel bulb

½ cup (120 ml) torn fresh mint

¼ cup (60 ml) finely chopped fresh chives

MARINATE: Put the cheese in the freezer for 20 minutes to make it easier to slice. Wet a knife and cut the cheese into 8 slices, rewetting the knife whenever the cheese starts to stick. (Sometimes I like to cut each slice into half-moons for a different look.) In a small bowl, combine the cheese, olive oil, and thyme. Cover and marinate in the refrigerator for at least 8 hours and up to 24.

START OUT: When you're ready to prepare the salad, preheat the oven to 375°F (190°C) and use convection mode if that's an option. Line a baking sheet with parchment paper or a silicone baking mat. Lightly oil a small baking dish and set aside.

In a large bowl, toss the beet wedges, oil, and salt until evenly coated. Pour the beets onto the baking sheet and spread out evenly in a single layer. Roast, tossing halfway through, until you can pierce through the beets with a fork with light pressure, 35 to 40 minutes (longer for a regular oven). Remove from the oven and cool. Raise the oven temperature to 425°F (220°C).

Put the bread crumbs on a small plate. Remove the cheese from the marinade and coat all over with bread crumbs. Place the coated cheese on the oiled baking dish. Bake until the cheese is golden brown, about 6 minutes (longer for a regular oven). Keep warm.

WHISK: In a large salad bowl, whisk together the oil, lemon juice, vinegar, honey, salt, pepper, and zest until well combined.

TOSS: In the bowl with the dressing, add the arugula, blood orange, fennel, mint, chives, and beets. Toss until all the ingredients are evenly combined and coated with dressing. Top with the warm goat cheese and serve.

ENJOY: I'm having it with sparkling rosé or homemade lemonade.

Winter Wedge

I have experienced many of Lake Tahoe's winters. After shoveling snow or skiing for what feels like a never-ending day, this is the salad I crave. With that sprinkling of steak, bacon, and blue cheese, it's one hearty meal. Find a blue cheese or Gorgonzola you love; they are not all created equal and that flavor sets the tone for this salad. Sometimes it can be hard to find the produce you need for a salad in the winter, especially in snow country. This salad has only two fresh ingredients (okay, and three fresh herbs; but you can always substitute dried) but still has that crisp crunch you hunger for.

EXPERIMENT:
There have been all kinds of weird produce viruses and unusual weather issues creating shortages and increased prices for different types of lettuce. If your market is out of iceberg, experiment with butter lettuce, romaine, frisée, escarole, napa cabbage, or any other head-style green.

START OUT

1 pound (450 g) sirloin steak

½ cup (120 ml) Quick Pickled Onions (page 256)

½ cup (120 ml) Chopped Bacon (use applewood bacon if possible; page 258)

1½ cups (360 ml) Classic Homemade Croutons (page 232)

4 cups (950 ml) cherry tomatoes

4 tablespoons (60 ml) extra-virgin olive oil

1 teaspoon (5 ml) granulated sea salt, plus more as needed

2 teaspoons (10 ml) freshly cracked black pepper, plus more as needed

4 Perfect Boiled Eggs (page 257)

1 tablespoon (15 ml) pressed garlic

WHISK

¼ cup (120 ml) buttermilk

¼ cup (120 ml) crumbled blue cheese (see page 43)

2 tablespoons (30 ml) extra-virgin olive oil

2 tablespoons (30 ml) mayonnaise

2 tablespoons (30 ml) finely chopped fresh chives or 2 teaspoons (10 ml) dried chives

1 tablespoon (15 ml) finely chopped fresh dill or 1 teaspoon (5 ml) dried dill

1 tablespoon (15 ml) red wine vinegar

1 teaspoon (5 ml) fresh lemon juice

1 teaspoon (5 ml) Tabasco or other hot sauce

½ teaspoon (2.5 ml) Worcestershire sauce

Flaky sea salt and freshly cracked black pepper

TOSS

1 head of iceberg lettuce

⅔ cup (160 ml) crumbled blue cheese

¼ cup (60 ml) finely chopped fresh flat-leaf parsley

START OUT: This one takes some prep! Take the steak out of the refrigerator and let it come to room temperature. Prepare the pickled onions 30 minutes or up to 1 day ahead of time.

Prepare the bacon. Prepare the croutons, and when they're cool place them in a freezer bag, seal, and gently crush them with a rolling pin or the back of a skillet into ¼- to ½-inch (6-mm to 1.3-cm) pieces.

Preheat the oven to 425°F (220°C) and use convection mode if it's an option. Line a baking sheet with parchment paper or a silicone baking mat. Add the tomatoes and 2 tablespoons (30 ml) of the oil to the prepared pan and season with granulated sea salt and pepper. Toss to coat. Bake until the tomatoes have started to collapse, wrinkle, and brown, 15 to 20 minutes (longer in a regular oven). Transfer the parchment paper with the tomatoes to the counter, being careful to retain the caramelized juices, and let the tomatoes cool. Make the eggs, and when they're cool enough to handle, chop them into ½-inch (1.3-cm) pieces.

Preheat the grill to 450°F (230°C) or for high-heat grilling, or heat a grill pan over medium high.

Mix the remaining 2 tablespoons (30ml) oil with the garlic and rub it all over the steak. Generously season the steak with 2 teaspoons (10 ml) black pepper and 1 teaspoon (5 ml) salt.

Place the steak on the grill and cook until grill marks appear, then rotate and repeat for crosshatched grill marks. Flip the steak and repeat on the other side. Remove the steak from the grill when the internal temperature reaches 140 to 145°F (60 to 63°C) on an instant-read thermometer for medium (timing will depend on the thickness of your steak, so check often). Transfer the steak to a plate and let it rest for 10 minutes before cutting it into ½-inch cubes.

WHISK: In a large beaker (if using an immersion blender) or small glass bowl, add the buttermilk, blue cheese, oil, mayonnaise, chives, dill, vinegar, lemon juice, Tabasco, and Worcestershire sauce and season with flaky sea salt and pepper. Blend or whisk until well combined, then taste and adjust the seasoning if needed.

TOSS: On a large cutting board, trim the stem off the head of iceberg lettuce, keeping the core intact. Cut the head vertically into 4 to 8 wedges (depending on how many people you're serving) and gently rinse, drain, and dry with a clean dish towel or paper towel.

In a large salad bowl, pour ¼ cup (60 ml) dressing onto the bottom. Gently place the iceberg wedges on top and drizzle over the rest of the dressing, or to taste (this will help the rest of the ingredients stick to the wedge). Next sprinkle the onions, tomatoes, bacon, croutons, eggs, steak, cheese, and finally sprinkle parsley on top. If you'd like to plate the salads individually, pour a little bit of the dressing on each plate, top with a wedge, then divide the toppings evenly among the plates. Serve immediately.

ENJOY: I'm having it with a glass of cabernet or hot apple cider.

Supreme Citrus Season Salad

SERVES 6 TO 10 AS A SIDE

When my kids were little, Jacques Pépin and his daughter, Claudine, hosted our favorite cooking show, and we would all sit together and watch. That's where I learned how to supreme citrus, prep pineapple, and many other fun skills. I'm sorry if you ever get "Welcome to The Salad Lab, where we're making fabulous salads every day" stuck in your head; I still hear his voice saying "Happy cooking" every time I supreme an orange.

EXPERIMENT:
If you can't find all the different citrus, simply add more of what you can. Some tangerines separate into segments easily, but if you can find firm ones, it's nice to slice them into wheels like the blood orange and Sumo Citrus.

START OUT

2 cups (475 ml) sliced blood orange, rind, pith, and seeds removed (¼-inch/6-mm crosswise slices; about 2 oranges)

2 cups (475 ml) tangerine segments, membranes and seeds removed (about 3 tangerines)

1 cup (240 ml) sliced Sumo Citrus, rind, pith, and seeds removed (¼-inch/6-mm crosswise slices; about 1 Sumo Citrus), or substitute navel orange

1 cup (240 ml) supremed pomelo segments (about 1 pomelo; see page 195)

1 cup (240 ml) supremed pink grapefruit segments (about 1 grapefruit; see page 195)

¼ cup (60 ml) mixed citrus juice

½ cup (120 ml) coarsely chopped, toasted (see page 257) pistachios

WHISK

⅓ cup (80 ml) avocado oil

2 tablespoons (30 ml) honey

2 tablespoons (30 ml) finely chopped fresh mint

1 tablespoon (15 ml) fresh lime juice

2 teaspoons (10 ml) grated fresh ginger

¼ teaspoon (1.5 ml) flaky sea salt

TOSS

1 cup (240 ml) shaved fennel

1 cup (240 ml) pomegranate seeds

½ cup (120 ml) crumbled feta cheese (see page 43)

START OUT: Prepare the citrus, and collect the ¼ cup (60 ml) citrus juice while doing so. You can use any juices from the cutting board after slicing the blood orange, tangerine, and Sumo Citrus and squeeze what's left of the pomelo and grapefruit after removing the segments.

Toast the pistachios.

WHISK: In a large salad bowl, whisk together the citrus juice, oil, honey, mint, lime juice, ginger, and salt until well combined.

TOSS: In the bowl with the dressing, add all of the prepared citrus, the fennel, and the pomegranate. Toss gently until well combined and evenly coated with dressing. Sprinkle the pistachios and feta over the top and serve.

ENJOY: I'm having it with a citrus mimosa or the extra collected juices served chilled.

HOW TO SUPREME

If you're new to supreme-ing, no worries—it's easy. Slice a bit off the top and bottom of your citrus so it can stand upright on the cutting board. Starting at the top, guide your chef's knife down to the bottom of the fruit, following the curve of the fruit with your knife and trying to remove only the rind and pith. Trim off any white pith left on the outside. Once all the pith is removed, you'll be able to see the membranes between each wedge. Use a small paring knife to slice along both sides of the membranes and lift out your supreme citrus wedges and remove any seeds. Do this last part over a bowl and collect all the juices while you prep the citrus for this salad.

New Year's Celebration Salad

SERVES 3 TO 4 AS A LIGHT MEAL OR 6 TO 8 AS A SIDE

December 31: It's time to celebrate! Our tradition is to go to a friend's beach house, have fresh crab (if the weather co-operates), artichokes, and a good salad for dinner, and then, at the stroke of midnight, spew a little champagne over the balcony, run as fast as we can to the ocean, dip our toes in, and then run back before our feet go numb. Looking for a simple yet fancy salad for your own New Year's celebration? This is it. It was originally inspired by Restoration Hardware's café at their compound in Yountville, California. With its crystal chandeliers, stone fountains, and "lifestyle" galleries, it makes you feel like you have been teleported from Napa County to the elegant European countryside. This salad is fab when you want to bring that elegance to the table, and with a few farm-fresh ingredients, it's a perfect way to end the year (or any day).

WHISK

½ cup (120 ml) buttermilk

3 tablespoons (45 ml) heavy cream, or substitute sour cream

2 tablespoons (30 ml) extra-virgin olive oil

2 tablespoons (30 ml) finely chopped fresh flat-leaf parsley

2 tablespoons (30 ml) finely chopped fresh dill

2 tablespoons (30 ml) finely chopped fresh basil

2 tablespoons (30 ml) finely chopped fresh chives

1 tablespoon (15 ml) finely chopped fresh mint

1 tablespoon (15 ml) champagne vinegar

1 tablespoon (15 ml) fresh lemon juice

1 tablespoon (15 ml) honey

1 teaspoon (5 ml) anchovy paste, or substitute about 2 chopped anchovy fillets

Flaky sea salt and freshly cracked black pepper

TOSS

8 cups (1,900 ml) lightly packed whole gem lettuce leaves (about 4 small heads)

1 cup (240 ml) cubed avocado (½-inch/1.3-cm pieces)

½ cup (120 ml) crumbled feta cheese (see page 43)

⅓ cup (80 ml) shaved radish, such as Easter egg or watermelon radish (see Note)

Mixed fresh herb sprigs, such as flat-leaf parsley, dill, basil, or mint, for serving (optional)

2 to 3 tablespoons (30 to 45 ml) Osetra caviar, to taste, for serving (optional)

WHISK: In a small bowl or beaker (if using an immersion blender), add the buttermilk, cream, oil, parsley, dill, basil, chives, mint, vinegar, lemon juice, honey, and anchovy paste and season with salt and pepper. Whisk or blend just until well combined, then taste and adjust the seasoning if needed.

TOSS: In a large salad bowl, add the lettuce, avocado, feta, and radish and drizzle with dressing to taste. Toss until all the ingredients are evenly combined and coated with dressing. Top with a few sprigs of fresh herbs or dollop caviar in the center, if you like, and serve.

ENJOY: I'm having it with Champagne or sparkling water.

NOTE: I like to use my food processor rather than a mandoline to shave vegetables. If you're going to use a mandoline, though, please be smart and safe! Wear protective gloves and use a holder to swipe the food across the blade, and when you get to the point where you think you can get just one more slice, stop.

EXPERIMENT:
Gem lettuce is essentially a mini delicate romaine lettuce—with more flavor, in my opinion. It is trendy and not always easy to find. Experiment with any greens you like, as this one is about the dressing. If you are feeling extra, go for it and top with more of your favorite caviar (or edible gold leaf!) and serve with fresh crusty bread. Finish it off with a finely grated hard-boiled egg (see my Kale Salad on page 60 for directions) too, or if you are not a caviar fan, top with more egg, a tablespoon or two of capers, or a few giant caper berries for garnish. For a cheaper caviar alternative, I enjoy salmon roe.

Lox and Bagel Salad
(page 203)

Everything
Is a Salad

Breakfast Burrito Salad

SERVES 4 TO 6 AS A MEAL OR 8 TO 10 AS A SIDE

I like to think of breakfast burritos as the "biscuits and gravy" of the West Coast. This Mexican-influenced salad is great for brunches, lunches, breakfast-for-dinner, or meal prep for the week. It satisfies that craving for a spicy, hearty burrito. Even my picky eater devours this one. Seek out fresh Mexican chorizo, which you'll find in the refrigerated meat or butcher section in a grocery store, unlike cured Spanish chorizo, which is more like a very hard salami and is kept at room temperature.

START OUT

3 cups (720 ml) cubed Yukon gold potatoes (peel if you like; ½-inch/1.3-cm pieces)

2 cups (475 ml) cubed zucchini (½-inch/1.3-cm pieces)

1 medium red bell pepper, halved, stemmed, and seeded

1 medium yellow bell pepper, halved, stemmed, and seeded

2 tablespoons (30 ml) extra-virgin olive oil

Flaky sea salt and freshly cracked black pepper

1½ cups (360 ml) Cheesy Tortilla Croutons (page 238)

8 ounces (225 g) fresh Mexican chorizo (not cured), casings removed if necessary

Ice water

½ cup (120 ml) diced red onion (¼-inch/6-mm pieces)

1½ cups (360 ml) diced Roma tomatoes, or substitute what looks best at the market (¼-inch/6-mm pieces)

WHISK

¼ cup (60 ml) fresh lime juice

¼ cup (60 ml) finely chopped fresh cilantro

3 tablespoons (45 ml) very finely diced seeded and deveined fresh jalapeño

½ teaspoon (2.5 ml) ground cumin

Flaky sea salt and freshly cracked black pepper

TOSS

4 large eggs

1 tablespoon (15 ml) avocado oil or unsalted butter

Granulated sea salt and freshly cracked black pepper

1 cup (240 ml) cubed avocado (½-inch/1.3-cm pieces)

½ cup (120 ml) chopped scallions (green and white parts)

START OUT: Preheat the oven to 425°F (220°C) and use convection mode if that's an option. Line two baking sheets with parchment paper or a silicone baking mat.

Put the potatoes on one baking sheet and the zucchini, red pepper, and yellow pepper on the other. Toss the potatoes with 1 tablespoon (15 ml) of the oil and season with salt and pepper. Toss the zucchini and peppers with the remaining 1 tablespoon (15 ml) oil and season with salt and pepper. Bake until the vegetables are golden brown and crispy on the outside, stirring or flipping halfway through, 12 to 15 minutes (longer for a regular oven) for the zucchini and 15 to 20 minutes (longer in a regular oven) for the potatoes. Gently lift the parchment with the vegetables off the baking sheet and transfer to the counter to cool. Once the peppers have cooled, chop them into ½-inch (1.3-cm) pieces.

Meanwhile, prepare the croutons. Then, heat a medium well-seasoned cast-iron skillet over medium-high heat. Line a plate with paper towels. When the pan is hot, add the chorizo and cook, stirring occasionally and breaking the meat up into small, bite-size pieces with a spatula, until well browned and cooked through, 6 to 9 minutes. Transfer to the prepared plate with a slotted spoon to drain. Wipe out the skillet and reserve.

Fill a 500-ml beaker or a small glass bowl halfway with ice water and add the onion. Soak for 10 minutes, then drain and pat the onion dry. Place the tomatoes for the dressing in a colander and gently press down with a spoon to drain off excess liquid.

WHISK: In a large salad bowl, add the drained tomatoes, onion, lime juice, cilantro, jalapeño, and cumin and season with flaky sea salt and pepper. Stir until well combined, then taste and adjust the seasoning if needed.

TOSS: In a medium bowl, crack the eggs one at a time. Whisk vigorously, trying to incorporate as much air as possible. Put the reserved skillet over medium-high heat, heat the oil or melt the butter until foaming subsides, and swirl to coat the entire inside surface of the pan. Pour the eggs into the center of the pan and reduce the heat to medium. Gently scramble and, using a rubber spatula, continue to slowly move the eggs from one side of the pan to the other just until cooked through, about 3 minutes. Remove immediately, and season with granulated sea salt and pepper.

In the bowl with the dressing, add the roasted vegetables, croutons, chorizo, eggs, avocado, and scallions. Toss until all the ingredients are evenly combined and coated with dressing and serve.

ENJOY: I'm having it with a tangerine margarita or horchata.

EXPERIMENT: It's delicious with breakfast sausage or vegan chorizo. If prepping ahead of time, keep the pico dressing and avocados separate until serving. Save a little prep time and use 1 cup (240 ml) chopped jarred roasted peppers instead of making them yourself.

Lox and Bagel Salad

SERVES 4 AS A MEAL OR 6 TO 8 AS A SIDE

I created this salad because bagels are my daughter's lucky pre-competition meal. No matter where we were in the world, I would be scoping out the area as soon as we landed. Sometimes we had to get creative, but I always found one. This recipe came to life when I got a whiff of freshly baked bagels as I walked past the bagel shop and thought, "Hmm . . ." An everything bagel with lox and the works is the best—so salty, rich, and satisfying. Combined, all the components make a fun brunch main or breakfast-for-dinner salad that everyone will love.

EXPERIMENT: Double the dressing recipe and use the leftovers to dip vegetables in for a snack, or to serve alongside a vegetable tray or bagel board. If you don't like lox, experiment with crumbled breakfast sausage. Vegetarians can double the jammy boiled eggs to two per person and vegans can skip them and try plant-based sausage.

START OUT

1½ cups (360 ml) Everything Bagel Croutons (page 236)

4 Perfect Boiled Eggs (page 257)

Ice water

1 cup (240 ml) halved and thinly sliced red onion

2 cups (475 ml) halved and sliced Roma tomatoes, or substitute what looks best at the market

WHISK

½ teaspoon (2.5 ml) pressed garlic

¼ cup (60 ml) cream cheese, softened

¼ cup (60 ml) buttermilk

2 tablespoons (30 ml) fresh lemon juice (remember to zest first)

2 tablespoons (30 ml) water

2 tablespoons (30 ml) avocado oil

1 heaping tablespoon (20 ml) everything bagel seasoning

1 tablespoon (15 ml) finely chopped fresh dill

1 tablespoon (15 ml) finely chopped fresh chives

1 tablespoon (15 ml) drained and finely chopped capers

2 teaspoons (10 ml) honey

1 teaspoon (5 ml) lightly packed grated lemon zest

TOSS

8 cups (1,900 ml) lightly packed spring mix (baby lettuce blend)

1½ cups (360 ml) halved lengthwise and sliced English cucumber

4 ounces (115 g) chopped lox (1-inch/2.5-cm pieces)

¼ cup (60 ml) drained capers

START OUT: Prepare the croutons and eggs. When the eggs are cool enough to handle, slice them into 8 wedges each.

Meanwhile, fill a 500-ml beaker or a small glass bowl halfway with ice water and add the onion. Soak for 10 minutes, then drain and pat the onion dry. Place the tomatoes in a colander and gently press down with a spoon to drain off excess liquid.

WHISK: Rinse the pressed garlic in a very fine mesh strainer and shake off any excess water. In a large salad bowl, whisk together the garlic, cream cheese, buttermilk, lemon juice, water, oil, bagel seasoning, dill, chives, capers, honey, and lemon zest until well combined.

TOSS: In the bowl with the dressing, combine the spring mix, cucumber, lox, capers, croutons, eggs, tomatoes, and onion. (If you're not serving right away, keep the croutons separate and add right before serving.) Toss until all the ingredients are evenly combined and coated with dressing, making sure the lox isn't sticking together, and serve.

ENJOY: I'm having it with a sparkling brut rosé.

Avocado Bruschetta

This is the recipe my daughter asks for more than any other, and she's the one who sparked this great adventure, so this is my "ode to Athena" in this book. This is not your typical salad—if I'm honest, it's more of a dip—but it is the perfect way to start off a meal, and is best followed by a fabulous salad and your favorite beverage. I have been making this for girlfriend gatherings and it's my go-to for spring and summer.

EXPERIMENT: If you want to get fancy, add a clove of pressed garlic to the oil and sprinkle Parmigiano-Reggiano over the baguette slices before toasting. Or add croutons to the salad and you have an avocado panzanella, yum! You can also double the tomato and reduce the avocado for a lighter version.

START OUT

1 baguette, sliced into crostini (¼ inch/6 mm thick)

Extra-virgin olive oil, for brushing

1½ cups (360 ml) quartered cherry tomatoes, or substitute what looks best at the market

WHISK

1 tablespoon (15 ml) pressed garlic

¼ cup (60 ml) extra-virgin olive oil

¼ cup (60 ml) fresh lemon juice (remember to zest first)

1 tablespoon (15 ml) balsamic vinegar

1 teaspoon (5 ml) lightly packed grated lemon zest

½ teaspoon (2.5 ml) flaky sea salt

¼ teaspoon (1.5 ml) freshly cracked black pepper

Pinch of red pepper flakes

TOSS

6 cups (1,400 ml) cubed avocado (½-inch/1.3-cm pieces; about 6 avocados)

¾ cup (175 ml) coarsely chopped fresh basil

⅔ cup (160 ml) chopped scallions (green and white parts)

START OUT: Preheat the oven to 400°F (200°C) and use convection mode if that's an option. Line a baking sheet with parchment paper or a silicone baking mat.

Brush the baguette slices with oil on one side. Bake until the edges start to brown, 8 to 10 minutes (longer for a regular oven).

Meanwhile, place the tomatoes in a colander and gently press down with a spoon to drain off excess liquid.

WHISK: Rinse the pressed garlic in a very fine mesh strainer and shake off any excess water. In a large salad bowl, whisk together the garlic, oil, lemon juice, vinegar, zest, salt, black pepper, and red pepper flakes until well combined.

TOSS: In the bowl with the dressing, combine the avocado, basil, scallions, and tomatoes. Gently toss until all the ingredients are evenly combined and coated with dressing. Serve with the crostini.

ENJOY: I'm having it with a pinot noir or a lemonade–iced tea.

Doradito Salad

Who doesn't love Doritos? Called "a swinging Latin sort of snack" when first advertised in the 1960s, Doritos are still the number one chip in the United States today. Fun fact: the name combines the Spanish words *doradito* and *dorado*, both of which describe fried golden things. They are considered comfort food for some and almost everyone has some sort of teenage flashback related to these cheesy corn chips. This salad recipe is a little trip down memory lane. I put the Salad Lab twist on the dressing and replaced the traditional bottled, syrupy Catalina dressing (yikes) with this lighter homemade one (yum). We also enjoy a little more spice in our house, so I used chorizo and pickled jalapeños instead of the classic "taco meat."

EXPERIMENT: Try substituting this dressing with the Cilantro Lime Dressing on page 251. There are so many canned beans available now; experiment with black beans, Great Northern beans, or black-eyed peas. Use any lettuce you like or already have. If you don't like spicy or are not a chorizo fan, substitute ground turkey or beef prepared with taco seasoning. If you like to eat the salad as a dip, don't crush the chips and toss them in; use them as your spoon instead.

START OUT

1½ cups (360 ml) fresh Mexican chorizo (not cured), casings removed if necessary

Ice water

¼ cup (60 ml) diced red onion (¼-inch/6-mm pieces)

1 cup (240 ml) quartered cherry tomatoes, or substitute what looks best at the market

WHISK

1 teaspoon (5 ml) pressed garlic

⅓ cup (80 ml) avocado oil

¼ cup (60 ml) red wine vinegar

¼ cup (60 ml) ketchup

3 tablespoons (45 ml) grated yellow or red onion

2 tablespoons (30 ml) sugar

1 teaspoon (5 ml) Worcestershire sauce

1 teaspoon (5 ml) celery seed

1 teaspoon (5 ml) sweet paprika

1 teaspoon (5 ml) chili powder

Flaky sea salt and freshly cracked black pepper

TOSS

4 cups (950 ml) chopped iceberg lettuce (bite-size pieces)

4 cups (950 ml) chopped romaine lettuce (bite-size pieces)

1½ cups (360 ml) crushed Nacho Cheese Doritos (bite-size pieces)

1 cup (240 ml) cooked or rinsed and drained canned pinto beans

1 cup (240 ml) cubed avocado (½-inch/1.3-cm pieces)

⅓ cup (80 ml) grated Monterey Jack cheese

⅓ cup (80 ml) grated medium-sharp cheddar cheese

¼ cup (60 ml) drained pickled jalapeño slices

Nacho Cheese Doritos, for serving (optional)

START OUT: Heat a medium skillet over medium-high heat. Line a plate with paper towels. When the pan is hot, add the chorizo. Cook, stirring occasionally and breaking up the meat in small, bite-size pieces using a spatula, until well browned and cooked through, 6 to 9 minutes. Transfer to the prepared plate with a slotted spoon to drain.

Meanwhile, fill a 500-ml beaker or a small glass bowl halfway with ice water and add the diced onion. Soak for 10 minutes, then drain and pat the onion dry. Place the tomatoes in a colander and gently press down with a spoon to drain off excess liquid.

WHISK: Rinse the pressed garlic in a very fine mesh strainer and shake off any excess water. In a large salad bowl, combine the garlic, oil, vinegar, ketchup, grated onion, sugar, Worcestershire sauce, celery seed, paprika, and chili powder and season with salt and pepper. Whisk until well combined, then taste and adjust the seasoning if needed.

TOSS: In the bowl with the dressing, add the iceberg lettuce, romaine lettuce, crushed Doritos, beans, avocado, jack cheese, cheddar cheese, jalapeños, chorizo, diced onion, and tomatoes. Toss until all the ingredients are evenly combined and coated with dressing and serve. If you want to get fancy, garnish with extra chips around the bowl.

ENJOY: I'm having it with a merlot or soda.

Potato Skin Salad

SERVES 4 TO 6 AS A MEAL OR 6 TO 10 AS A SIDE

"Cheesy bacon fries!" my kids would cheer when they saw the bag of potatoes on the counter. Potato skins or cheesy potato wedges (what my kids called fries) topped with bacon and scallions are making a comeback on appetizer menus at steakhouses these days. Why not the salad menu too? Living in Santa Rosa, California, you hear the name Luther Burbank a lot. There are gardens, a theater, and parks named after him, but do you know what he's most famous for? The Russet Burbank potato. Almost every fast-food French fry or bag of brown potatoes you see at the grocery store descends from the hybridization Burbank created in the nineteenth century. These potatoes grew better, and larger, than other varieties. The hybrid even helped Ireland after the Great (Potato) Famine. Now more than half the potatoes grown and consumed in the United States are Burbank russets. This one is fun for tailgating, watch parties, or a family gathering.

EXPERIMENT:
Like a little heat? Experiment with adding a tablespoon of hot sauce to the dressing and/or pepperoncini or pickled jalapeños. Need protein? Top with cubed steak, chili, or buffalo chicken/vegan chicken. To lighten it up, use nonfat sour cream or Greek yogurt and skip the extra cheddar and avocado.

START OUT	WHISK	TOSS
1 tablespoon (15 ml) Roasted Garlic Purée (page 256)	½ cup (120 ml) buttermilk	4 cups (950 ml) chopped romaine lettuce (bite-size pieces), or substitute any combination of greens you like
3 medium Russet potatoes	½ cup (120 ml) sour cream	
1 tablespoon (15 ml) extra-virgin olive oil	2 tablespoons (30 ml) extra-virgin olive oil	4 cups (950 ml) torn butter lettuce (1-inch/2.5-cm pieces)
⅔ cup (160 ml) grated extra-sharp cheddar cheese	2 tablespoons (30 ml) finely chopped fresh flat-leaf parsley	1 cup (240 ml) cubed avocado (½-inch/1.3-cm pieces)
Flaky sea salt and freshly cracked black pepper	2 tablespoons (30 ml) finely chopped fresh chives, or substitute scallion greens	⅔ cup (160 ml) chopped scallions (green and white parts)
½ cup (120 ml) Chopped Bacon (page 258)	1 tablespoon (15 ml) apple cider vinegar	½ cup (120 ml) grated extra-sharp cheddar cheese
1 cup (240 ml) quartered cherry tomatoes or chopped Roma tomatoes (½-inch/1.3-cm pieces)	1 tablespoon (15 ml) finely chopped fresh dill	
	Flaky sea salt and freshly cracked black pepper	

START OUT: Prepare the roasted garlic purée for the dressing up to 3 days in advance (or you can make it at the same time as the potatoes; it may take a little longer at the slightly lower temperature). Preheat the oven to 400°F (200°C) and use convection mode if that's an option. Line a baking sheet with foil.

Clean and dry the potatoes and rub lightly with the oil. Bake on the prepared baking sheet until the skin is crispy and the potatoes are fork-tender, 50 to 60 minutes (longer for a regular oven). Transfer the potatoes to a wire rack until cool enough to handle. Reserve the baking sheet.

Set the oven to broil. Once the potatoes are cool, cut them in half lengthwise and scoop out the flesh from each half, leaving ¼ inch (6 mm) or more of the flesh. Return the potato skins to the foil-lined baking sheet, skin side down. Sprinkle the cheese evenly over the potatoes and place under the broiler until the cheese is melted, bubbling, and beginning to brown, 30 seconds to 2 minutes, checking every 10 seconds. Remove from the oven and return to the wire rack. Season with salt and pepper, then cut into ¾-inch (2-cm) cubes.

Meanwhile, prepare the bacon and let it drain. Place the tomatoes in a colander and gently press down with a spoon to drain off excess liquid.

WHISK: In a large salad bowl, add the roasted garlic purée, buttermilk, sour cream, oil, parsley, chives, vinegar, and dill and season with salt and pepper. Whisk until well combined, then taste and adjust the seasoning if needed.

TOSS: In the bowl with the dressing, add the romaine lettuce, butter lettuce, avocado, scallions, cheese, tomatoes, potato skins, and bacon. Toss until all the ingredients are evenly combined and coated with dressing and serve.

ENJOY: I'm having it with an IPA or a lemonade–iced tea.

_____

Spring Roll Salad

SERVES 4 AS A MEAL OR 6 TO 8 AS A SIDE

I was craving spring rolls one day, didn't have any sheets of rice paper, but did have some vermicelli rice noodles in the pantry, and voilà: Spring Roll Salad. It is so sweet, tangy, and flavorful. I love the freshness of mint and cilantro paired with the rich crunch of the peanut dressing. It's just what you need on a hot summer day when you'd rather be anywhere besides the kitchen. And if you start with precooked shrimp, it's even *less* time from boiling the noodles to enjoying.

EXPERIMENT:
Don't like shrimp? This salad is excellent with thinly shredded poached chicken or Roasted Tofu (page 258). Try it with bean sprouts or sliced radishes, or replace the cilantro with basil—even better, purple Thai basil if you can find it.

START OUT

3 ounces (85 g) dried vermicelli rice noodles

8 ounces (225 g) medium (U31-40) peeled and deveined shrimp

1 tablespoon (15 ml) extra-virgin olive or avocado oil

1 teaspoon (5 ml) fresh lemon juice, plus more for serving

Flaky sea salt and freshly cracked black pepper

WHISK

½ teaspoon (2.5 ml) pressed garlic

¼ cup (60 ml) smooth natural (unsweetened) peanut butter

¼ cup (60 ml) full-fat coconut milk, or substitute light coconut milk

3 tablespoons (45 ml) water

3 tablespoons (45 ml) Vietnamese sweet chili sauce

2 tablespoons (30 ml) fresh lime juice (remember to zest first)

2 tablespoons (30 ml) chopped, toasted (see page 257) peanuts

1 tablespoon (15 ml) hoisin sauce

½ teaspoon (2.5 ml) lightly packed grated lime zest

TOSS

6 cups (1,400 ml) torn curly leaf lettuce (bite-size pieces)

1½ cups (360 ml) peeled and shredded carrots

1½ cups (360 ml) julienned (see page 143) seeded English cucumber

½ cup (120 ml) coarsely chopped fresh mint

½ cup (120 ml) coarsely chopped fresh cilantro

½ cup (120 ml) chopped scallions (green and white parts)

Chopped, toasted (see page 257) peanuts, for serving

START OUT: Soak 6 bamboo skewers in water for 30 to 60 minutes to prevent burning.

Meanwhile, cook the noodles according to the package directions, then rinse with cold water until cool enough to handle. Chop into 1-inch (2.5-cm) pieces.

Preheat the grill to 375°F (190°C) or for medium-high heat, or heat a grill pan over medium high. Rinse the shrimp and pat dry. In a medium bowl, combine the shrimp, oil, and lemon juice and season with salt and pepper. Evenly place a few shrimp on each skewer, leaving a little space in between. Grill the skewers until the shrimp are bright pink and cooked through, 1 to 2 minutes per side. Remove from the grill, squeeze over a little more lemon juice, and let rest for 5 minutes. Coarsely chop the shrimp.

WHISK: Rinse the pressed garlic in a very fine mesh strainer and shake off any excess water. In a large salad bowl, whisk together the garlic, peanut butter, coconut milk, water, chili sauce, lime juice, peanuts, hoisin, and lime zest until smooth.

TOSS: In the bowl with the dressing, add the lettuce, carrots, cucumber, mint, cilantro, scallion, shrimp, and noodles. Toss until all the ingredients are evenly combined and coated with dressing, top with as many chopped roasted peanuts as you like, and serve.

ENJOY: I'm having it with Vietnamese iced tea or green bubble tea.

Soba Noodle Salad

Buckwheat in general, and soba noodles in particular, are underrated. Buckwheat has a gently nutty flavor that enhances the overall flavor of a noodle-based salad. I like to keep some in my pantry for just this recipe. It comes together quickly and is a good one to use up all the bits of vegetables you have left in the refrigerator, so feel free to experiment with what you have. You get a lot of flavor "bang for your buck" with every bite. Use the slicing attachment on a food processor or a mandoline—carefully!—to very thinly slice the vegetables quickly and evenly.

EXPERIMENT: Can't find furikake? Crumpling up a seaweed snack and adding a tablespoon of black and/or white sesame seeds is an easy substitute in a pinch. If you do not like it spicy, skip the wasabi in the dressing, or if you want your nose to tingle, add more. If you need more protein, add teriyaki chicken, a few jammy eggs (see page 257), or Roasted Tofu (page 258).

START OUT

1 cup (240 ml) frozen shelled edamame

Flaky sea salt

8 ounces (225 g) dried soba noodles

2 teaspoons (10 ml) avocado oil

1 cup (240 ml) thinly sliced stemmed shiitake mushrooms

WHISK

¼ cup (60 ml) avocado oil

2 tablespoons (30 ml) fresh lime juice

2 tablespoons (30 ml) mirin, or substitute 2 tablespoons (30 ml) rice vinegar with 2 teaspoons (10 ml) sugar

2 tablespoons (30 ml) white miso paste

2 tablespoons (30 ml) water

2 teaspoons (10 ml) toasted sesame oil

1 teaspoon (5 ml) grated fresh ginger

¼ teaspoon (1.5 ml) wasabi, or substitute red pepper flakes

TOSS

1 cup (240 ml) peeled and shredded carrots

1 cup (240 ml) thinly shredded red cabbage (a food processor is helpful)

½ cup (120 ml) halved and shaved watermelon radish or daikon radish (a food processor is also helpful here)

½ cup (120 ml) cubed seeded cucumber (½-inch/1.3-cm pieces)

½ cup (120 ml) thinly sliced red and/or orange bell pepper

¼ cup (60 ml) chopped scallions (greens only)

2 tablespoons (30 ml) furikake, for serving

START OUT: Thaw the edamame. Meanwhile, fill a large pot with water and lightly salt it. Bring to a rolling boil, then add the soba noodles, return to a boil, and cook, uncovered and stirring occasionally, until soft with a slight chew in the center, 4 to 6 minutes. Strain, lightly rinse the noodles, and let cool.

Heat the avocado oil in a small skillet over medium-high heat. When the oil is hot, add the mushrooms and cook, stirring often, until soft, about 5 minutes. Transfer to a plate to cool.

WHISK: In a large salad bowl, whisk together the avocado oil, lime juice, mirin, miso, water, sesame oil, ginger, and wasabi until smooth.

TOSS: In the bowl with the dressing, add the carrots, cabbage, radish, cucumber, bell pepper, scallions, edamame, noodles, and mushrooms. Toss until all the ingredients are evenly combined and coated with dressing. Top with furikake and serve.

ENJOY: I'm having it with cold sake or iced green tea.

Fish Taco Salad

Fish Taco Salad

So good! Fish tacos always remind me of being in school or on vacation. I spent my college years in Southern California where almost every weekend we would head down to the beach for some fish tacos. Anywhere you go along the coast of California or Mexico, you are sure to find a stand or taqueria. Even as I write this I start to think of warm beaches, free time, and sandy feet. No matter where you are or what weather you are in, this salad is sure to bring a little sunshine to your day. I live by the mantra "everything's better with mangos" and I especially love them in this salad.

EXPERIMENT:
Replace the mango with pineapple or with diced orange supremes (see page 195). It's blasphemy, but you do you. Add your favorite red or green salsa and omit the cilantro or replace it with parsley if you don't like the flavor. This salad is yummy made with salmon, shrimp or prawns, or other seafood. When you're in a hurry, brush a few frozen battered fried fish fillets with a coat of the chipotle oil combo, pop them in the oven, and you're good to go.

START OUT

½ cup (120 ml) Quick Pickled Onions (page 256)

⅔ cup (160 ml) quartered cherry tomatoes or chopped Roma tomatoes (½-inch/1.3-cm pieces)

WHISK

½ cup (120 ml) smashed avocado

¼ cup (60 ml) sour cream or Mexican crema

¼ cup (60 ml) avocado oil

2 tablespoons (30 ml) very finely diced seeded and deveined fresh jalapeño

2 tablespoons (30 ml) fresh lime juice (remember to zest first)

1 tablespoon (15 ml) finely chopped fresh cilantro

2 teaspoons (10 ml) Mexican hot sauce

½ teaspoon (2.5 ml) lightly packed grated lime zest

Flaky sea salt and freshly cracked black pepper

TOSS

4 cups (950 ml) thinly shredded green cabbage or savoy cabbage (a food processor is helpful)

3 cups (720 ml) thinly shredded red cabbage

⅔ cup (160 ml) cubed peeled (see page 119) mango (½-inch/1.3-cm pieces)

1½ cups (360 ml) Cheesy Tortilla Croutons (page 238)

2 teaspoons (10 ml) chipotle chile powder or chili powder

1 tablespoon plus 1 teaspoon (20 ml) avocado oil

½ teaspoon (2.5 ml) granulated sea salt

1 pound (450 g) white fish such as mahimahi, cod, or tilapia, cut into 1-inch (2.5-cm) cubes

½ cup (120 ml) crumbled Cotija cheese, or substitute grated jack cheese

¼ cup (60 ml) finely chopped fresh cilantro

Lime wedges, for serving

START OUT: Prepare the pickled onions 30 minutes or up to 1 day in advance. Place the tomatoes in a colander and gently press down with a spoon to drain off excess liquid.

WHISK: In a large salad bowl, add the avocado, sour cream, oil, jalapeño, lime juice, cilantro, hot sauce, and zest and season with flaky sea salt and pepper. Whisk until well combined, then taste and adjust the seasoning if needed.

TOSS: In the bowl with the dressing, add the green and red cabbage, mango, pickled onions, and tomatoes. Toss until all the ingredients are evenly combined and coated with dressing. Let the salad marinate while you finish the toppings.

Prepare the croutons and keep warm.

In a small bowl, whisk together the chipotle powder, 1 teaspoon (5 ml) of the avocado oil, and the granulated sea salt. Add the fish and gently toss until well combined.

Heat a large well-seasoned cast-iron skillet over medium-high heat, then add the remaining 1 tablespoon (15 ml) avocado oil and tilt the pan to entirely coat the bottom. Add the fish and cook for 2 minutes. Flip the fish and cook for another 2 minutes. Flip and continue cooking for 1 to 2 minutes longer if needed until the fish is opaque all the way through. Gently remove from the pan.

Add the warm fish directly to the bowl of tossed cabbage mixture. Sprinkle the top with the warm croutons, cheese, and cilantro and serve immediately with lime wedges on the side for squeezing over the salad.

ENJOY: I'm having it with a Mexican beer or glass bottle of cola.

Grinder Salad

SERVES 4 TO 6 AS A MEAL OR 6 TO 10 AS A SIDE

I love a good deli sandwich with all the fixings—don't you? This salad was inspired by the Italian deli sandwiches originally made for ship workers or "grinders" during World War Two. The signature shredded lettuce lightly dressed with an Italian dressing was the key component. I grew up on a street that had a deli/convenience store at the end of it and spent many hours of my childhood hanging out with friends, sharing a sandwich and soda out front. This salad takes me back to fond memories of a simple life where time seemed to stand still.

EXPERIMENT:
What's your favorite sandwich combination? I make a "California" version of this with turkey, avocado, and Swiss cheese—so good. Skip the croutons if you're low carb. High carb? Make it a pasta salad by adding 4 cups (950 ml) of your favorite shape (cooked) and omit the croutons and iceberg.

START OUT

2 cups (475 ml) Sourdough Garlic Croutons (page 235)

Ice water

½ cup (120 ml) very finely diced red onion

2 cups (475 ml) halved and sliced Roma tomatoes

WHISK

1 tablespoon (15 ml) pressed garlic

1 cup (240 ml) mayonnaise

½ cup (120 ml) finely chopped banana peppers or pepperoncini

3 tablespoons (45 ml) red wine vinegar

½ teaspoon (2.5 ml) red pepper flakes

½ teaspoon (2.5 ml) dried oregano

Flaky sea salt and freshly cracked black pepper

TOSS

8 cups (1,900 ml) shredded iceberg lettuce

1½ cups (360 ml) halved lengthwise, seeded, and thinly sliced English cucumber

1 cup (240 ml) chopped red bell pepper (½-inch/1.3-cm pieces)

½ cup (120 ml) cubed thick-sliced salami (½-inch/1.3-cm pieces)

½ cup (120 ml) cubed thick-sliced ham (½-inch/1.3-cm pieces)

½ cup (120 ml) cubed thick-sliced roast beef (½-inch/1.3-cm pieces)

½ cup (120 ml) cubed thick-sliced smoked turkey (½-inch/1.3-cm pieces)

½ cup (120 ml) freshly grated Parmigiano-Reggiano (use a Microplane)

START OUT: Prepare the croutons. Meanwhile, fill a 500-ml beaker or a small glass bowl halfway with ice water and add the onion. Soak for 10 minutes, then drain and pat the onion dry. Place the tomatoes in a colander and gently press down with a spoon to drain off excess liquid.

WHISK: Rinse the pressed garlic in a very fine mesh strainer and shake off any excess water. In a large salad bowl, combine the garlic, onion, mayonnaise, peppers, vinegar, red pepper flakes, and oregano and season with salt and pepper. Whisk together until well combined, then taste and adjust the seasoning if needed.

TOSS: In the bowl with the dressing, add the lettuce, cucumber, bell pepper, salami, ham, roast beef, turkey, cheese, croutons, and tomatoes. Toss until all the ingredients are evenly combined and coated with dressing and serve.

ENJOY: I'm having it with a pilsner or diet cola.

Burger and Fries Salad

Trying to cook and prepare meals to meet the nutrition requirements for an elite athlete can be a challenge, especially when that athlete is your teenage daughter in a weight-class sport. Once in a while we all want pizza or a burger and fries, which definitely *don't* meet those requirements. This recipe is based on the burger salad I would make for her weekly. I have added a couple extra ingredients for a deluxe kind of meal, since we don't need to clean and jerk 250 pounds.

EXPERIMENT:
Try iceberg lettuce for a more classic burger combo. I went through a paleo phase and still try to use grass-fed beef when available, and it's becoming easier to find at grocery stores. The flavor is a little different, but once you try it, there's no going back. This is my favorite burger combo but it doesn't have to be yours. Other combos include grilled mushrooms and Swiss cheese, cheddar and fresh red onions, Mexican spices with the beef plus Cotija cheese and pickled jalapeños—the options are endless. Get creative!

START OUT

1 pound (450 g) lean (80–90 percent) ground beef

½ cup (120 ml) Chopped Bacon (page 258)

1 cup (240 ml) chopped beefsteak tomatoes (½-inch/1.3-cm pieces)

2½ cups (590 ml) cubed Yukon gold potatoes (½-inch/1.3-cm pieces)

1 tablespoon (15 ml) extra-virgin olive oil

1 tablespoon (15 ml) unsalted butter, melted

½ teaspoon (2.5 ml) granulated sea salt

4 teaspoons (20 ml) Cajun spice blend (optional)

Flaky sea salt and freshly cracked black pepper

1 cup (240 ml) diced yellow onion (¼-inch/6-mm pieces)

WHISK

2 tablespoons (30 ml) extra-virgin olive oil

2 tablespoons (30 ml) mayonnaise

2 tablespoons (30 ml) ketchup

2 tablespoons (30 ml) pickle relish

1 heaping tablespoon (20 ml) yellow mustard

1 tablespoon (15 ml) fresh lemon juice

½ teaspoon (2.5 ml) flaky sea salt

½ teaspoon (2.5 ml) freshly cracked black pepper

TOSS

8 cups (1,900 ml) torn romaine lettuce (bite-size pieces)

1 cup (240 ml) cubed avocado (½-inch/1.3-cm pieces)

½ cup (120 ml) crumbled blue cheese (see page 43), or substitute grated sharp cheddar

½ cup (120 ml) diced refrigerated dill pickles, such as Claussen (¼-inch/6-mm pieces)

¼ cup (60 ml) sliced pepperoncini

START OUT: Preheat the oven to 425°F (220°C) and use convection mode if that's an option. Line a baking sheet with parchment paper or a silicone baking mat. Remove the beef from the refrigerator and let it come to room temperature. Prepare the bacon and let it drain. Place the tomatoes in a colander and gently press down with a spoon to drain off excess liquid.

In a medium bowl, combine the potatoes, oil, melted butter, and granulated sea salt and stir until the potatoes are evenly coated. Spread the mixture out on the baking sheet. Bake, stirring and flipping the potato cubes every 10 minutes or so, until golden brown and crisp, 30 to 40 minutes total (longer for a regular oven). Remove from the oven and let cool slightly.

Meanwhile, form the beef into four 4-inch (10-cm) square patties ½ inch to ¾ inch (1.3 to 2 cm) thick. Sprinkle with Cajun spice (if using) and season with salt and pepper. Heat a large cast-iron skillet or griddle on medium-high heat. Add the onion and cook, stirring often, until the onions start to turn translucent, about 2 minutes, then push to the edge of the pan.

Add the patties to the center of the pan, cook until crispy and browned, 5 to 7 minutes, then flip. Cook until the internal temperature reads 160°F (70°C) and the other side is crisp, another 5 to 7 minutes. While the burgers are cooking, stir the onions every few minutes while keeping them to the edges of the skillet. The onions are done when they are dark brown and translucent. Remove the onions and patties from the skillet and transfer to a plate to cool for 5 minutes. Cut the hamburgers into 1-inch (2.5-cm) cubes.

WHISK: In a large salad bowl, whisk together the oil, mayonnaise, ketchup, relish, mustard, lemon juice, flaky sea salt, and pepper until well combined.

TOSS: In the bowl with the dressing, add the lettuce, avocado, cheese, pickles, pepperoncini, beef, potatoes, sautéed onions, bacon, and tomatoes. Toss until all the ingredients are evenly combined and coated with dressing and serve.

ENJOY: I'm having it with a zinfandel or lemonade.

THE PERFECT AVOCADO: I use avocado quite often in my salads. When picking "camera-ready" avocados you want to be able to push lightly with your thumb near the top and feel a little give (but it shouldn't feel completely soft). Long skinny ones have smaller pits than the round ones, usually. Bagged avocados are less likely to be bruised than loose ones. Use them before they get too ripe and mushy. You want distinct chunks of the fruit in your salad, not a guacamole dressing! Any very ripe avocados can be used for Avocado Bruschetta (page 205). If you're making your salad more than 30 minutes before serving, toss the avocado in a squeeze of fresh lemon juice or diluted citric acid to prevent it from browning.

Pizza Salad

In the United States, 40 percent of Americans eat pizza at least once a week. But according to another survey, the average American eats four salads every week, and 62 percent surveyed said salad is part of their regular diet. Take that, pizza! Let's corner the market and make a pizza salad. Humans are drawn to foods that are fatty, sweet, rich, chewy, crunchy, and complex, and this one has all that and more. Enjoy!

EXPERIMENT:
Have fun with this and turn it into your usual order by adding your favorite toppings and subtracting the ones that aren't. If you have fresh pizza dough or a prepared crust, you can make it a piadina and serve the salad on top of a warm pizza crust. It's fabulous!

START OUT

1 tablespoon (15 ml) Roasted Garlic Purée (page 256)

1¼ cups (300 ml) chopped green bell pepper (½-inch/1.3-cm pieces)

1¼ cups (300 ml) quartered button mushrooms

1 cup (240 ml) chopped red onion (½-inch/1.3-cm pieces)

2 tablespoons (30 ml) extra-virgin olive oil

Flaky sea salt and freshly cracked black pepper

1½ cups (360 ml) Sourdough Garlic Croutons (page 235), for serving (optional)

1 cup (240 ml) quartered cherry tomatoes or chopped Roma tomatoes (½-inch/1.3-cm pieces)

⅓ cup (80 ml) sweet Italian sausage, casings removed

WHISK

⅓ cup (80 ml) extra-virgin olive oil

2 tablespoons (30 ml) balsamic vinegar

1 tablespoon (15 ml) tomato paste

1 teaspoon (5 ml) dried oregano

1 teaspoon (5 ml) honey

¼ teaspoon (1.5 ml) red pepper flakes

Flaky sea salt and freshly cracked black pepper

TOSS

4 cups (950 ml) chopped romaine lettuce (bite-size pieces)

1 cup (240 ml) lightly packed arugula

1 cup (240 ml) thinly sliced lacinato kale, ribs removed, or substitute your greens of choice

½ cup (120 ml) grated mozzarella cheese (preferably fresh)

½ cup (120 ml) drained and chopped canned water-packed artichoke hearts (½-inch/1.3-cm pieces)

⅓ cup (80 ml) chopped sliced pepperoni

⅓ cup (80 ml) drained and sliced canned pitted black olives

¼ cup (60 ml) freshly grated Parmigiano-Reggiano (use a Microplane)

¼ cup (60 ml) coarsely chopped fresh basil

START OUT: Prepare the roasted garlic purée for the dressing up to 3 days in advance (or you can make it at the same time as the vegetables). Preheat the oven to 425°F (220°C) and use convection mode if that's an option. Line a baking sheet with parchment paper or a silicone baking mat.

Put the green pepper, mushrooms, and onion onto the prepared sheet pan, toss with the oil, and season with salt and pepper. Bake until the vegetables are golden brown and crispy on the outside, stirring or flipping halfway through, 12 to 15 minutes (longer for a regular oven). Gently lift the parchment with the vegetables off the baking sheet and transfer to the counter to cool.

Prepare the croutons (if using). Place the tomatoes in a colander and gently press down with a spoon to drain off excess liquid.

Meanwhile, heat a medium skillet over medium-high heat. Line a plate with a paper towel. When the pan is hot, add the sausage. Cook, stirring occasionally and breaking up the meat into small, bite-size pieces using a spatula, until well browned and cooked through, 6 to 9 minutes. Transfer to the prepared plate with a slotted spoon to drain.

WHISK: In a very large salad bowl, combine the roasted garlic purée, oil, vinegar, tomato paste, oregano, honey, and pepper flakes and season with salt and pepper (the salad has several salty components so you may want to go easy on the salt). Whisk until well combined, then taste and adjust the seasoning if needed.

TOSS: In the bowl with the dressing, add the romaine lettuce, arugula, kale, mozzarella, artichokes, pepperoni, olives, Parmigiano-Reggiano, basil, roasted vegetables, sausage, and tomatoes. Toss until everything is coated with dressing and well combined, garnish with croutons if desired, and serve.

ENJOY: I'm having it with a glass of zinfandel or a bottle of root beer.

Corned Beef and Cabbage Salad

SERVES 4 TO 6 AS A MEAL OR 8 TO 12 AS A SIDE

Just starting out after college, my then-fiancé worked with an Irish engineer who had just moved from Dublin to Southern California. We spent many evenings with him and his Irish girlfriend at the local pub singing Irish folk songs (or quietly humming and pretending to know the words) late into the night. We had our Irish friends over for dinner one Saint Patrick's Day and of course, I had to make them corned beef and cabbage. I was so excited to share it and to make them feel at home, only to find out they had never heard of it. I was embarrassed at the time, but we all laughed and enjoyed it nonetheless. Like many "ethnic" traditions in the United States, it stems from a population of immigrants at a particular time in history. "Corned" actually refers to the size of the salt crystals used to preserve the beef; there was no refrigeration in the eighteenth and nineteenth centuries when they immigrated. This is a tasty fun favorite I make whenever I'm craving a not-so-Irish meal. If you don't want to make your own corned beef, skip the first step and use 1½ cups (360 ml) cubed prepared corn beef.

EXPERIMENT:
I prefer the taste of naturally preserved corned beef and avoid the ones with sodium nitrates and nitrites. They may cost a little more but you can find them at almost any grocery store in March. Like your salads gooey? Double the dressing; this one is on the lighter side. I know it's salad blasphemy, but experiment with heating up leftovers of this salad the second day if it's cold outside—it's delicious warm, too.

START OUT

2 pounds (900 g) corned beef, with included seasoning packet

1 (355-ml) bottle or can dark beer (such as Guinness or a nonalcoholic variety)

1 pound (450 g) baby red potatoes, boiled (see page 260)

Ice water

¼ cup (60 ml) thinly sliced shallot (about 1 medium)

WHISK

6 tablespoons (90 ml) buttermilk

2 tablespoons (30 ml) extra-virgin olive oil

2 tablespoons (30 ml) finely chopped fresh flat-leaf parsley

1 tablespoon (15 ml) mayonnaise

1 teaspoon (5 ml) prepared horseradish

½ teaspoon (2.5 ml) caraway seeds

Flaky sea salt and freshly cracked black pepper

TOSS

4 cups (950 ml) thinly shredded green cabbage (a food processor is helpful)

4 cups (950 ml) thinly shredded red cabbage

1½ cups (360 ml) peeled and shredded carrots

1 cup (240 ml) grated white cheddar

START OUT: Place the corned beef in a large stockpot. Add the seasoning packet, beer, and enough water to cover the beef completely. Bring it to a boil, then cover and cook, adjusting the heat as needed to keep it at a gentle simmer, until fork-tender, 1½ to 2½ hours (about 50 minutes per pound/450g). Cooking time will vary depending on the size and shape of the corned beef, so check regularly (you can also follow the directions on the package). Set aside on a plate

to cool. Cut enough into ½-inch (1.3-cm) cubes to measure 1½ cups (360 ml) for the salad and save the rest for sandwiches.

Meanwhile, boil the potatoes and when cool, cut them into ¾-inch (2-cm) pieces. (You need 2 cups/475 ml for the salad; save any extra for another use.) Fill a 250-ml beaker or a small glass bowl halfway with ice water and add the shallot. Soak for 10 minutes, then drain and pat the shallot dry.

WHISK: In a large salad bowl, combine the buttermilk, oil, parsley, mayonnaise, horseradish, and caraway seeds and season with salt and pepper. Whisk until well combined, then taste and adjust the seasoning if needed.

TOSS: In the bowl with the dressing, add the shredded green and red cabbage, carrots, cheddar, corned beef, potatoes, and shallot. Toss until all the ingredients are evenly combined and coated with dressing and serve right away (or store for up to 3 days in the refrigerator).

ENJOY: I'm having it with a Guinness or an iced Irish breakfast tea.

Everything
Bagel Croutons
(page 236)

Sourdough
Garlic
Croutons
(page 235)

Cheesy Tortilla
Croutons (page 238)

Pita Croutons
(page 233)

Classic Homemade
Croutons (page 232)

Salad Lab
Elements

Classic Homemade Croutons

MAKES ABOUT 5 CUPS (1,200 ML)

Good croutons are all about the bread. Well, that and not burning them. My local bakery always puts their extra bread on sale after two p.m. That's when I stock up, wait a day, and make an ovenful. This simple recipe is quick and satisfies that homemade crouton flavor and crunch to elevate all your salads—even ones not in this book.

2 tablespoons (30 ml) extra-virgin olive oil

2 tablespoons (30 ml) unsalted butter, melted

½ teaspoon (2.5 ml) granulated sea salt

½ teaspoon (2.5 ml) freshly cracked black pepper

6 cups (1,400 ml) cubed day-old bread (¾- to 1-inch/2- to 2.5-cm pieces; from 1 loaf French bread or 1 large baguette)

Preheat the oven to 400°F (200°C) and use convection mode if that's an option. Line a baking sheet with parchment paper or a silicone baking mat.

In a medium bowl, whisk together the olive oil, melted butter, salt, and pepper. Add the bread cubes and toss until evenly coated. Pour the bread cubes onto the prepared baking sheet and spread out so the cubes can brown on all sides. Bake until golden brown and crispy on the outside, stirring halfway through, 10 to 15 minutes (longer for a regular oven).

Cool on the counter, add to a salad, or store in an airtight container at room temperature and use within a few days. You can also freeze them for up to 2 months. When you're ready to serve them, defrost them for 30 minutes and pop them into a 300°F (150°C) oven for 5 to 10 minutes and you have delicious "freshly made" croutons.

EXPERIMENT:
Try different breads like seeded sourdough, walnut, olive, or whole-grain varieties. As with all ingredients, taste your bread before adding more salt. Vegans: Use double the olive oil or the excellent Miyoko's Creamery vegan cultured butter instead.

Polenta Croutons

MAKES ABOUT 1½ CUPS (360 ML)

Crispy on the outside, chewy on the inside, these give a hint of corn flavor without overpowering salads. If you're a purist, you can make your polenta from scratch. I always say pick your battles, and homemade polenta for croutons is not one of mine. If you cannot find the tubes, there are boxed instant varieties. You may want to double the recipe if you have people walking through the kitchen; these croutons disappear quickly.

1 (1-pound/450-g) tube precooked polenta

2 tablespoons (30 ml) extra-virgin olive oil

2 tablespoons (30 ml) freshly grated Parmigiano-Reggiano (use a Microplane), or substitute Cotija cheese

¼ teaspoon (1.5 ml) granulated sea salt

¼ teaspoon (1.5 ml) freshly cracked black pepper

Preheat the oven to 400°F (200°C) and use convection mode if that's an option. Line a baking sheet with parchment paper or a silicone baking mat.

Pat the polenta dry if necessary and cut into ½-inch (1.3-cm) cubes. In a large bowl, gently toss the cubed polenta, olive oil, cheese, salt, and pepper until evenly coated. Spoon the cubes onto the baking sheet in a single layer. Bake, flipping after 15 minutes, until the croutons are brown on the edges, 35 to 40 minutes (longer for a regular oven).

Use right away, or cool and store extras in an airtight container for up to 3 days or freeze and reheat when ready to use.

 EXPERIMENT: When made with Cotija cheese, they're a great addition to a Mexican-inspired salad.

Pita Croutons

MAKES ABOUT 4 CUPS (950 ML)

These croutons are the base for my version of Fattoush (page 138), but they are wonderful in *any* salad and can easily replace just about any crouton in a recipe. Use a good-quality large pita, and make sure it has a pocket!

3 tablespoons (45 ml) extra-virgin olive oil

1 teaspoon (5 ml) ground sumac

1 teaspoon (5 ml) za'atar

½ teaspoon (2.5 ml) granulated sea salt

½ teaspoon (2.5 ml) freshly cracked black pepper

4 cups (960 ml) torn or chopped pita (bite-size pieces)

3 tablespoons (45 ml) ghee or unsalted butter

In a medium bowl, whisk together the oil, sumac, za'atar, salt, and pepper until well combined. Toss the pita with the mixture to coat.

Heat a large saucepan or skillet over medium heat and add the ghee. Once the ghee has melted, add the seasoned pita and fry, stirring occasionally, until toasted golden brown on both sides, about 5 minutes. Remove from the skillet and transfer to a plate to cool.

Add to a salad, or cool completely and store in an airtight container at room temperature and use within a few days.

 EXPERIMENT: Extras are a great accompaniment for hummus or tzatziki. If you only have sumac or za'atar, double up instead of running out to the store.

Sourdough Garlic Croutons

Sourdough bread was one of the key inspirations for starting the Salad Lab, but not in the way you might think. At the beginning of my social media journey when everyone was making sourdough starters and many subsequent loaves, I asked: "Where's the good salad content? I can't keep eating all this bread!" These sourdough croutons are my go-to. But we won't be making the bread from scratch here. They are family-tested and approved, and they cannot be left on the counter without supervision!

2 tablespoons (30 ml) unsalted butter, melted

2 tablespoons (30 ml) extra-virgin olive oil

2 tablespoons (30 ml) freshly grated Parmigiano-Reggiano (use a Microplane)

2 teaspoons (10 ml) pressed garlic

½ teaspoon (2.5 ml) sweet paprika

¼ teaspoon (1.5 ml) flaky sea salt

¼ teaspoon (1.5 ml) freshly cracked black pepper

4 cups (950 ml) cubed sourdough bread (1-inch/2.5-cm pieces)

Preheat the oven to 400°F (200°C) and use convection mode if that's an option. Line a baking sheet with parchment paper or a silicone baking mat.

In a medium bowl, whisk together the melted butter, oil, cheese, garlic, paprika, salt, and pepper. Add the bread cubes and toss until evenly coated. Pour the bread cubes onto the prepared baking sheet and spread out so the cubes can brown on all sides. Bake until golden brown and crispy on the outside, stirring halfway through, 10 to 15 minutes (longer for a regular oven).

Add to a salad, or cool completely and store in an airtight container at room temperature and use within a few days.

EXPERIMENT:
Are you a "Garlic Girl" or "Garlic Addict"? Replace the 2 teaspoons (10 ml) of garlic with 1 tablespoon (15 ml) or more. I am notorious for putting bread in the oven and leaving the room just for a second, only to suddenly smell burning toast. If you have that habit, when in doubt, stay close by in the kitchen when making croutons, set a timer, and check them every few minutes.

Everything Bagel Croutons

Full of flavor from the garlic, onion, poppy seeds, and salt, these croutons really do go with everything. These are best made right before serving; your house will smell like your favorite New York City bagel shop. If your bagels are particularly small, use three.

2 everything bagels

¼ cup (60 ml) extra-virgin olive oil

¼ teaspoon (1.5 ml) flaky sea salt (optional)

Preheat the oven to 375°F (190°C) and use convection mode if that's an option. Line a baking sheet with parchment paper or a silicone baking mat.

Split the bagels in half and cut into 1-inch (2.5-cm) pieces. Toss in a bowl with the oil to coat, add the salt if the bagels don't have salt on them, then pour the croutons onto the prepared baking sheet in an even layer. Bake, stirring halfway through, until golden brown, 10 to 12 minutes (longer in a regular oven). Carefully lift the parchment paper with the croutons off the baking sheet and transfer to the counter to cool.

Add to a salad, or store in an airtight container at room temperature and use within a few days.

EXPERIMENT:
Have plain bagels and a jar of everything bagel seasoning? Add 2 tablespoons (30 ml) to the oil before tossing, skip the salt, and you're good to go.

Parmesan Crisp "Croutons"

Homemade Parmesan crisps are a great way to get a salty crunch in your salad without the bread. They are easy to make and come together in minutes with just four ingredients. Please don't leave the kitchen while they are in the oven, or the smoke alarm may remind you that you burned them. Warning: Leftovers disappear quickly.

1½ cups (360 ml) lightly packed finely grated Parmigiano-Reggiano (use a Microplane; about 4 ounces/115g)

1 tablespoon (15 ml) pressed garlic

½ teaspoon (2.5 ml) lightly packed grated lemon zest or Meyer lemon zest

½ teaspoon (2.5 ml) freshly cracked black pepper

EXPERIMENT: If you're looking for a vegan option, I hear Trader Joe's has a vegan Parmesan that crisps up like the original.

Preheat the oven to 400°F (200°C) and use convection mode if that's an option. Arrange two oven racks in the middle. Line two baking sheets with silicone baking mats or parchment paper.

In a medium bowl, mix the cheese, garlic, lemon zest, and pepper until well combined. Place tightly packed heaping teaspoons of the mixture 2 inches (5 cm) apart, in 4 rows of 3, and lightly pinch each one together. Repeat with the other baking sheet.

Bake both baking sheets until the crisps are flat with little holes in the middle and the edges have started to turn golden brown, rotating the pans halfway through, 3 to 5 minutes (longer for a regular oven but keep an eye on them; depending on your oven, it could be a little more or less time). Let cool for a few minutes before transferring to a plate. Repeat with the remaining cheese in two batches.

Transfer to an airtight container and use within 5 days.

Cheesy Tortilla Croutons

MAKES ABOUT 1½ CUPS (360 ML)

One of my favorite trends is to fry a layer of grated cheese on the grill and then wrap your burrito with crispy fried cheese. So delicious! I had to figure out a way of incorporating it into the salads. This was the result of that experiment, and what a successful one it was! You may want to double the recipe for snacking.

¼ cup (60 ml) crumbled Cotija cheese, or substitute grated Monterey Jack

¼ cup (60 ml) grated sharp cheddar cheese

2 (6-inch/15-cm) flour tortillas

In a small bowl, mix the Cotija and cheddar cheese. Heat a skillet over medium-high heat until you see faint wisps of smoke.

Place half of the cheese mixture in the center of the pan and spread out evenly in a circle the same size as the tortillas. Place a tortilla on top and cook, flipping once the cheese is melted, crispy, and browned, 2 to 3 minutes. Heat the other side of the tortilla until starting to brown, another minute or so. Transfer to a wire rack to cool. Repeat with the remaining cheese and tortilla. Cut into ½-inch (1.3 cm) cubes and use right away.

EXPERIMENT:
Cut the tortillas into triangles instead and use them to scoop up Cowboy Caviar (page 116) or Esquites Salad (page 126).

238   THE SALAD LAB

Vinaigrette

MAKES ABOUT 1¼ CUPS (300 ML)

My first experience with salad dressed with vinaigrette was in college, when my "French" roommate (who had family from Lyon) swore it would make the best salad I'd ever had. The dressing consisted of Dijon mustard, oil, vinegar, salt, and cracked pepper and was poured over a head of butter lettuce. The result was delicious and probably planted a seed for where I am now, writing a book about salads. Here is my elevated version of the classic vinaigrette.

EXPERIMENT:
I swap out herbs depending on my mood, what's in season, and what I've got at home, or what I'm using with other parts of the meal. As I always say: use what you have.

2 tablespoons (30 ml) very finely diced shallot

2 tablespoons (30 ml) white balsamic or sherry vinegar

2 tablespoons (30 ml) hot water

½ teaspoon (2.5 ml) pressed garlic

1 tablespoon (15 ml) finely chopped fresh flat-leaf parsley

2 teaspoons (10 ml) honey

2 teaspoons (10 ml) Dijon mustard

2 teaspoons (10 ml) whole-grain mustard

1 teaspoon (5 ml) fresh thyme

½ teaspoon (2.5 ml) flaky sea salt, or more as needed

½ teaspoon (2.5 ml) freshly cracked black pepper, or more as needed

½ cup (120 ml) extra-virgin olive oil

In a medium bowl, combine the shallot, vinegar, and hot water. Let sit for a few minutes to lightly pickle. Rinse the pressed garlic in a very fine mesh strainer and shake off any excess water.

To the bowl with the shallot, add the garlic, parsley, honey, Dijon mustard, whole-grain mustard, thyme, salt, and pepper. With a whisk, blend the ingredients while slowly drizzling in the oil until the dressing is emulsified, then taste and adjust the seasoning as needed. Store in an airtight container in the refrigerator for up to 1 week.

Caesar Dressing

MAKES ABOUT 2 CUPS (475 ML)

I do not recall how I came up with my version; it is one I have made for years for most holidays, ever since I was a teenager. My mother was not a garlic girl and couldn't stand the smell of it, but she loved this dressing. It was also the only salad dressing my teenage son would eat. I hope you enjoy it as much as we do. The coddled eggs in the dressing are optional and you can use regular yolks. The purpose is just to sterilize the eggshell, but leave the yolk as is so it can be easily emulsified.

START OUT (CODDLED EGGS)

2 large eggs

WHISK

1 tablespoon (15 ml) pressed garlic

¼ cup (60 ml) freshly grated Parmigiano-Reggiano (use a Microplane)

2 tablespoons (30 ml) fresh lemon juice (remember to zest first)

2 tablespoons (30 ml) chopped oil-packed anchovy fillets (about 5 fillets)

1 tablespoon (15 ml) Dijon mustard

1 tablespoon (15 ml) lightly packed grated lemon zest

2 teaspoons (10 ml) balsamic vinegar

2 teaspoons (10 ml) red wine vinegar

1 teaspoon (5 ml) Worcestershire sauce

¼ teaspoon (1.5 ml) flaky sea salt

¼ teaspoon (1.5 ml) freshly cracked black pepper

½ cup (120 ml) extra-virgin olive oil

EXPERIMENT:
Don't like anchovies? Skip the Worcestershire and instead of anchovies, use 2 tablespoons (30 ml) chopped capers or a sprinkle of nori for a salty/briny flavor, or make the vegan Caesar on page 248. Want a more lemony version? Omit the balsamic and add another 1 tablespoon (15 ml) lemon juice.

START OUT: To make the coddled eggs, fill a small pan halfway with water and bring to a boil. Carefully place the whole eggs into the boiling water, adjust the heat so the water gently boils, and cook for 1 minute. Remove the eggs immediately and rinse under cold water to stop the cooking. When the eggs are cool enough to handle, crack and reserve the yolks for the dressing.

WHISK: Rinse the pressed garlic in a very fine mesh strainer and shake off any excess water. In a blender, small food processor, or beaker (if using an immersion blender), add the garlic, coddled egg yolks, cheese, lemon juice, anchovies, mustard, zest, balsamic vinegar, red wine vinegar, Worcestershire, salt, and pepper and blend until smooth. With the machine running, slowly drizzle in the oil until emulsified. Serve immediately, or store in an airtight container in the refrigerator for up to 1 day.

Ranch Dressing

Everybody loves ranch dressing: it's been the best-selling dressing in the United States since 1992. Hidden Valley Ranch dressing was created by Steve Henson, a plumber that did so well in the Alaskan bush that he was able to retire at thirty-five and move to Santa Barbara. He then purchased a ranch and re-named it Hidden Valley, where they served visitors salads with the dressing made in their ranch kitchen. Soon they were selling packets of the seasonings and, well, the rest is history. Whether it's the tang of the buttermilk, the herb combination, or the creaminess of the sour cream and mayonnaise combination that makes it so popular, I am not sure; but this is my version of ranch-style dressing with fresh buttermilk and herbs, minus the artificial flavors and stabilizers in the bottled versions you find in stores.

EXPERIMENT:
I love to dip my pizza crust . . . I mean carrot and cucumber sticks in this as a crunchy snack; so good.

2 teaspoons (10 ml) pressed garlic

⅔ cup (160 ml) buttermilk

½ cup (120 ml) mayonnaise

½ cup (120 ml) sour cream

¼ cup (60 ml) finely chopped fresh dill

3 tablespoons (30 ml) finely chopped fresh chives

2 tablespoons (30 ml) finely chopped fresh flat-leaf parsley

2 tablespoons (30 ml) finely chopped fresh basil

½ teaspoon (2.5 ml) mustard powder

¼ teaspoon (1.5 ml) red pepper flakes

Flaky sea salt and freshly cracked black pepper

Rinse the pressed garlic in a very fine mesh strainer and shake off any excess water.

In a blender, small food processor, or beaker (if using an immersion blender), combine the garlic, buttermilk, mayonnaise, sour cream, dill, chives, parsley, basil, mustard powder, and red pepper flakes and season with salt and black pepper. Blend until smooth, then taste and adjust the seasoning if needed. Store in an airtight container in the refrigerator for up to 1 week.

Blue Cheese Dressing

Not only is this dressing perfect for salads, it is my go-to for wings and as a crudité dip. Blue cheese is made with Penicillium cultures, giving it spots or veins of greenish blue. Roquefort or Gorgonzola in the fridge? Both are blue cheeses: Roquefort is a French sheep's milk cheese and Gorgonzola is Italian made from cow's milk. I usually use Point Reyes Blue, a local cow's milk blue. You can blend all the cheese in the dressing, but I prefer the rich, salty, sharp hit of the crumbled chunks, so I blend half with the dressing and add the rest at the end.

EXPERIMENT:
You are making homemade mayonnaise in the beginning of this recipe. If you're in a hurry, you can replace the egg, lemon juice, Dijon, water, salt, and oil with 1 cup (240 ml) mayonnaise.

START OUT

Ice water

2 tablespoons (30 ml) very finely diced shallot

1 coddled egg yolk (see page 243)

WHISK

2 teaspoons (10 ml) fresh lemon juice (remember to zest first)

1 teaspoon (5 ml) Dijon mustard

1 teaspoon (5 ml) water

½ teaspoon (2.5 ml) flaky sea salt

¾ cup (175 ml) avocado oil

1 cup (240 ml) crumbled blue cheese (see page 43)

½ cup (120 ml) buttermilk

2 tablespoons (30 ml) finely chopped fresh flat-leaf parsley

½ teaspoon (2.5 ml) lightly packed grated lemon zest

½ teaspoon (2.5 ml) freshly cracked black pepper

START OUT: Fill a 250-ml beaker or a small glass bowl halfway with ice water and add the shallot. Soak for 10 minutes, then drain and pat the shallot dry. Prepare the coddled egg and separate the yolk.

WHISK: In a small blender, food processor, or large beaker (if using an immersion blender), combine the lemon juice, mustard, water, and ¼ teaspoon (1.5 ml) of the salt. Drop in the coddled egg yolk and begin blending. Slowly pour in the oil while blending to make mayo.

Once the mixture is emulsified, add the shallot, half the cheese, the buttermilk, parsley, zest, pepper, and remaining ¼ teaspoon (1.5 ml) salt. Run the mixer for a few more seconds, then stir in the rest of the cheese. Store in an airtight container in the refrigerator for up to 1 week.

Balsamic Dressing

Balsamic vinegar is made by cooking down and reducing unfermented grape juice and aging it in wooden barrels to create a delicate flavor that balances both sweet and sour. It comes from Italy, and vinegars that are produced in the Modena or Reggio Emilia regions are considered to be the highest quality. For this recipe, I like to use vinegar that has been aged for at least ten years in red oak kegs, then chestnut, mulberry, and juniper barrels. Good thing the bottles last for a few years in the pantry, because I still haven't found my favorite.

EXPERIMENT:
Balsamic dressing is great for vegetable marinades before grilling, especially for portobellos and summer squash. I also enjoy it as a dip for vegetables or bread, or even a sandwich condiment.

START OUT

1 tablespoon (15 ml) Roasted Garlic Purée (page 256), or substitute 2 teaspoons (10 ml) pressed garlic

WHISK

¼ cup (60 ml) Italian balsamic vinegar

1 tablespoon (15 ml) finely chopped fresh basil

1 tablespoon (15 ml) finely chopped fresh flat-leaf parsley

1 tablespoon (15 ml) honey or maple syrup

1½ teaspoons (7.5 ml) Dijon mustard

1 teaspoon (5 ml) whole-grain mustard

½ teaspoon (2.5 ml) flaky sea salt, or more as needed

Pinch of red pepper flakes

½ cup (120 ml) extra-virgin olive oil

START OUT: Prepare the roasted garlic purée (up to 3 days in advance if you like). If using pressed garlic, rinse it in a very fine mesh strainer and shake off any excess water.

WHISK: In a small bowl, beaker, or large jar, combine the garlic, vinegar, basil, parsley, honey, Dijon mustard, whole-grain mustard, salt, and red pepper flakes. Whisk until combined, then slowly drizzle the oil into the mixture while whisking to emulsify. Taste and adjust the seasoning as needed. Serve right away or refrigerate in an airtight container for up to 1 week.

Ginger Miso Tahini Dressing

One of my go-to dressings, this is especially good with kale salads—and sometimes I throw leftovers with a can of chickpeas and a couple cloves of garlic in the food processor to make an instant hummus. Check the consistency of the tahini (sesame seed butter), as it can vary in thickness. Some are oilier and others are a thicker paste. Don't worry if you need to add a little extra water to thin this one out; it will not affect the delicious flavor.

EXPERIMENT:
For a speedier dressing, use 1 teaspoon (5 ml) pressed garlic, rinsed, in place of the roasted garlic purée.

START OUT

2 tablespoons (30 ml) Roasted Garlic Purée (page 256)

2 teaspoons (10 ml) sesame seeds, toasted (see page 257)

WHISK

⅔ cup (160 ml) tahini

¼ cup (60 ml) water, plus more as needed

2 tablespoons (30 ml) rice vinegar

2 tablespoons (30 ml) low-sodium soy sauce or tamari

2 tablespoons (30 ml) grated fresh ginger

1 tablespoon (15 ml) fresh lemon juice (remember to zest first)

1 tablespoon (15 ml) white miso paste

1 tablespoon (15 ml) maple syrup or honey

1 teaspoon (5 ml) lightly packed grated lemon zest

½ teaspoon (2.5 ml) flaky sea salt

½ teaspoon (2.5 ml) red pepper flakes

START OUT: Prepare the roasted garlic purée (up to 3 days ahead if you like) and toast the sesame seeds.

WHISK: In a small bowl, beaker, or mason jar, add the garlic, sesame seeds, tahini, water, vinegar, soy sauce, ginger, lemon juice, miso, maple syrup, zest, salt, and red pepper flakes. Whisk until well combined, adding more water 1 tablespoon (15 ml) at a time as needed to reach your desired consistency. Store in an airtight container in the refrigerator for up to 1 week.

Vegan Better-than-
Caesar Caesar

Whether you're vegan or not, this dressing is a winner. In a side-by-side test with the regular Caesar Dressing (page 243), you may even prefer this one. The secret is the nori, Meyer lemon zest, and rinsing the crushed garlic before adding it to the blender (my secret for *every* dressing). It's fun to add to sandwiches and roasted vegetable bowls, and tossed with a bowl of greens, of course.

EXPERIMENT:
Substitute roasted seaweed snacks for the nori sheet if you already have them at home. They may be a little saltier, so taste before adding salt.

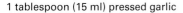

1 tablespoon (15 ml) pressed garlic

⅓ cup (80 ml) extra-virgin olive oil

¼ cup (60 ml) water

3 tablespoons (45 ml) nutritional yeast

2 tablespoons (30 ml) drained capers

2 tablespoons (30 ml) fresh Meyer lemon juice,
or substitute regular lemon juice (remember to zest first)

1 tablespoon plus 1 teaspoon (20 ml) Dijon mustard

1 teaspoon (5 ml) lightly packed grated Meyer lemon zest,
or substitute regular lemon zest

1 teaspoon (5 ml) freshly cracked black pepper

½ (10-inch/25-cm) sheet dried nori

Flaky sea salt

Rinse the pressed garlic in a very fine mesh strainer and shake off any excess water.

In a small blender, small food processor, or large beaker (if using an immersion blender), combine the garlic, oil, water, nutritional yeast, capers, lemon juice, mustard, zest, and pepper, and crumble in the nori. Blend until smooth. Taste and add salt if necessary (it might not be with some of the salty ingredients). Store in an airtight container in the refrigerator for up to 1 week.

Green Goddess Dressing

My favorite dressing for a simple side salad. The original dressing was developed in the 1920s at the beautiful Palace Hotel in San Francisco for a theater actor, in honor of his play *The Green Goddess*, a big hit at the time. You can still go to the Palace Hotel and order the salad today. My recipe inspired by the original uses a fraction of the mayonnaise, but retains the classic tarragon and buttermilk flavor. Be sure to use a good-quality, mild vinegar that you love in this dressing, and if you're unsure of tarragon, this is a wonderful use for it.

EXPERIMENT: If you cannot find fresh tarragon, or any other fresh herb, you can always substitute 1 teaspoon (5 ml) dried for 1 tablespoon (15 ml) fresh. Try making your own mayonnaise using the directions on page 245.

2 teaspoons (10 ml) pressed garlic

½ cup (120 ml) buttermilk

½ cup (120 ml) cubed avocado (½-inch/1.3-cm pieces)

¼ cup (60 ml) mayonnaise

¼ cup (60 ml) sour cream

3 tablespoons (45 ml) tarragon or champagne vinegar

2 tablespoons (30 ml) finely chopped fresh flat-leaf parsley

2 tablespoons (30 ml) finely chopped fresh chives

2 tablespoons (30 ml) finely chopped fresh tarragon

1 tablespoon (15 ml) chopped oil-packed anchovies (about 3 fillets)

1 tablespoon (15 ml) fresh lemon juice

Flaky sea salt and freshly cracked black pepper

Rinse the pressed garlic in a very fine mesh strainer and shake off any excess water.

In a small blender, small food processor, or large beaker (if using an immersion blender), combine the garlic, buttermilk, avocado, mayonnaise, sour cream, vinegar, parsley, chives, tarragon, anchovies, and lemon juice and season with salt and pepper. Blend until smooth, then taste and adjust the seasoning if needed. Store in an airtight container in the refrigerator for up to 5 days.

Carrot Ginger Dressing

MAKES ABOUT 2¼ CUPS (530 ML)

I receive requests for a Japanese steakhouse–style dressing all the time and it has taken me a few years to get my version, inspired by the restaurant classic, right. Fresh carrots are key—try to find ones with the tops still attached, to make the fresh carrot flavor shine through. This dressing has a slight kick, no doubt from the sriracha. I love it, but if you don't, skip it.

EXPERIMENT:
If you are using seasoned rice vinegar or mirin you may need to adjust the amounts of salt and sugar. Leave the salt and sugar out when you blend, then taste and add as needed.

START OUT

Ice water

½ cup (120 ml) diced yellow onion (½-inch/1.3-cm pieces)

WHISK

2 cups (240 ml) peeled and shredded carrots

½ cup (120 ml) rice vinegar, or substitute mirin or seasoned rice vinegar (see Experiment)

⅓ cup (80 ml) Kewpie mayonnaise, or substitute any mayonnaise

2 tablespoons (30 ml) grated fresh ginger

2 tablespoons (30 ml) sugar

2 tablespoons (30 ml) low-sodium soy sauce or tamari

1 tablespoon (15 ml) sriracha, or more to taste

2 teaspoons (10 ml) white or red miso paste

1 teaspoon (5 ml) fresh lemon juice

1 teaspoon (5 ml) toasted sesame oil

½ teaspoon (2.5 ml) flaky sea salt

START OUT: Fill a 500-ml beaker or small glass bowl halfway with ice water and add the onion. Soak for 10 minutes, then drain and pat the onion dry.

In a blender, food processor, or large beaker (if using an immersion blender), combine the onion, carrots, vinegar, mayonnaise, ginger, sugar, soy sauce, sriracha, miso, lemon juice, sesame oil, and salt. Blend until smooth. Store in an airtight container in the refrigerator for up to 5 days.

Cilantro Lime Dressing

I love the South American vibe of this dressing. Roasting the garlic and chiles, combined with the tang of lime and cilantro, gives it a delightful combination of fresh and deeper, rich flavors. If you have the "soap gene" and can't stand cilantro, experiment with fresh parsley or basil.

EXPERIMENT:

Use this dressing in more than just salads. It's excellent as a salsa with burritos, as a topping for street tacos, or as a marinade for grilled meat.

START OUT

1 large fresh serrano chile

1 large fresh jalapeño

4 garlic cloves, unpeeled

1 teaspoon (5 ml) extra-virgin olive oil

WHISK

⅓ cup (80 ml) extra-virgin olive oil

1 cup (240 ml) coarsely chopped fresh cilantro

1 cup (240 ml) cubed avocado (½-inch/1.3-cm pieces)

¼ cup (60 ml) fresh lime juice (remember to zest first)

¼ cup (60 ml) water

2 teaspoons (10 ml) agave syrup

1 teaspoon (5 ml) lightly packed grated lime zest

½ teaspoon (2.5 ml) ground cumin

¼ teaspoon (1.5 ml) flaky sea salt, or more as needed

START OUT: Preheat the oven to 425°F (220°C) and use convection mode if that's an option. In a square of aluminum foil, combine the serrano, jalapeño, garlic, and oil. Close it up so everything is tightly sealed in the foil. Roast until the skin on the chiles blisters, about 15 minutes (a little longer for a regular oven), then set aside to cool. Remove the veins and seeds from the chiles (or leave some in if you want more heat) and coarsely chop them. Peel the garlic.

WHISK: In a food processor, blender, or beaker (if using an immersion blender) add the oil, cilantro, avocado, lime juice, water, agave, zest, cumin, salt, roasted chiles, and garlic. Purée until smooth. Taste and add more salt if you'd like. If your dressing is very thick, stir in water 1 tablespoon (15 ml) at a time until it is your desired consistency. Store in an airtight container in the refrigerator for up to 5 days.

Thousand Island Dressing

MAKES ABOUT 1¼ CUPS (300 ML)

Nothing beats a good Thousand Island dressing on crisp butter lettuce with a few tomatoes. This dressing is so American that a University of Wisconsin professor and graduate students have done extensive research to determine who originally created it. Was it a hunting and fishing lodge owner's wife in the Thousand Island region between the United States and Canada who created it in the 1900s? Or was it George Boldt, castle owner in the same region and proprietor of the Waldorf Astoria in New York City? The hotel's head chef? We may never know (the researchers never came to a conclusion). I do know it's a hearty dressing, and a fun substitute for mayonnaise in egg salad or tuna salad. Use leftover dressing to top hard-boiled eggs, burgers, or sandwiches like a BLT. Yum!

EXPERIMENT:
I was raised on Best Foods mayonnaise and this dressing is quite good as it stands, but there are healthier versions of mayonnaise these days or—even better—make your own (see the recipe for Blue Cheese Dressing on page 245). There are always ways to change things up in the kitchen!

START OUT

Ice Water

1 tablespoon (15 ml) very finely diced shallot

WHISK

⅔ cup (160 ml) mayonnaise

2 tablespoons (30 ml) ketchup

1 tablespoon (15 ml) cocktail sauce

1 tablespoon (15 ml) white balsamic vinegar, or substitute white wine vinegar

1 tablespoon (15 ml) sweet pickle relish

1 tablespoon (15 ml) finely chopped fresh flat-leaf parsley

Flaky sea salt and freshly cracked black pepper

START OUT: Fill a 250-ml beaker or a small glass bowl halfway with ice water and add the shallot. Soak for 10 minutes, then drain and pat the shallot dry.

WHISK: In a small bowl, combine the shallot, mayonnaise, ketchup, cocktail sauce, vinegar, relish, and parsley and season with salt and pepper. Whisk until well combined, then taste and adjust the seasoning if needed. Store in an airtight container in the refrigerator for up to 5 days.

Creamy Peanut Dressing

MAKES 1½ CUPS (360 ML)

I'm not saying you will lick the bowl in which you make this dressing, but you might think about it. It's excellent with kale, cabbage, and quinoa salads. Superb as a sauce over grilled or pan-fried chicken, tofu, or pork—or even fried rice. Basically, this dressing is always a hit.

2 teaspoons (10 ml) pressed garlic

⅓ cup (80 ml) creamy natural (unsweetened) peanut butter

3 tablespoons (45 ml) rice vinegar

3 tablespoons (45 ml) water

2 tablespoons (30 ml) low-sodium soy sauce

2 tablespoons (30 ml) honey

2 tablespoons (30 ml) fresh lime juice (remember to zest first)

1 tablespoon (15 ml) grated fresh ginger

1 tablespoon (15 ml) sesame seeds

1 teaspoon (5 ml) toasted sesame oil

1 teaspoon (5 ml) sambal oelek, or substitute sriracha

½ teaspoon (2.5 ml) lightly packed grated lime zest

Flaky sea salt and freshly cracked black pepper

Rinse the pressed garlic in a very fine mesh strainer and shake off any excess water.

In a small bowl, combine the garlic, peanut butter, vinegar, water, soy sauce, honey, lime juice, ginger, sesame seeds, sesame oil, sambal oelek, and lime zest and season with salt and pepper. Whisk together until smooth and well combined, then taste and adjust the seasoning if needed. Store in an airtight container in the refrigerator for up to 1 week.

EXPERIMENT:
I was introduced to sambal oelek when I wanted to impress my boyfriend with my cooking skills. A way to a person's heart is through their stomach . . . and it worked! He's now my husband. (My mother-in-law, who introduced me to the chile paste, has taught Indonesian-style cooking classes in the Netherlands.) Sambal oelek is an Indonesian hot sauce that has a depth of flavor different from sriracha that gives a dish that wow factor. You can find it at your local Asian market or near the hot sauce or Asian section of larger grocery stores.

Basil Mustard Dressing

I enjoyed this dressing once a week for almost ten years and it is still one of my favorites. Chloe's, a French-style café in Santa Rosa, California, served it on the side of many of their salads, and we always asked for double dressing. The café was run by two brothers from Saint-Tropez, part of a family that owned a bakery there. They were always smiling, working hard in the back, with a cute antique Citroën delivery truck parked out front. The owners are retired now, but this version of the dressing inspired by them lives on in my heart, in my kitchen, and now in this book.

EXPERIMENT:
This one is a family favorite and I use it throughout the year. It's great for everything from a salmon marinade to a vegetable dip or even drizzled atop avocado toast.

1 teaspoon (5 ml) pressed garlic

1 cup (240 ml) finely chopped fresh basil

2 tablespoons (30 ml) balsamic vinegar

2 tablespoons (30 ml) whole-grain mustard

2 tablespoons (30 ml) fresh lemon juice (remember to zest first)

1 tablespoon (15 ml) honey

½ teaspoon (2.5 ml) lightly packed grated lemon zest

Flaky sea salt and freshly cracked black pepper

½ cup (120 ml) extra-virgin olive oil

Rinse the pressed garlic in a very fine mesh strainer and shake off any excess water.

In a small bowl or beaker (if using an immersion blender), combine the garlic, basil, vinegar, mustard, lemon juice, honey, and lemon zest and season with salt and pepper. Whisk, or lightly blend with an immersion blender, while slowly drizzling in the olive oil until emulsified. Taste and adjust the seasoning if needed. Store in an airtight container in the refrigerator for up to 1 week.

A Few More Salad Lab Elements

These are elements you'll find in many of my salads. They can easily be made in large batches and stored for even quicker salad-making throughout the week.

Roasted Garlic Purée

MAKES ABOUT ¼ CUP (60 ML)

This is one recipe that rewards doubling, or even tripling. The cooking time will be the same no matter what.

2 large garlic bulbs
1 teaspoon (5 ml) extra-virgin olive oil

Preheat the oven to 425°F (220°C) and use convection mode if that's an option.

Cut about ½ inch (1.3 cm) off the top of the garlic bulbs to remove the tips and discard. Drizzle the tops with the oil and wrap the whole bulbs in aluminum foil. Roast until the outer skin turns golden and slightly translucent (and your house smells like a pizza parlor), 30 to 45 minutes (longer for a regular oven). Place on the counter to cool in the foil, then squeeze out the roasted garlic cloves from bottom to top. Use the side of a chef's knife to thinly spread the cloves along a cutting board to smash, then finely chop to make sure there are no long fibers left. Store in an airtight container in the refrigerator for up to 3 days, or freeze for up to 1 month.

NOTE: When I'm short on time, I'll put a few cloves of unpeeled garlic onto a square of aluminum foil, drizzle with a bit of oil, seal, and roast until soft, 15 to 20 minutes (longer in a regular oven). The outer layer is a little tougher so my purée isn't as smooth, but it takes half the time.

Quick Pickled Onions

MAKES ABOUT 1¼ CUPS (300 ML)

¾ cup (175 ml) white distilled vinegar, or substitute apple cider vinegar
¾ cup (175 ml) water
1 tablespoon (15 ml) sugar
½ teaspoon (2.5 ml) granulated sea salt
1½ cups (360 ml) quartered and sliced red onion (about 1 medium)

In a small pan, combine the vinegar, water, sugar, and salt and cook over medium heat until the sugar and salt have dissolved, about 4 minutes. Pour the brine into a large glass jar or beaker and add the onion slices, stirring and pressing them down in the liquid until they are evenly coated. Let sit for 30 minutes at room temperature or refrigerate overnight.

Perfect Boiled Eggs

MAKES 4

I like my yolks to be vibrant and creamy, but not runny. To me, these are the ideal eggs for salad.

Ice water

4 large eggs

Fill a small pot halfway with water and bring to a boil. Prepare a bowl of ice water.

Gently lower the eggs into the boiling water. Once the pot returns to a boil, adjust the heat so the water simmers, cover, and cook for 10 minutes (9 if the eggs were room temperature). Remove with a slotted spoon and transfer to the ice bath for a few minutes before peeling and rinsing.

Honey-Roasted Sliced Almonds

MAKES 2 CUPS (475 ML)

2 cups (475 ml) sliced almonds

1 tablespoon (15 ml) avocado oil

2 tablespoons (30 ml) honey

½ teaspoon (2.5 ml) granulated sea salt

Preheat the oven to 325°F (165°C) and use convection mode if that's an option. Line a baking sheet with parchment paper or a silicone baking mat.

Add the almonds to the prepared baking sheet and toss them in the avocado oil. Drizzle them with the honey, sprinkle them with the salt, and stir until the almonds are coated.

Place in the oven and roast until golden brown, stirring gently every few minutes, 10 to 15 minutes (longer for a regular oven). Transfer the parchment paper with the almonds on it to the counter to cool. Store in an airtight container for up to 1 week.

Toasted Nuts and Seeds

MAKES ½ CUP (120 ML)

This step improves the flavor and texture of nuts, even if you purchase roasted nuts. Heating them draws the natural oils to the surface, intensifying the rich nutty essence and creating a deeper color, and the nuts are crunchier.

½ cup (120 ml) any type nut or seed

Heat a skillet on the stovetop over medium heat. Once heated, add a single layer of nuts (or seeds). Stir frequently with a spatula until the nuts turn golden brown and aromatic, 3 to 4 minutes. Immediately remove the nuts from the pan and transfer to a small bowl to stop the cooking. Let cool for a few minutes before using. Store extras in an airtight container for up to 3 days at room temperature or 3 months in the freezer.

Roasted Tofu

MAKES 2 CUPS (475 ML)

1 (12-ounce/340-g) block extra-firm tofu

3 tablespoons (45 ml) fresh orange juice

1 tablespoon (15 ml) white miso paste

1 tablespoon (15 ml) extra-virgin olive oil

½ teaspoon (2.5 ml) toasted sesame oil

1 tablespoon (15 ml) sesame seeds

Preheat the oven to 425°F (220°C) and use convection mode if that's an option. Line a baking sheet with parchment paper or a silicone baking mat.

Cut the block of tofu horizontally into thirds and firmly pat dry all sides with a clean kitchen towel or paper towel, then cut the slices into ½-inch (1.3-cm) cubes.

In a medium bowl, mix together the orange juice, miso, olive oil, and sesame oil until well combined. Add the tofu and gently fold the marinade onto the tofu until evenly coated, trying not to break up the cubes. Spread out the tofu cubes on the prepared baking sheet so they are not touching and sprinkle with the sesame seeds.

Bake for 15 minutes. Flip the tofu over and bake until it starts to turn golden brown, another 12 to 20 minutes (longer for a regular oven). Remove from the oven and transfer the parchment paper with the tofu to the counter to cool for at least 5 minutes.

Chopped Bacon

MAKES ABOUT ½ CUP (120 ML)

1 (12-ounce/340-g) package sliced bacon
(nitrate free if possible)

Slice the bacon into small matchsticks. Line a plate with paper towels.

Heat a large skillet over high heat and sprinkle the bacon evenly into the pan. Cook undisturbed for 3 minutes, then stir. Cook, stirring occasionally, until crisp and golden brown, another 3 to 5 minutes depending on the thickness. Remove with a slotted spoon and drain on the paper towel–lined plate.

Grilled Chicken Breast

MAKES ABOUT 2 CUPS (475 ML)

2 boneless skinless chicken breasts
(about 1¼ pounds/570 g)

1 tablespoon (15 ml) extra-virgin olive or avocado oil

1 teaspoon (5 ml) pressed garlic

¼ teaspoon (1.5 ml) sweet paprika

Flaky sea salt and freshly cracked black pepper

Remove the chicken from the refrigerator and let it come to room temperature.

Preheat the grill to 475°F (245°C) or for high-heat grilling, or heat a griddle pan or cast-iron skillet on high heat.

In a medium bowl, combine the chicken with the oil, garlic, and paprika and season with salt and pepper.

Place the chicken on the grates or in the hot pan and sear until char marks are visible or the chicken is golden brown, about 1 minute per side. Turn the heat down to medium high and continue cooking until the internal temperature reads 165°F (75°C) on an instant-read thermometer, 4 to 5 minutes per side. Set the chicken aside on a plate to rest for 5 minutes before cutting into ½-inch (1.3-cm) cubes.

NOTE: You may want to add seasonings that are also in the salad you're making with the chicken, such as spices like red pepper flakes, or herbs like oregano or basil, to create depth of flavors.

Periodic Table of Salad

Do you ever come home from the market with bags full of vegetables you had no intention of buying? Usually because they were beautiful, were on sale, or triggered an inspiration? Don't let them sit in the back of the vegetable drawer; a fabulous salad is just a few steps away! Check out the charts below, decide how you want to prepare your vegetables, then whisk up a dressing (pages 242–55), toss with greens and croutons (pages 232–38) or a cooked grain (page 264), and enjoy!

Blanched Vegetables

Fill a large bowl two-thirds full with **ice water** and set near the cooktop. Fill a large pot with **about 1 gallon (3.8 liters) of water per pound (450 g) of vegetables** and **lightly salt** it. Bring the water to a boil, then add the **washed and trimmed veggies**, and adjust the heat so the water boils softly. Cook the vegetables until they become bright and vibrant; see the times below. With a slotted spoon, transfer the vegetables immediately into the ice water. Chill for the same amount of time they are boiled, then drain in a colander, removing any pieces of ice.

VEGETABLE	SIZE	TIME
Asparagus	1- to 1½-inch (2.5- to 4-cm) pieces, woody ends removed	2 to 3 minutes
Broccoli and Cauliflower	1-inch (2.5-cm) florets	3 minutes
Carrots	¼-inch- (6-mm-) thick slices, cut at an angle, (peel first)	3 to 5 minutes
Beans (Green, Italian, Snap)	1-inch (2.5-cm) pieces	3 to 4 minutes
Edamame, Peas (English or Green)	Whole	1½ minutes

Boiled Vegetables

Put the **vegetables** in a large pot and cover with **2 inches (5 cm) of water** and **lightly salt** the water. Bring to a boil over high heat and adjust the heat so the water boils softly. Cook, topping up the water level if too much boils off, until fork-tender all the way to the center. With a slotted spoon, transfer the vegetables to a strainer and let cool. I recommend only boiling one type of vegetable at a time.

VEGETABLE	SIZE	TIME (ONCE THE WATER HAS COME TO A BOIL)
Potatoes	Whole, unpeeled	15 to 30 minutes (depending on size)
Beets	Whole, unpeeled	20 to 40 minutes (depending on size)

Grilled Vegetables

Preheat the grill to 375°F (190°C) or for medium-high-heat grilling. In a large bowl combine the **vegetables**, **1 teaspoon (5 ml) extra-virgin olive oil or avocado oil per 1 cup (240 ml) vegetables** (or enough to lightly coat), **salt and pepper to taste**, and **any other seasonings** (pressed garlic, chopped rosemary, lemon zest and juice, etc., depending on the salad) and toss until the vegetables are evenly coated. Place on the hot grill and cook, undisturbed, until grill marks appear. Flip halfway through; see times below. If you have a grill basket for vegetables, preheat it on the grill before adding the vegetables; or soak wooden skewers for 30 minutes, then thread the vegetables on them. (This will keep small vegetables from falling through the grill.)

VEGETABLE	SIZE	TIME
Asparagus	Whole (woody ends removed)	5 to 7 minutes
Corn	Whole, husks removed	10 to 15 minutes (turn often)
Eggplant	½-inch- (1.3-cm-) thick slices	15 to 20 minutes
Mushrooms	Whole	10 to 20 minutes (depending on size)
Onion	½-inch (1.3-cm) thick slices	10 to 12 minutes
Peppers and Chiles	Whole	8 to 12 minutes
Summer Squash	½-inch (1.3-cm) thick slices	6 to 8 minutes

Oven-Roasted Vegetables

Preheat the oven to 425°F (220°C) and use convection mode if it's an option. Line a baking sheet with parchment paper or a silicone baking mat. Start with **twice the amount of raw vegetables as you'll need roasted**. (Fun fact: Vegetables are 90 to 96 percent water, and up to half of that is lost when it converts to steam during roasting.) Add the vegetables, **2 tablespoons (30 ml) oil per full baking sheet**, **seasoning of choice**, and toss. Spread out evenly so the vegetables brown on all sides. Bake until golden brown and crispy on the outside, stirring or flipping halfway through; see the times below. Gently lift the parchment paper or silicone mat with the vegetables off the baking sheet to cool.

VEGETABLE	SIZE	TIME (ALL TIMES ARE FOR CONVECTION AND WILL BE LONGER FOR A REGULAR OVEN)
Root Vegetables (Potatoes, Sweet Potatoes, Peeled Beets, Peeled Carrots)	½- to 1-inch (1.3- to 2.5-cm) cubes	25 to 45 minutes
Winter Squash (Butternut, Acorn, Delicata)	1-inch (2.5-cm) cubes or ¼-inch (6-mm) thick slices	25 to 35 minutes for cubes; 20 minutes for slices
Crucifers (Broccoli, Cauliflower, Brussels Sprouts)	1-inch (2.5-cm) florets, halved; halved Brussels sprouts	20 to 30 minutes
Soft Vegetables (Zucchini, Summer Squash, Bell Peppers)	½-inch (1.3-cm) pieces	10 to 20 minutes
Thin Vegetables (Asparagus, Green Beans)	Whole	10 to 20 minutes
Onions	Whole or ½-inch (1.3-cm) wedges	30 to 45 minutes for whole; 15 to 20 minutes for wedges

VEGETABLE	SIZE	TIME (ALL TIMES ARE FOR CONVECTION AND WILL BE LONGER FOR A REGULAR OVEN)
Tomatoes	Whole (grape and cherry); halved (all others)	15 to 20 minutes
Eggplant	½- to 1-inch (1.3-cm to 2.5-cm) cubes	15 to 25 minutes
Mushrooms (Button, Shiitake, and Portobello)	Quartered (button); whole and stemmed (shiitake); ¾-inch (2-cm) cubes (portobello)	20 to 25 minutes
Beans (Chickpeas, Cannellini, Black-Eyed Peas)	Whole	15 to 20 minutes

Cooked Grains

Rinse the **grains**, then add to a pot with the **water** and **salt**. Bring to a boil, then cover (or keep uncovered; check specific grains below) and reduce the heat and cook until the water has been absorbed; see times below. Keep covered and let steam for 5 to 10 minutes, then fluff and cool if necessary.

GRAIN	AMOUNT	WATER	FLAKY SEA SALT	TIME	MAKES
Short-Grain White Rice	3 cups (720 ml)	3⅓ cups (800 ml)	½ teaspoon (2.5 ml)	15 to 20 minutes (covered)	6 cups (1,400 ml)
Short-Grain Brown Rice	3 cups (720 ml)	6 cups (1,400 ml)	½ teaspoon (2.5 ml)	About 30 minutes (covered)	6 cups (1,400 ml)
Quinoa (any color)	1 cup (240 ml)	1¾ cups (415 ml)	½ teaspoon (2.5 ml)	About 15 minutes (uncovered)	About 3 cups (720 ml)
Medium- to Long-Grain White Rice	1 cup (240 ml)	1⅓ cups (315 ml)	½ teaspoon (2.5 ml)	About 15 minutes (covered)	About 2 cups (475 ml)
Medium- to Long-Grain Brown Rice	1 cup (240 ml)	1¾ cups (415 ml)	½ teaspoon (2.5 ml)	About 30 minutes (covered)	About 2 cups (475 ml)

Acknowledgments

A huge thank-you to everyone below and to all of you who helped me get here.
I'm overwhelmed with appreciation, and you know I will hug you when
I see you, but for now, let's tell everyone how fabulous you are.

First and foremost, I have to thank our Salad Lab community: My heart is filled with gratitude. If it weren't for all the love, support, and encouragement from each of you, I would not—could not—be here typing these words. I'm so excited to have found this group of like-minded salad "scientists."

To Athena Schrijver, my daughter, who sparked this whole journey when she asked for my recipes: You continue to inspire me to keep creating, looking at things with a different perspective, and unapologetically going for it! Thank you for squeezing in a few recipe tests with Tara in the middle of finals.

To Morgan Schrijver, my son, who taught me to trust my heart and pursue a passion that is true to myself, no matter the "social norm": Thank you for inspiring me to explore what's possible. And to his wife, Amanda, for her support.

To Bart Schrijver, my husband: Thank you for tolerating, somewhat willingly, living in the "lab" and eating all the experiments for dinner and lunch the next day and for the foreseeable future, even the soggy ones. "Don't eat that cheese, it's for a salad."

To my mother, Sandy Hunkapiller, who now cannot remember but who set the standard and poured the foundation by teaching me independence, work ethic, creativity, and how to start a business, all from a very young age. And to my late father, Marshall Hunkapiller, who taught me that life is short, so live large while you can.

To Justin Schwartz, my editor, for taking me under your wing and guiding me through it all. Your professionalism, kindness, and patience have made this the most amazing experience. To Gina Navaroli, for always fielding all my questions. To Kristina Juodenas: I'm deeply grateful for the beautiful design.

To Emily Stephenson: Your calming voice, organization, and, most of all, creative writing talent made this experience special. You have been so lovely to work with; I can't imagine writing this book with anyone else. You made this book dream a reality. Thank you for last-minute recipe testing, and to your parents for being willing "lab rats."

To Erin Kunkel: I am forever grateful that you took on this project; working with you was a dream come true. All your magical photography made this book so beautiful. To Glenn Jenkins: You are a gem—love your props and your energy. To Vanessa Solis, who was always there to help: We are Duran Duran forever-fans! To Amanda Anselmino: You have style—and not just with food! And to the prep crew, Harumi Shimizu and Cole

Church: I still can't figure out how you were able to make all the recipes look so beautiful in just eight days!

To Grace Rosanova and Scott Hocker, for testing so many recipes. You know the true meaning of "Fabulous Salads Every Day."

To Susan Baldwin, Eric Stevens, and Stephen Amber, the "NC Crew," for being in my corner from the beginning and through every step on the way. Susan, for being my biggest cheerleader, planting the seed to write a book, and supporting me through the whole process. Stephen, for inspiring and supporting me when I questioned what I was doing. Eric, for the countless hours of contract negotiations, and preparing salads for your family.

Andi Barzvi and Carrie Howland: Thank you for being my literary agents, educating and guiding me through this whole process, helping me create this incredible team, and being there for me.

Leilani Cooper, my sister from another mother: "Why don't you film the recipes and put them on TikTok?" Your words changed my life forever. You have always been there, encouraging and supporting me through all my different life journeys, including this crazy one, with creative, logical, inspiring ideas. Shout-out to Ashley Fairchild (Leilani's daughter), for cheering me on every step of the way.

To Gail Stanley, Janet Kendrick, Elizabeth Ross, Kim Peterson, and Karen Carlo-Salinger, my childhood friends, who are really sisters without the shared DNA. Thank you for your endless support, help, and encouragement with life, this book, recipe testing, and bouncing around ideas, and for being my sous chefs for cooking demonstrations.

To Mitzi Tzujihara: Thank you for going through it with me. Your continuous support, researching, and wine tastings made this journey so fun.

To Cory Nguyen, for recipe testing on your days off when you were working eighteen-hour shifts in the restaurant. To Suzy, for always talking me off the ledge, liking all my videos even when they weren't vegan, and convincing Cory to test my salads.

To Laurel Hannon, for your vegan palate and help with testing all the way in NJ.

To Eileen Fumire, for being there for my first cooking demonstration and stepping up to test recipes for this book.

To the ladies at iLeoni, my favorite local kitchen store: Thank you for taking me under your wing, hosting my first live demonstration, and lending all your support, encouragement, and girl power. You are the best!

To the Fountaingrove Tennis Team Ladies, nothing but love, encouragement, and support from the most incredible group of friends and teammates, especially Judith Mattingly and Ann Rogalski.

And to Midnight, my fifteen-year-old fluffy "therapy cat" who's always ready to purr and cuddle when I've had a hard day, and to Beast, my wild calico who wants to talk and see what's in the salads while I'm trying to film.

Index

almond butter, in Waldorf Salad, 182
almonds. *See also* Honey-Roasted
    Sliced Almonds
    Across-the-Pond Irish Salad, 128–30
    Fall Chopped Salad, 178–79
    Not-So-Chinese Chicken Salad, 62–63
    Vegan Cobb, 54–55
    Viral Sesame Chicken, 82
American Potato Salad, 48–49
apples
    Autumn Fruit Salad, 176–77
    BBQ Salad, 112–13
    Fall Chopped Salad, 178–79
    Waldorf Salad, 182
Arizona Chopped Salad, 92–93
artichoke hearts
    Chicken Pesto Pasta Salad, 170–72
    Pizza Salad, 225–26
arugula
    Arizona Chopped Salad, 92–93
    Arugula Salad, 36
    Beet Salad, 187–89
    Brunch Salad, 158–59
    Grilled Peach Salad, 160–61
    Pizza Salad, 225–26
    Southern Hemisphere Sweet Potato
        Salad, 147–49
    Steak and Chimichurri, 120–22
    Supermodel's Arugula Salad, 72
Asiago cheese, in Arizona Chopped
    Salad, 92–93
asparagus
    blanching, 260
    First Lady's Spring Pea Salad with
        Asparagus and Pea Shoots, 74–75
    grilling, 262
    oven-roasted, 262
    Steak and Chimichurri, 120–22
    Summer Wedding Salad, 166–67
avocado
    Avocado Bruschetta, 205
    Beverly Hills McCarthy Salad, 88–89
    Breakfast Burrito Salad, 200–202
    Brunch Salad, 158–59
    Burger and Fries Salad, 222–24

Chicken and Avocado with Honey Hot
    Sauce Vinaigrette, 86
Chopped Salad, 66–67
Cilantro Lime Dressing, 251
Cowboy Caviar, 116–17
Doradito Salad, 206–8
Fish Taco Salad, 218–19
My First Celebrity's Creamy, Lemony
    Cobb, 80
New Year's Celebration Salad, 196–97
Original Cobb Salad, 68–69
Poke Bowl Salad, 108
Potato Skin Salad, 209–11
Smoked Jalapeño Mexican Grill,
    94–96
Southern Hemisphere Sweet Potato
    Salad, 147–49
Steak and Chimichurri, 120–22
Summer Wedding Salad, 166–67
Supermodel's Arugula Salad, 72
Vegan Cobb, 54–55
West African Avocado and Citrus
    Salad, 140

bacon. *See* Chopped Bacon
bagels, in Everything Bagel Croutons,
    236
baguette
    Avocado Bruschetta, 205
    Classic Homemade Croutons, 232
Balsamic Dressing, 246
Basil Mustard Dressing, 255
beakers, 26
beans
    Controversial Fake Cobb Salad, 76–77
    Cowboy Caviar, 116–17
    Doradito Salad, 206–8
    oven-roasted, 263
    Smoked Jalapeño Mexican Grill,
        94–96
beef. *See also* steak
    Burger and Fries Salad, 222–24
    Corned Beef and Cabbage Salad,
        228–29
    French Fry Salad, 102–4
    Grinder Salad, 220–21
    Steak and Chimichurri, 120–22
    Winter Wedge, 190–92
beer, in Corned Beef and Cabbage
    Salad, 228–29

beets
    Beet Salad, 187–89
    Beverly Hills McCarthy Salad, 88–89
    boiling, 260
    Harvest Salad, 180
    in House Salad, 39
    oven-roasted, 262
    Vegan Cobb, 54–55
bell pepper(s)
    Arizona Chopped Salad, 92–93
    Breakfast Burrito Salad, 200–202
    Chicken Pesto Pasta Salad, 170–72
    Cowboy Caviar, 116–17
    Fall Chopped Salad, 178–79
    French Fry Salad, 102–4
    Greek Salad, 40
    Grinder Salad, 220–21
    Hot Girl Salad, 164–65
    Not-So-Chinese Chicken Salad,
        62–63
    oven-roasted, 262
    Pizza Salad, 225–26
    Roasted Vegetable Salad, 173–75
    Smoked Jalapeño Mexican Grill,
        94–96
    Soba Noodle Salad, 214–15
    Southern Hemisphere Sweet Potato
        Salad, 147–49
    Supermodel's Arugula Salad, 72
berries
    Grilled Peach Salad, 160–61
    Spinach Salad, 42
    Strawberry Jicama Salad, 156
    Summer Wedding Salad, 166–67
beverages, 32
black-eyed peas, in Cowboy Caviar,
    116–17
blanched vegetables, 260
blue cheese, 43
    Blue Cheese Dressing, 245
    Burger and Fries Salad, 222–24
    Chopped Salad, 66–67
    My First Celebrity's Creamy, Lemony
        Cobb, 80
    Original Cobb Salad, 68–69
    substitute, 33
    Wedge salad, 64–65
    Winter Wedge, 190–92
boiled vegetables, 260
Boston lettuce, in Niçoise, 56–57

broccoli
  blanching, 260
  oven-roasted, 262
  Poke Bowl Salad, 108
Brussels sprouts
  All in One Thanksgiving Salad, 184–86
  Harvest Salad, 180
  oven-roasted, 262
bulgur wheat
  Controversial Fake Cobb Salad, 76–77
  Tabbouleh, 44–45
butter lettuce
  House Salad, 38–39
  Niçoise, 56–57
  Potato Skin Salad, 209–11
  Pub Salad, 157
  Viral Sesame Chicken, 82

cabbage
  BBQ Salad, 112
  Coleslaw, 46
  Corned Beef and Cabbage Salad,
    228–29
  Fisherman's Wharf Shrimp Louie,
    97–98
  Fish Taco Salad, 218–19
  Jamaican Coleslaw, 118–19
  Not-So-Chinese Chicken Salad, 62–63
  Soba Noodle Salad, 214–15
  Viral Sesame Chicken, 82
Caesar Dressing, 243
Caesar salad, 58
carrot(s)
  Bibimbap Salad, 144–46
  Carrot Ginger Dressing, 250
  Corned Beef and Cabbage Salad,
    228–29
  Famous Sisters-with-a-K's Favorite,
    78–79
  Fisherman's Wharf Shrimp Louie, 97–98
  Jamaican Coleslaw, 118–19
  Kani (Kanikama) Salad, 142
  Not-So-Chinese Chicken Salad,
    62–63
  oven-roasted, 262
  Poke Bowl Salad, 108
  Soba Noodle Salad, 214–15
  Spring Roll Salad, 212–13
  Summer Wedding Salad, 166–67
  Vegan Cobb, 54–55

cauliflower
  All in One Thanksgiving Salad, 184–86
  blanching, 260
  oven-roasted, 262
caviar, in New Year's Celebration Salad,
  196–97
Ceviche, 123–25
cheddar cheese
  Beverly Hills McCarthy Salad, 88–89
  Cheesy Tortilla Croutons, 238
  Corned Beef and Cabbage Salad,
    228–29
  Doradito Salad, 206–8
  French Fry Salad, 102–4
  House Salad, 38–39
  Pea Salad, 152
  Potato Skin Salad, 209–11
  Pub Salad, 157
  Smoked Jalapeño Mexican Grill,
    94–96
Cheesy Tortilla Croutons
  Breakfast Burrito Salad, 200–202
  recipe, 238
cherry tomatoes
  Avocado Bruschetta, 205
  Brunch Salad, 158–59
  Chicken Pesto Pasta Salad, 170–72
  Doradito Salad, 206–8
  Fisherman's Wharf Shrimp Louie,
    97–98
  Fish Taco Salad, 218–19
  Greek Salad, 40
  Kale Salad, 60–61
  Niçoise, 56–57
  Orzo Pasta Salad, 50
  Panzanella, 132
  Pizza Salad, 225–26
  Potato Skin Salad, 209–11
  Pub Salad, 157
  Roasted Vegetable Salad, 173–75
  Steak and Chimichurri, 120–22
  Tapas Salad, 136–37
  Vegan Cobb, 54–55
  Winter Wedge, 190–92
chicken. *See also* Grilled Chicken Breast
  Chicken and Avocado with Honey Hot
    Sauce Vinaigrette, 86
  Famous Sisters-with-a-K's Favorite,
    78–79
  Kale Salad, 60–61

  Smoked Jalapeño Mexican Grill,
    94–96
  Tropical Salad with Fruit and Creole
    Chicken, 105–7
chickpeas, in Controversial Fake Cobb
  Salad, 76–77
Chimichurri, Steak and, 120–22
Chopped Bacon, 258
  Brunch Salad, 158–59
  Burger and Fries Salad, 222–24
  Chopped Salad, 66–67
  My First Celebrity's Creamy, Lemony
    Cobb, 80
  Original Cobb Salad, 68–69
  Pea Salad, 152
  Potato Skin Salad, 209–11
  Wedge salad, 64–65
  Winter Wedge, 190–92
Chopped Salad, 66–67
Classic Homemade Croutons
  All in One Thanksgiving Salad, 184–86
  recipe, 232
  Winter Wedge, 190–92
cobb salad
  Controversial Fake Cobb Salad, 76–77
  My First Celebrity's Creamy, Lemony
    Cobb, 80
  Original Cobb Salad, 68–69
  Vegan Cobb, 54–55
coconut flakes
  Waldorf Salad, 182
  West African Avocado and Citrus
    Salad, 140
Coleslaw, 46, 118–19
condiments, 20
corn
  Arizona Chopped Salad, 92–93
  Ceviche, 123–25
  Cowboy Caviar, 116–17
  Esquites Salad, 126–27
  grilling, 262
  Southern Hemisphere Sweet Potato
    Salad, 147–49
Corned Beef and Cabbage Salad,
  228–29
Cotija cheese
  Cheesy Tortilla Croutons, 238
  Cowboy Caviar, 116–17
  Esquites Salad, 126–27
  Fish Taco Salad, 218–19

couscous, in Arizona Chopped Salad, 92–93

Cowboy Caviar, 116–17

cream cheese, in Lox and Bagel Salad, 203–4

crouton recipes, 232–38. See also specific names of croutons

cucumber(s)
  Chopped Salad, 66–67
  Controversial Fake Cobb Salad, 76–77
  Famous Sisters-with-a-K's Favorite, 78–79
  Fattoush, 138–39
  French Fry Salad, 102–4
  Greek Salad, 40
  Grinder Salad, 220–21
  Hot Girl Salad, 164–65
  House Salad, 38–39
  Kale Salad, 60–61
  Kani (Kanikama) Salad, 142
  Lox and Bagel Salad, 203–4
  Poke Bowl Salad, 108
  Pub Salad, 157
  Soba Noodle Salad, 214–15
  Spring Roll Salad, 212–13
  Strawberry Jicama Salad, 156
  Summer Wedding Salad, 166–67
  Supermodel's Arugula Salad, 72
  Tabbouleh, 44–45
  Vegan Cobb, 54–55
  Watermelon Feta Salad, 162

curly leaf lettuce, in Spring Roll Salad, 212–13

dairy and dairy substitutes, 21

deli meats, in Grinder Salad, 220–21

dressing
  fundamentals on making, 30–31
  recipes, 242–55

edamame
  blanching, 260
  Poke Bowl Salad, 108
  Soba Noodle Salad, 214–15
  Spinach Salad, 42

eggplant
  Across-the-Pond Irish Salad, 128–30
  grilling, 262
  oven-roasted, 263
  Roasted Vegetable Salad, 173–75

eggs. See also Perfect Boiled Eggs
  Bibimbap Salad, 144–46
  Breakfast Burrito Salad, 200–202
  Brunch Salad, 158–59
  Kale Salad, 60–61

Everything Bagel Croutons
  Lox and Bagel Salad, 203–4
  recipe, 236

Fattoush, 138–39

fennel bulb
  Beet Salad, 187–89
  Supreme Citrus Season Salad, 193

feta cheese, 43
  Chicken and Avocado with Honey Hot Sauce Vinaigrette, 86
  Controversial Fake Cobb Salad, 76–77
  Greek Salad, 40
  Kale Salad, 60–61
  Orzo Pasta Salad, 50
  Spinach Salad, 42
  Supreme Citrus Season Salad, 193
  Watermelon Feta Salad, 162

fish and seafood
  Arizona Chopped Salad, 92–93
  Ceviche, 123–25
  Fisherman's Wharf Shrimp Louie, 97–98
  Fish Taco Salad, 218–19
  Kani (Kanikama) Salad, 142
  Niçoise, 56–57
  Poke Bowl Salad, 108
  Tapas Salad, 136–37

French-Style Potato Salad
  Niçoise, 56–57
  recipe, 134

gem lettuce
  Caesar, 58
  Fancy Italian Caesar, 90–91
  House Salad, 38–39
  My First Celebrity's Creamy, Lemony Cobb, 80
  New Year's Celebration Salad, 196–97
  Viral Sesame Chicken, 82

goat cheese, 43
  Across-the-Pond Irish Salad, 128–30
  Beet Salad, 187–89
  Tapas Salad, 136–37

Tropical Salad with Fruit and Creole Chicken, 105–7

Gorgonzola cheese
  Chopped Salad, 66
  Windy City–Style Chopped, 114–15

Gouda cheese
  All in One Thanksgiving Salad, 184–86
  Harvest Salad, 180

grains, 20. See also specific grains

grapes
  Tropical Salad with Fruit and Creole Chicken, 105–7
  Waldorf Salad, 182

Greek Salad, 40

green beans
  All in One Thanksgiving Salad, 184–86
  blanching, 260
  Niçoise, 56–57
  oven-roasted, 262
  pickled, in Pub Salad, 157
  Pub Salad, 157
  Vegan Cobb, 54–55

Green Goddess Dressing, 249

Grilled Chicken Breast
  BBQ Salad, 112–13
  Beverly Hills McCarthy Salad, 88–89
  Chicken Pesto Pasta Salad, 170–72
  My First Celebrity's Creamy, Lemony Cobb, 80
  Not-So-Chinese Chicken Salad, 62–63
  Original Cobb Salad, 68–69
  recipe, 258
  Viral Sesame Chicken, 82
  Windy City–Style Chopped, 114–15

grilled vegetables, 261

ham
  Grinder Salad, 220–21
  Maurice Salad, 100

Hawaii, Poke Bowl Salad from, 108

hemp seeds, in Vegan Cobb, 54–55

Honey-Roasted Sliced Almonds
  Grilled Peach Salad, 160–61
  recipe, 257
  Spinach Salad, 42
  Tropical Salad with Fruit and Creole Chicken, 105–7
  Waldorf Salad, 182

House Salad, 38–39

iceberg lettuce
    Beverly Hills McCarthy Salad, 88–89
    Doradito Salad, 206–8
    Famous Sisters-with-a-K's Favorite, 78–79
    French Fry Salad, 102–4
    Grinder Salad, 220–21
    Maurice Salad, 100
    Not-So-Chinese Chicken Salad, 62–63
    Original Cobb Salad, 68–69
    Wedge salad, 64–65
    Windy City–Style Chopped, 114–15
    Winter Wedge, 190–92
Ireland, Across-the-Pond Irish Salad from, 128–30
Italy, Panzanella salad from, 132

Jamaican Coleslaw, 118–19
jicama
    Cowboy Caviar, 116–17
    Strawberry Jicama Salad, 156
julienned vegetables, 143

kale, 33
    Across-the-Pond Irish Salad, 128–30
    Chicken and Avocado with Honey Hot Sauce Vinaigrette, 86
    Fall Chopped Salad, 178–79
    Harvest Salad, 180
    Kale Salad, 60–61
    Pizza Salad, 225–26
    varieties of, 60
    Vegan Cobb, 54–55
Kardashian salad, 78–79
kimchi, in Bibimbap Salad, 144–46
kitchen equipment and tools, 26–27

legumes, 20. See also beans; peas and pea shoots
lettuces, preparing, 30. See also specific types of lettuces
lox, in Lox and Bagel Salad, 203–4

Maldon flaky sea salt, 19
Manchego cheese, in Tapas Salad, 136–37
mandarin oranges
    Not-So-Chinese Chicken Salad, 62–63
    Tropical Salad with Fruit and Creole Chicken, 105–7

mango
    Fish Taco Salad, 218–19
    how to prep, 119
    Jamaican Coleslaw, 118
    Kani (Kanikama) Salad, 142
    Poke Bowl Salad, 108
    West African Avocado and Citrus Salad, 140
measurements, 37
meat substitutes, 33
Mexican chorizo
    Breakfast Burrito Salad, 200–202
    Doradito Salad, 206–8
microgreens
    Summer Wedding Salad, 166–67
    Waldorf Salad, 182
mixed greens, in All in One Thanksgiving Salad, 184–86
Monterey Jack cheese
    Cheesy Tortilla Croutons, 238
    Smoked Jalapeño Mexican Grill, 94–96
mozzarella balls/cheese
    Chicken Pesto Pasta Salad, 170–72
    Grilled Peach Salad, 160–61
    Pizza Salad, 225–26
mushrooms
    All in One Thanksgiving Salad, 184–86
    Bibimbap Salad, 144–46
    Fisherman's Wharf Shrimp Louie, 97–98
    grilling, 262
    Harvest Salad, 180
    oven-roasted, 263
    Pizza Salad, 225–26
    Soba Noodle Salad, 214–15
    Steak and Chimichurri, 120–22
mustard, 19

Nacho Cheese Doritos, in Doradito Salad, 206–8
Niçoise, 56–57
nonalcoholic beverages, 21
nut butters, 21. See also peanut butter/ peanuts
nutritional yeast, 33, 178, 186
    Vegan Better-than-Caesar Caesar, 248
    Vegan Cobb, 54–55

nuts and seeds. See also specific nuts and seeds
    toasted, 257
    types of, 21

Obama, Michelle, 74
olives, 21
    Fisherman's Wharf Shrimp Louie, 97–98
    Greek Salad, 40
    Maurice Salad, 100
    Niçoise, 56–57
    Orzo Pasta Salad, 50
    Pizza Salad, 225–26
    Tapas Salad, 136–37
orange(s). See also mandarin oranges; tangerine segments
    Beet Salad, 187–88
    Supreme Citrus Season Salad, 193–94
    Tropical Salad with Fruit and Creole Chicken, 105–7
Orzo Pasta Salad, 50
oven-roasted vegetables, 262–63

pantry items, shopping for, 18–23
Panzanella, 132
Parmesan cheese, 73. See also Parmigiano-Reggiano cheese
Parmesan Crisp "Croutons," 237
Parmigiano-Reggiano cheese
    Arugula Salad, 36
    Caesar, 58
    Caesar Dressing, 243
    Chicken Pesto Pasta Salad, 170–72
    Fall Chopped Salad, 178–79
    Fancy Italian Caesar, 90–91
    Grilled Peach Salad, 160–61
    Grinder Salad, 220–21
    Lemon Basil Pasta Salad, 154
    Parmesan Crisp "Croutons," 237
    Pizza Salad, 225–26
    Polenta Croutons, 233
    Sourdough Garlic Croutons, 235
    Supermodel's Arugula Salad, 72
pasta and noodles, 20
    Chicken Pesto Pasta Salad, 170–72
    Lemon Basil Pasta Salad, 154
    Orzo Pasta Salad, 50
    Soba Noodle Salad, 214–15

Spring Roll Salad, 212–13
Windy City–Style Chopped, 114–15
peaches, in Grilled Peach Salad, 160–61
peanut butter/peanuts
Creamy Peanut Dressing, 253
Spring Roll Salad, 212–13
pears, in Autumn Fruit Salad, 176–77
peas and pea shoots
All in One Thanksgiving Salad, 184–86
blanching, 260
First Lady's Spring Pea Salad with
Asparagus and Pea Shoots, 74–75
Pea Salad, 152
pecans
Autumn Fruit Salad, 176–77
BBQ Salad, 112–13
Harvest Salad, 180
Kale Salad, 60–61
Pecorino Romano cheese, 73
Arizona Chopped Salad, 92–93
Fall Chopped Salad, 178–79
pepitas, in Arizona Chopped Salad,
92–93
pepperoncini
Burger and Fries Salad, 222–24
Grinder Salad, 220–21
Hot Girl Salad, 164–65
pepperoni, in Pizza Salad, 225–26
Perfect Boiled Eggs
American Potato Salad, 48–49
Beverly Hills McCarthy Salad, 88–89
Chopped Salad, 66–67
Fisherman's Wharf Shrimp Louie,
97–98
Hot Girl Salad, 164–65
House Salad, 38–39
Lox and Bagel Salad, 203–4
Maurice Salad, 100
My First Celebrity's Creamy, Lemony
Cobb, 80
Niçoise, 56–57
Original Cobb Salad, 68–69
Pea Salad, 152
Pub Salad, 157
recipe, 257
Tapas Salad, 136–37
Wedge salad, 64–65
Winter Wedge, 190–92
persimmons, in Autumn Fruit Salad,
176–77

Pesto Pasta Salad, 170–72
petri dishes, 26
pineapple, in Tropical Salad with Fruit
and Creole Chicken, 105–7
pine nuts
Chicken Pesto Pasta Salad, 170–72
Lemon Basil Pasta Salad, 154
pistachios
Arugula Salad, 36
Controversial Fake Cobb Salad, 76–77
Supreme Citrus Season Salad, 193
Pita Croutons
Fattoush, 138–39
recipe, 233
Pizza Salad, 225–26
plantain, in Vegan Cobb, 54–55
Polenta Croutons, 233
pomegranate seeds
Arugula Salad, 36
Autumn Fruit Salad, 176–77
Supreme Citrus Season Salad, 193
Tabbouleh, 44–45
potatoes
All in One Thanksgiving Salad, 184–86
American Potato Salad, 48–49
boiling, 260
Breakfast Burrito Salad, 200–202
Burger and Fries Salad, 222–24
Corned Beef and Cabbage Salad,
228–29
French Fry Salad, 102–4
French-Style Potato Salad, 134
oven-roasted, 262
Potato Skin Salad, 209–11
Red, White, and Blue Potato Salad,
168–69
Power Greens mix, in Harvest Salad, 180
prosciutto, in Grilled Peach Salad,
160–61

Quick Pickled Onions
Fish Taco Salad, 218–19
Grilled Peach Salad, 160–61
recipe, 256
Winter Wedge, 190–92
quinoa
cooking, 263
Harvest Salad, 180
Kale Salad, 60–61
Vegan Cobb, 54–55

radish
Fattoush, 138–39
New Year's Celebration Salad, 196–97
Ranch Dressing, 244
rice
Bibimbap Salad, 144–46
cooking, 264
Poke Bowl Salad, 108–9
Smoked Jalapeño Mexican Grill,
94–96
Roasted Garlic Purée
Across-the-Pond Irish Salad, 128–30
All in One Thanksgiving Salad, 184–86
Beverly Hills McCarthy Salad, 88–89
Fancy Italian Caesar, 90–91
Ginger Miso Tahini Dressing, 247
Harvest Salad, 180
Not-So-Chinese Chicken Salad,
62–63
Pizza Salad, 225–26
Potato Skin Salad, 209–11
recipe, 256
Roasted Vegetable Salad, 173–75
Roasted Tofu
recipe, 258
Spinach Salad, 42
Vegan Cobb, 54–55
romaine lettuce
Beverly Hills McCarthy Salad, 88–89
Burger and Fries Salad, 222–24
Caesar salad, 58
Chicken and Avocado with Honey Hot
Sauce Vinaigrette, 86
Chopped Salad, 66–67
Doradito Salad, 206–8
Famous Sisters-with-a-K's Favorite,
78–79
Fancy Italian Caesar, 90–91
Fattoush, 138–39
Fisherman's Wharf Shrimp Louie,
97–98
House Salad, 38–39
Maurice Salad, 100
My First Celebrity's Creamy, Lemony
Cobb, 80
Original Cobb Salad, 68–69
Pizza Salad, 225–26
Potato Skin Salad, 209–11
Smoked Jalapeño Mexican Grill,
94–96

romaine lettuce (*cont.*)
  Tapas Salad, 136–37
  Viral Sesame Chicken, 82
Roquefort cheese, 245
  Chopped Salad, 66–67
  Original Cobb Salad, 68–69

salad toppings, 20
salami, in Grinder Salad, 220–21
sausage, in Pizza Salad, 225–26
seed butters, 21
shopping for pantry items, 18–23
shrimp
  Fisherman's Wharf Shrimp Louie,
    97–98
  Spring Roll Salad, 212–13
sourdough bread, in Across-the-Pond
    Irish Salad, 128–30. *See also*
    Sourdough Garlic Croutons
Sourdough Garlic Croutons
  Caesar salad, 58
  Fisherman's Wharf Shrimp Louie,
    97–98
  Grinder Salad, 220–21
  Harvest Salad, 180
  House Salad, 38–39
  Panzanella, 132
  Pizza Salad, 225–26
  recipe, 235
  Wedge salad, 64–65
spinach
  Bibimbap Salad, 144–46
  Harvest Salad, 180
  Spinach Salad, 42
spring mix
  Brunch Salad, 158–59
  Grilled Peach Salad, 160–61
  Lox and Bagel Salad, 203–4
  Spinach Salad, 42
  Steak and Chimichurri, 120–22
  Summer Wedding Salad,
    166–67

Tropical Salad with Fruit and Creole
    Chicken, 105–7
Vegan Cobb, 54–55
squash. *See also* zucchini
  Fall Chopped Salad, 178–79
  oven-roasted, 262
  Summer Wedding Salad, 166–67
steak
  Bibimbap Salad, 144–46
  French Fry Salad, 102–4
  Steak and Chimichurri, 120–22
  Winter Wedge, 190–92
substitutions, 21, 33
sun-dried tomatoes, in Orzo Pasta
    Salad, 50
sunflower seeds
  Hot Girl Salad, 164–65
  Vegan Cobb, 54–55
sweet potatoes
  All in One Thanksgiving Salad, 184–86
  Ceviche, 123–25
  Harvest Salad, 180
  oven-roasted, 262
  Southern Hemisphere Sweet Potato
    Salad, 147–49
Swiss cheese, in Maurice Salad, 100

Tabbouleh, 44–45
tahini
  Ginger Miso Tahini Dressing, 247
  Viral Sesame Chicken, 82
tangerine segments
  Autumn Fruit Salad, 176–77
  Tropical Salad with Fruit and Creole
    Chicken, 105–7
Tapas Salad, 136–37
test tubes, 26
Thousand Island Dressing, 252
tofu. *See* Roasted Tofu
tomatoes. *See also* cherry tomatoes
  Across-the-Pond Irish Salad, 128–30
  Beverly Hills McCarthy Salad, 88–89

Breakfast Burrito Salad, 200–202
Burger and Fries Salad, 222–24
Chopped Salad, 66–67
Cowboy Caviar, 116–17
Fattoush, 138–39
Grinder Salad, 220–21
House Salad, 38–39
Lemon Basil Pasta Salad, 154
Lox and Bagel Salad, 203–4
Original Cobb Salad, 68–69
oven-roasted, 263
Panzanella, 132
Smoked Jalapeño Mexican Grill,
  94–96
Tabbouleh, 44–45
turkey
  All in One Thanksgiving Salad, 184–86
  Grinder Salad, 220–21
  Maurice Salad, 100

Vegan Better-than-Caesar Caesar, 248
Vegan Cobb, 54–55
Vinaigrette, 242
vinegar, 18–19

Waldorf Salad, 182
walnuts, in Chicken and Avocado with
    Honey Hot Sauce Vinaigrette, 86
Watermelon Feta Salad, 162
watermelon radish
  New Year's Celebration Salad,
    196–97
  Soba Noodle Salad, 214–15
  Summer Wedding Salad, 166–67
Wedding Salad, Summer, 166–67
wines, 21
  Doradito Salad, 206–8
  French-Style Potato Salad, 134

zucchini
  Bibimbap Salad, 144–46
  Breakfast Burrito Salad, 200–202

Darlene Schrijver grew up in Los Altos, California. She worked in market research and as a financial analyst before focusing on raising her two children, volunteering in classrooms, and competing in triathlons, including an Iron Man. She raised her son, Morgan, and daughter, Athena, while managing her daughter's athletic career as a youth and Junior Team USA Olympic weight lifting athlete. The Salad Lab was born in 2020 when a friend suggested Darlene post her recipes on TikTok. In addition to growing a community of salad fans, Darlene found creating salads on social media to be therapeutic as well. She enjoyed doing research for recipes and learning the history of each salad and its sometimes unfamiliar ingredients. Her following soon grew into the millions, and she continues to strive to celebrate all fresh ingredients through her recipes. Darlene lives in Sonoma County, California.